Wholeness is Living

WHOLENESS IS LIVING

SCIENTIFIC THINKING AND RELIGIOUS EXPERIENCE

by

A. GRAHAM IKIN

PUBLISHERS
GEOFFREY BLES · LONDON
1970

SBN; 7138 0274 X

Printed in Great Britain
by Cox & Wyman Ltd
Reading

Published by
GEOFFREY BLES LTD
52 Doughty Street, London, W.C.1
36–38 Clarence Street, Sydney 2000, N.S.W.
353 Elizabeth Street, Melbourne C.1
246 Queen Street, Brisbane
CML Building, King William Street, Adelaide
Lake Road, Northcote, Auckland
100 Lesmill Road, Don Mills, Ontario
P.O. Box 8879, Johannesburg
P.O. Box 834, Cape Town
P.O. Box 2800, Salisbury, Rhodesia

CONTENTS

ACKNOWLEDGEMENTS

My thanks are due to the editors of *Science of Mind*, California, and *The Science of Thought Review*, as well as of *Faith and Freedom*, for permission to include articles published in their respective journals.

Some extracts have been taken from books of my own which are now out of print, the copyright of which has reverted to me.

Others have not appeared in print previously.

I also wish to thank the following authors and publishers for permission to quote extracts from the works mentioned below:

Allen & Unwin: *Narcissus*, Grace Stuart.

Routledge & Kegan Paul: *Between Man and Man*, Martin Buber; and *Essays on Contempory Events*, C. G. Jung.

PREFACE

'What is man that thou art mindful of him? and the son of man that thou visitest him?'[1]

This quotation from the Psalms shows how far back the query as to the nature of man in the midst of a creation which included the sun and the moon and the stars of heaven arose. Yet recently in *Man the Unknown* Dr Alexis Carrel showed how great man's ignorance of his true nature still is, and the distortion that this brings into the image of the world in which he lives as he sees it, and not as it is in itself, as well as into his image of God.

At first man can only make God in his own image. Yet the fact of the development of religious insight in the development of man may be taken to imply that God has actually been in the process of making man into His image—making man to reflect His nature increasingly, until in some measure real communion, a real interchange could occur. Man could then begin to co-operate in the creative process consciously instead of unconsciously.

For the further development of this, man needs to know himself, not just superficially but in the depths of the prolonged human experience that has shaped and is shaping human beings within the context of all life, whether below or above the everyday level of any stage of achievement.

Man's researches into nature and outer space reveal immensities which seem to dwarf him into insignificance. Yet it is the mind of man that has brought awareness of these immensities within its range through experiment and exploration. The direction in which he looks, the tools

[1] Psalm 8, 4.

9

he uses with which to explore, whether microscopic or telescopic, decide what he will see in that particular cross section of a Reality that still transcends all we as yet know of it. Since the days of the psalmist who was moved to wonder and awe at the sight of the canopy of stars, man has developed tools and machinery capable of revealing more and more of the complicated processes that not only bring the stars within the sight of man, but impart something of the very substance of the sun into our tissues, through our food and some absorption of its light through our skins. The framework of life in a 'boundless creation' has extended beyond the range of our full comprehension, and our image of God must expand accordingly.

We are only on the fringe of realising the possibilities for a fuller life ahead of us. Not just a life cluttered up with more and more gadgets to save us from the skill involved in true living: but a life that is increasingly lived from its own true centre, with insight, initiative, responsibility and enjoyment blended into a unity that also enriches the life of our fellows.

Many books are being written with 'Man' in the title, as this need for self-knowledge is being borne in on us. This book gathers together some of the strands which are thus being woven in order to give us glimpses into a deeper self than our surface consciousness reveals. Some glimpses open a vista of further explorations of an inner reality which undergirds our daily life in touch with nature, mankind and God, in a unity that is given in the very structure of Reality. The images of Nature, of Man and of God, all three change when any one of them is seen more truly as it is: Man's stature increases and life becomes fuller as a result.

Each age and generation has to face fundamental problems for itself, seeing them in the perspective of its own type of experience and cultural background. Always there is some tension between those who seek to conserve the form of the past at the expense of the growing spirit, which needs to clothe itself afresh to be appropriate to the present, and those who tend to disown the past. The creative elements within the past when recognised can lead to a *continuity of development* in which all that is of permanent value from the past is conserved, while the changing needs of a different age are also met.

We cannot undo the scientific revolution but we can learn to harmonise it with the deepest needs of our souls which are rooted in the very nature of reality. As allies, life can be enriched—as enemies it may be more unliveable on earth.

Shangri La
Eskdale Green
Cumberland
1970

I

SCIENTIFIC THINKING AND RELIGIOUS EXPERIENCE

Once, as I was travelling through a long tunnel, when a waiter approached me, bowed deferentially and said 'Will you have plain cake or currant cake, Madam?' I thought of Aladdin's lamp and that not all the wealth of Eastern imagination could have conjured up anything more wonderful than being offered the choice of plain cake or currant cake in a small room, beautifully upholstered, well warmed and lighted, travelling at a great speed right under a mountain. Yet this had become such a commonplace of everyday activity that it was taken for granted.

The possibility of such a marvellous happening was the result of much co-operation, involving the pooling of knowledge in many inter-related subjects, as well as its practical application by engineers and workmen, as well as railway officials, not to mention confectioners and salesmen.

The whole of our everyday life is permeated with the products of scientific thinking. If all scientific thinking were suddenly removed, we should not only be unable to live the *good* life, but we should be unable to live *any* life at all. I read a novel some time ago in which the collapse of civilisation was pictured, when some rapid intra-atomic dissolution of metals took place, and all the iron, steel or other metal machinery broke down. In a few weeks only a few hordes of savages, reduced to cannibalism to live at all, were left of our modern world, except for a few scientists

who, like Noah of old, had seen what was coming and prepared a modern ark, stored with food enough to last twelve
months; while they strove to use their scientific thinking to
produce a substitute metal that would not rot, in the hope of
saving a fraction of mankind to carry life forward. Since
then the discovery of atomic bombs has brought the possibility of this phantasy into the realm of sober fact.

This brought home very forcibly how dependent we now
are upon this comparatively recently developed capacity
of man to think scientifically. Wherein does it differ from
another, much older capacity, which we call religious
experience? And what part does religious experience play
in a world so dependent upon scientific thinking? Is it to
be outgrown as childish and infantile, to be transcended by
scientific thinking? Some scientists would have us think so.
But one thing is sure—that scientific thinking makes it impossible to rest content with a superstitious and infantile
religion. Religious experience, which so far as we know is
as old as man himself, has developed through many strange
and often ugly and repelling forms. It bears the marks of
history within it, and the science that condemns its superstitions and childishness should challenge us to grow up
religiously as well as scientifically.

If so, can we use scientific thinking to clarify and purify
our religious experience?

In the succeeding chapters I hope to show that we can,
and that the consideration of all the religious problems involved in the various subjects is greatly illumined by insight gained by psychological workers, not all of whom
would call themselves religious. Psychotherapy, which
means the *healing of the mind*, is bringing many of the
Gospel miracles within the realm of present experience.
The application of some of the psychological principles
(discovered through practical therapeutic work in curing
patients) within the sphere of the mental health of the
community, and the effect of this on both physique and

culture, the attitude towards crime, delinquency and other forms of misconduct, together with insight into aids and hindrances in the realm of prayer, are a rich indication of the value of scientific thinking in deepening our religious experience and enabling it to bring forth fruit in the everyday world in which we live.

Before going into this application in detail, however, it is necessary to go back to a question raised near the beginning, namely, what is the difference between scientific thinking and religious experience? And how can each play its part in the communal life of mankind?

But there is one difficulty which must first be considered. If, as some scientists have held, science leaves no room for the reality of God, then all religious experience, and any attempt to interpret history in the light of the unfolding of a Divine purpose, is illusory. Religious experience on this view is a flight from reality and not a closer approximation to it. So let us first see what evidence we can find, *apart from religious experience itself*, which makes another interpretation possible and which will allow for the reality of God and therefore for conceptions and *mis*conceptions of this Reality.

The question at some stage in the life of every genuine scientific thinker becomes a very real one, not just a matter of academic interest, but a life-and-death struggle within himself. Has the pursuit of Truth, which has illumined so much of his way and led him to realise its ultimate and absolute value, led him to where he must discard his religion? A genuine agnosticism, as Professor Malinowski pointed out, is a tragic and shattering state of mind. And those who have not had to face the issue have no right to find fault with those who have been unable to find a way of reconciling their scientific and religious activity.

The inability to distinguish between the product of our imagination and reality, marks the infancy of the individual and the race. This is at the root of many of the difficulties that arise when factual thinking and symbolic representation are confused. Both of these are involved in all our experience, and symbolic presentation may gather together many facts, the significance of which cannot be perceived by itemising them separately. Whether scientific thinking or religious experience is involved, we must have a clue or a key in our minds to correlate the impact of either sensory or extra-sensory experience. What we are and the state of our body-minds conditions what we can register from outside us, as well as our capacity to respond to the immediate impact of experience.

The query as to whether 'God is dead' illustrates this. When inadequate conceptions of God are seen to be the product of our human imagining, the first reaction may be to say there is no God, God is dead, or God is unreal. This may come with despair, or with relief at the apparent death of a bogey. But this is not an end point. The very nature of reality poses its question again. Can this vast panorama of life, of the starry heavens, the earth on which we live and the millions of our fellow men, really be a soulless, mechanical system, with no over-ruling intelligence, no creative purpose and we ourselves robots within it?

Once when this was a very real question in my own mind, I looked around my room. In it I saw signs of real co-ordination and co-operation instanced by my gas fire, my electric light, and some Japanese prints I love for their beauty. These had involved colour printing in Japan, and shipping to transport them to England, the shop from which they had been bought and the money which enabled me to buy them. This made me realise there is some intelligence available. The result of intelligent purposive and co-operative activity on the part of almost the whole world was actually expressed in my room. This included not only Japanese workmanship, but towels from Cyprus, prints from Egypt and India, chocolate from the cocoa plantations, as well as home products such as gas, electricity, curtains, carpet and furniture. This seemed to imply that *reality responds to the intelligence and good will of men* (the good will is instanced by the co-operation necessary for such a collection of international products of pooled intelligence —they had not just grown like a plant). This seemed to imply there was Reason at the heart of reality, and that a purposive orderly controlling intelligence correlated the forces of nature and the minds of men to make such creativity, productivity and distribution possible. And this surely is what we mean by God, a God who holds all that is together within a unitary purpose.

The words of the late King George V's broadcast at Christmas 1933 came into my mind. 'Unshakeable sanity, invincible patience and tireless good will' were, he said, 'the foundation for seeing us through the difficulties ahead.'

It is a short step to seeing this embodied in Christ on Calvary. For there was a sanity that no outward circumstance broke, a patience that saw it through, and a tireless good will that forgave his crucifiers, pardoned the penitent thief, and provided for his mother. These were real. The reality of Jesus of Nazareth guarantees the reality of human personality and with it the corollary that God cannot be less than that—however much He may transcend it. The reason, patience and good will embodied or incarnate in Christ, were incarnate in a real person. It was not just 'Universal Mind' (which may be a meaningless term) but the mind of Jesus expressing its reality in the process of living through the worst and showing it could not permanently defeat the fundamental purposes of God. In some way Christ seems to guarantee the reality of both God and man, or both dissolve into phantasy. If God is dead in the sense of the whole Universe being inanimate and soulless, a 'fortuitous concourse of atoms', then we could never have become aware of life, love or beauty—we could never have suffered or rejoiced, could never have found either fellowship or enmity with each other. And no sane mind would accept the complete unreality of *all* these.

So there are some grounds for thinking religious experience is not illusory—though illusions may occur within it—and that the Universe is not only fundamentally rational, but good.

Perhaps we can now get clear what is the difference between scientific thinking and religious experience.

Suppose for a moment we had achieved the miracle of universal good-will. Suppose throughout the world all men everywhere desired the good-will of their fellows and were prepared to work and suffer to achieve it, as the best men and women are now. Would that desire, in harmony with the mind of God, who has no favourites, be sufficient to clothe and educate the human race? Would a world that genuinely put personal values highest, a world on a religious basis, be able to dispense with 'scientific thinking' in its attempt to build the Kingdom of God on earth? No!

Throughout life under material conditions we need the kind of knowledge that comes from scientific thinking, which seeks to discover how things behave, and which learns to control the forces or energies we find in nature by understanding. But the attempt to be exact in scientific thinking introduces a definite limitation. If we knew everything about any one thing, we should also know something about everything else, as Tennyson pointed out with his 'flower in a crannied wall'. Since we cannot start by this, we take certain aspects of any object or phenomenon we wish to understand *and for the time being ignore other aspects*. The different natural sciences are the products of extensive knowledge of particular aspects of the universe. These aspects are never found separately in reality, but each of them is found *concurrently* throughout a whole section of experience. Chemistry and physics, for example, both deal with the material universe, though with different aspects of it. The trouble comes when scientists forget they have taken great trouble to isolate some particular aspect in order to investigate its nature. Because they can explain phenomena within the competence of their abstraction without life, consciousness or God, if they then say that life, consciousness and God have no real existence they go beyond their chosen subject matter.

For some purposes scientific knowledge is necessary and reliable, because those aspects which fall outside its range are relatively negligible. The beauty of a picture, for example, is negligible when considering how large a space to reserve for it in a luggage van. Its weight and size are essential. But for the artist, the beauty is primary, weight and size secondary.

This brings us to another way of responding to reality, another aspect of reality. The beauty of an opal is quite as real as its hardness and size; but in complete darkness, with no light to be refracted through it, though its hardness and size are unchanged, the beauty has gone. It does not reside only in itself, but *in itself in a suitable environment*, in this case light. It is not necessary for our purpose here to go into the vexed problem as to whether beauty is in the eye of the beholder, or in the illuminated opal, or the relation between them. It is sufficient to indicate that some elements in the beauty of the opal depend on its capacity for differential refraction of light and that that beauty can only be perceived when suitably illumined; though any beauty of form will still be apprehensible to touch, since shape, size and hardness remain in the absence of light.

Through an appreciation of beauty in nature the artist feels he too illumines an aspect of experience, as much a part of reality as that measured by the scientist. In various forms, poetry or prose, sculpture or painting, he seeks to portray something of the nature of reality as *he* sees it.

Does religious experience reveal yet another aspect? Can we, while utilising all that art and science can tell us, get even deeper into reality in religious experience?

We must take into account as a fundamental fact that human nature will not be satisfied without the expression of emotion and action based on some measure of contact with the unseen ground of our existence.

We might use this to illustrate the difference in the quality of life which responds to God consciously, and reveals by the fruits of that response other human qualities not revealed in the experience of the non-religious man. The latter cuts himself off from the stimulus of the Divine environment, in so far as it depends upon his conscious attitude, and limits himself to such human qualities as depend upon his unconscious dependence, apart from which he would not exist at all.

Otto stressed a unique element in our experience, continuous from grisly demonic horror in the presence of the *felt* unseen to awe in the Presence of the Unspeakably Holy as running throughout our religious experience. Though his emphasis on the supra-rational and wholly other (like all over-simplifications of so complex an experience as the religion of man) tends to ignore other elements equally essential to any mature religion, Otto has done us a great service in bringing to the fore this corrective to our modern tendency to defy our rationality at the expense of the integrity of human personality, which includes affective elements, impervious to reason, yet with a relevance essential to the harmonious development of the individual, as well as to healthy communal life. *Mysterium tremendum, mysterium fascinans*, expresses a deep religious attitude.

Jung also stresses the importance of harmony between these deep-seated affective tendencies and our conscious aims and ideals. Their divergence on the basis of a narrow intellectualism, which repressed the life of feeling as childish, is responsible for many nervous troubles, and for Jung, the problem of their cure is ultimately a religious one.

Whitehead points out that experience includes 'brute alogical fact'. Life is always wider than logic. Two and two only equals four in the realm of mathematical abstraction. The moment actuality is involved an irreducible surd is introduced, and unless insight can take this logically (but not necessarily intuitively) irrational element into account, prediction is always contradicted by experience.

It may be logically absurd to suggest that feeling is the warp that produces the curvature of space-time responsible for material existence:[1] but it is less absurd than suggesting that the fundamental reality on which this phenomenal world is based, or of which it is the expression, riddled as it is with distortions of logical procedure and mathematical inconsistencies, is a passionless mathematician. Feeling must be as integral a part of fundamental or ultimate reality as of the universe in which feeling, creative or destructive, in terms of love or hate, is the great dynamic. God as Father is a more adequate symbol for this than God as a mathematician: though the relation of this eternal ultimate reality to all that exists involves mathematical elements throughout. Love may not be exhaustively expressed by an equation, but it cannot exist apart from a nexus of interrelations which *can* be expressed in mathematical symbols. We falsify reality by ignoring the mathematical and therefore inevitable element in experience as much as by ignoring the qualitative apprehension of that fundamental order which is beauty, goodness or love. Reality is neither quantitative nor qualitative in isolation: but *both are aspects of a universal continuum, within which all that has been, is, or can be, is vitally interrelated*.

In *The Structure of Religious Experience*, Professor J. Macmurray works out very clearly the fundamental nature of the facts of experience on which religion is based. He points out that in science utility dominates; we seek to control and use the forces of nature by insight and understanding, whereas in art intrinsic values matter most. We

---

[1] This is not meant to be taken as a 'scientific' explanation; it is only an illustration to emphasise the absurdity of materialism.

appreciate, contemplate and enjoy things for themselves. But these two attitudes towards experience, both selecting from the world of everyday experience, are transcended in a third attitude which combines both, in which personal relations dominate or are central. This sphere according to Professor Macmurray is the sphere of religion.

When we organise our whole life so that personal relations are genuinely central, so that, in fact, we love our neighbour as ourselves and use our scientific thinking for the common good and dedicate our sense of beauty to bring it within the reach of all, we are living in touch with reality on the level of religion.

It is true, as Macmurray says, that science, art and religion alike claim the whole universe as their field; but it is as if out of this whole experience there are three centres of interest round which science, art and religion develop respectively. But, as he says, *religion is more comprehensive because it includes ourselves and our interrelations with each other, which transcend and transform the natural world considered independently of personal purposes.*

Because personal relations, while actually inescapable, are yet the most difficult to adjust adequately, religion often falls below its high estate and concentrates on tradition or ceremonial, becoming meticulous to fulfil the law, while leaving genuine human needs unsatisfied. Christ was crucified because He put human needs before tradition; because He healed on the Sabbath, for example; because He showed that love for God which was not expressed in the service of our fellow men, was not love of the real God He called Father; because He could take little children and say 'of such is the kingdom of Heaven' and could tell an elder of the Church of His day, a specialist in religion in the most religious nation, that he must be born again before he could even see the Kingdom of God; because He could say the publicans and harlots would go into the Kingdom of Heaven before the self-righteous superior Pharisee; because He spoke in terms of our common humanity, that made the needs of each one of us, however lowly, the concern of Almighty God, irrespective of rank or creed (witness the parable of the Good Samaritan); because He lived and worked within the common round of human toil, and instead of claiming exemption as leader, washed the feet of His disciples, which each was too proud to do for the other. In all this He showed that in meeting real human needs, in doing 'the job that is under our nose, with the tools that come to our hands, we find ourselves in fellowship with Christ, who was always moved to compassion by the sufferings of others; and find through this we are fellow workers with God, within the sphere of true religion.

Professor Macmurray points out the combination of utilitarian and intrinsic valuation in religion. He says:

'Religion has always been associated with the need that men have felt for help and assistance, and part of the religious attitude has always looked upon religion as a practical means of achieving its end. But it is equally certain that religion has always looked upon its activities as important in themselves, imbued with an intrinsic value of their own. Primitive religious ceremonial is both an expression of the sense of beauty and a means of securing the welfare of the tribe. The Lord who is to be worshipped in the beauty of holiness is also a very present help in times of trouble. Christianity has always insisted on the absolute intrinsic value of the individual. But it has also equally insisted that his value lies in doing the will of God and making himself the instrument of a divine purpose.'[1]

The field of religious experience is the sphere of personal relations. Where these are the centre of valuation, we ask not how much money will this produce, but what quality of manhood will it develop, what range of fellowship will it make possible? We then inevitably come into contact with God on the level of personality and cannot rest content

[1] J. Macmurray, *The Structure of Religious Experience* (Faber), p. 34.

with a God who is less than personal. We may bow defiantly before a god of Force: we can worship a God who loves. And in proportion as our worship is sincere, we combine the paradoxes we mentioned previously. For an apprehension of God, worshipped spontaneously, as the Supreme Value, brings with it a measure of communion which *is* the help in time of trouble and involves a realisation of fellowship which fulfils the will of God for men.

Scientific thinking, though it abstracts certain aspects of experience, is tested throughout by its correspondence with experience. When once it ceases to bring its abstractions and hypotheses to the test of experiment and experience, it ceases to be scientific thinking and becomes speculative.

So with religious experience. *Unless it illumines and is effective within the sphere of personal life and history, individual and racial, it fails to be religious.* Any speculations as to future life in another world that are not based upon genuine insight into experience and actuality in *this life* are doomed to an illusory existence within the mind of the dreamer who postulated them, because he had neither the courage nor the sincerity to find God within the everyday life of the world in which we are so placed that we may learn to know and love God as He is, and not as our childish phantasies may desire Him to be.

It is true that our ideas or images of God are inadequate and fall short of the Reality. Our ideas may be only symbolical, but the symbols refer to that which is real and the very ground from which our symbolism springs. We are hearing much about the importance of our image of God today. Our images may represent or misrepresent the inner reality of our experience of God. Even to say 'there is no God' is to have an image of God in our minds which is being rejected as having no existence beyond or outside our minds. It is an image of something to which we deny any reality in its own right. Nevertheless, if we think this through, we find it involves contact with a deeper or truer expression of the mind of God which is destroying false or misleading images of its nature.

Hence such symbols may be dynamic, bridging the gulf between the finite and the infinite, so that they are not wholly and antithetically separated, but fall within a unitary comprehension; such dynamic symbolism, for example, as that of the Kingdom of God allows for the dependence of created being and the supremacy of God in perfect harmony. Such symbolism Plato considered to be essential to express the nature of ultimate realities, beyond the grasp of the discursive intellect. For him effective symbolism, while it could not express exhaustively the nature of reality involved, was essentially related to it and thus was a medium for revelation.

If Plato had lived after Christ and carried this idea further in the light of personality, he would have found in the Incarnation the completion of the process of symbolism, through which the Divine Mind revealed itself at last as perfectly personal. The religious response to Reality would then find its fulfilment in communion with the Christ, who had thus embodied the symbol in life, and not merely in thought, and thus united men with the God to whom they owed their origin.

THE SCIENCE OF MEDICINE AND THE ART OF HEALING

Some years ago the late Professor J. Mackenzie wrote an article in the *British Weekly* on 'An Abuse of Religion'. In this he referred to the dangers of spiritual healing. He quoted Paul Tillich as having said 'Faith healing as practised by many groups, is one of the worst abuses of religion today. When faith becomes a medical tool, it is magic.'

Much that goes by the name of faith healing is due to suggestion, which is all the more effective if it is believed to be directly due to God. This may, as Professor Mackenzie rightly realises, mask the personal conflicts which were at the root of the disease; the last state may well then be worse than the first when the conflicts break through once more unresolved. Christ himself realised this, when he referred to the fact that unless the ground was well tilled between, after having cast out one devil others would come back into the empty, garnished house. Positive aims must replace the old ones for healing to be permanent.

If, however, religious faith is used as a medical tool, it betrays its real nature; *faith is not a tool, it is a quality of being which brings us into touch with spiritual resources which enhance personality and enable it to transcend some of the conflicts which on lower levels give rise to disease.* Any healing which follows this is not an 'adjunct to medicine'. It involves the re-orientation to life, which may produce as definite therapeutic results physically as the anger of a nursing mother may give rise to toxins which can upset the baby fed at her breast.

It is important to realise that the medical profession has not the monopoly of the healing and creative forces of the universe. We are *people*, not diseases. The structure of personality, as Professor Mackenzie points out, plays a vital part in health and in its breakdown leads to some forms of disease. Religion in its true form is vital to health. As Professor C. G. Jung, who was probably the world's best known psychiatrist, has said in his most quoted statement, 'Out of many hundreds of patients coming from all parts of the civilised world, there was not one among them whose problem was not, in the last resort, that of finding a religious outlook on life.' Still more significantly he adds, 'none of them has been really healed who did not regain his religious outlook'.[1]

If a healer can evoke this, he goes beyond the realm of magic and brings a spiritual health that goes beyond the frequent placebo use of barbiturates by doctors, which also mask personal conflicts instead of resolving them.

It is of course true that not everyone is willing to face up to their own personal conflicts, and the effect this has on their life and health. Ways of escape are just as frequent in appealing to a doctor as they are in going to a healer. Not all who apply for help either to doctor or to spiritual healer are really seeking health and wholeness. They are seeking relief from symptoms without the desire to change their way of life which gave rise to those symptoms. But it is necessary to recognise that this is just as true in the case of the great majority of those who go to doctors, as it is of any of those who seek the less orthodox means of cure. Some of the latter are, in fact, seeking newness of life and not mere relief from symptoms, and the results of healers with a big reputation show that some influence is being brought to bear upon them which does issue in a higher quality of

[1] *Modern Man in Search of a Soul* (Routledge), pp. 264–265.

life. If this were not so, numbers of people would not go to these particular people. It is because they find fresh life, even though all their symptoms may not be removed, that they realise something new has come into their experience, through a personality dedicated to mediate that particular quality of life to others. It is not always realised that training in healing work is undertaken seriously by those who seek to do more than help one or two individuals in their own immediate neighbourhood. Such training usually follows having discovered some capacity for relieving pain or helping a person to get better, bringing courage or hope, and then seeking to see, 'Well, how did that happen? What can I do to see that it happens more often?' And somehow, in this seeking, they find others have gone before them and have found various ways of tuning in to some level of their own psyche which is more open to the needs of others than the average ego-centred psyche of the individual. Such a capacity for being open to the needs of another in such a way that help can reach the other through them, is not an abnormality, as at some times it has been supposed to be. It is a very real level of the psyche which goes beyond the aim of mere self-preservation or social prestige. Those who are healers very rarely realise how their own personality plays a part in mediating healing forces—healing influences might perhaps be a better word—to others. In some this is below the level of self-consciousness, yet in others it is obviously very far ahead of the average degree of self-consciousness, which has a limited area of responsibility and a complete unawareness of the real needs of others who might be helped through them or who may be hindered through them. There is an art in healing, as well as a science.

There is at the present time a very real conflict within the medical profession itself as to two different ways of approaching the many problems involved in the health of communities who are inevitably affecting each other and affected by each other, by large-scale activities as well as by personal reaction. A polluted water supply, for example, may affect a whole population and nothing that they can do individually can avoid having this effect. The polluted water has to be cleansed and further pollution avoided if the health of that community is to be regained and then maintained. Another very important distinction here is that doctors have been trained to look for the specific element in any disease. A very great deal has come through researches which have involved tremendous patience and research to isolate the different types of germ that produced similar symptoms in different patients. There is no going back on this, medical work in this field has made discoveries that in some cases enable us to rule out certain types of disease if we are prepared to take the necessary steps to deal with the conditions which give rise to them. But this is not the whole story. It has been found throughout the ages that under somewhat similar external conditions, people will differ in their reactions to them, some will get better, and some will die, from an apparently similar infection or accident. The personal factor comes into play. Someone who wishes to get well as quickly as possible to get back to a job he wants to finish or to pick up the responsibilities of a family of whom he is genuinely fond and about whom he is concerned, will recover very much quicker than someone who is being taken out of a difficult environment by his illness and who dreads having to go back to it when he is better. These of course are commonplaces. The issue is rarely as simple as that, but it does show that under certain conditions personal reactions may influence the course even of physically caused disease.

It is to deal with these personal reactions that modern psychiatry developed, but it sometimes, like the Christian Scientists, has gone to other extremes and tended to conclude that all illness must come through these personal conflicts and personal differences, and has thrown too great a burden of responsiblity on the individual patients. We need here a middle way, a way that recognises that body, mind and spirit are a unity, they are not three separate entities, interacting with each other; the human being is a unity, a functional unity, with physical, mental and spiritual characteristics, with opportunities for interacting with and responding to a physical world, a mental world, and perceiving a spiritual significance in the whole of experience which includes these various worlds within a unity. This latter is a religious activity, it takes a whole man to realise it and respond to an element of wholeness in the universe.

The difference that is important is that doctors themselves differ as to the emphasis they lay upon these various factors. Some are certain that only the physical ones count, that all mental and spiritual phenomena, which they accept as phenomena, are by-products, so to speak, of physical functioning. To doctors of this school, any attempt to heal through either mind or spirit is doomed to failure; they cannot see that they can have any effect upon the physical situation or condition, they can only influence what to them is an unreal epiphenomenon, and thus act only within a narrow sphere within an individual and not in reality itself. On the other hand, those doctors who have found that most profound physical disturbances can be influenced and affected by mental and spiritual activities are sure that these are more fundamental in the long run than a physical substratum of personality through which our minds function within a universe which allows for and expresses the reality of spiritual experience. It is only from the context of this wider background that we can realise the difficulties there are today in real communication and understanding between people without medical training who have found in experience that their type of approach does produce results, but are not aware of how many complicated inter-relations they are bringing into play and which a doctor, trained in his own way, recognises. Each becomes to some extent a master of his own approach, his own cross section of reality, but just because of that his terminology is conditioned by the nature of that cross section, and it is very difficult even for medical specialists to understand each other—let alone those without a medical training. On certain points, of course, they will all agree, but on many others they will find divergence and differences of opinion which make for very different types of treatment, and which can help or hinder patients accordingly.

If then a healer can show that in a certain proportion of his cases given up on the medical side things do happen, we need to understand why this is so, and how to make such help available without the slur of dabbling in magic or losing one's balance in theories which may or may not be relevant to the actual fact of contact on a deeper level of the psyche, through the psyche of the healer, with forces that are available for all but not yet recognised or utilised by all.

A rather important point was raised also by Professor Mackenzie. He had read Harry Edwards' answer to some comments on his work from the British Medical Association and he had not been very much impressed by these. He also said that he was not impressed by his discussion on television with a leading medical specialist—his sincerity, he said, was obvious, but so also was his lack of knowledge of the diseases that he was treating. It seems to me that this was inevitable. Harry Edwards had tried to get medical co-operation with his work, he knew he was producing results that should be able to be recognised and vouched for by doctors, but no one who is not a doctor can diagnose certain physical diseases which are expressed much more precisely in a medical diagnosis than the symptomatic description which any patient can give. Harry Edwards therefore was not in a position of being able to produce cases that had been adequately vetted by doctors, and this is because the medical profession at present is very strongly against its members co-operating with non-medically trained people. A doctor who openly works with a spiritual healer of the type of Harry Edwards, does run a risk of being deprived of his practice in the sphere of medicine. This seems to me to be a real tragedy. The greatest need is to pool our knowledge from all angles of approach, and we can only eliminate the dangers and the superstitions attached to more primitive attempts when we are prepared to investigate those which very obviously go beyond the primitive and are actually producing cures that at present cannot be duplicated within the medical world in the precise way in which they are produced outside it. One of the very simplest of these which has become a commonplace is that a wart may disappear through the suggestion of some country woman with a private recipe for it, which will not be cured by a doctor except by actual cauterisation. We do not always realise that the vascular changes that have to take part to bring about the reduction and disintegration of a wart are probably equally capable of bringing about the reduction and disintegration of cancerous tissue. If this was more fully realised we would be turning far more of our energies into trying to see how to produce a curative effect without direct medication. It must come through some effect upon the mind of the person which is expressed within the organism which includes the wart or the cancer. If we could spend some of the vast sums that go into physical research on a study of such cases in conjunction with those who have some capacity for influencing this more primitive substratum of our being, we might find a clue that would lead not only to the cure of cancer, but what is much more important, to its prevention.

People like Harry Edwards and Elsie Salmon have, I think, jumped a gulf, and shown us that there is something on the other side which must be taken into account, without building the bridge across which would take a two-way traffic of mutual understanding and effective co-operation between their non-physical methods of healing, and the medical approach and diagnosis. The bridge for communication between them and orthodox doctors may take some time to build. Their pre-suppositions are different, and they also differ from each other and from many others who produce results which—to their patients at least— are satisfying and satisfactory. This difficulty of communication, however, does not only arise between qualified medical practitioners and unorthodox healers. Even within psychiatry itself schools of thought differ, and some rely on physical means, insulin and electric shock, and even lobotomy, where others lean towards psychological methods. Both, as we have seen, produce some results; all have many failures; but without experience of depth analysis their medical colleagues fail to understand what their analytical fellows mean by the very terms they use, so it is not surprising if they fail to understand the approach and terminology of a—to them—so alien philosophy of those who heal or seek to do so, through prayer, faith, or intuitive or telepathic contact with some non-incarnate but intelligent focus of spiritual life, with whom a measure of communication is actually possible.

Any doctor now who came from a post-mortem with unwashed hands and clothes to deliver an expected baby would be highly censured. Yet for a time doctors were themselves carrying in this way the infection which led to so many deaths from puerperal fever in childbirth, and they fought against the recognition that the way to prevention lay in utter cleanliness and the sterilisation of all instruments used. So perhaps now doctors may not realise that they sometimes produce chronic cases by closing the door to hope. I heard one doctor say to a patient, 'You are a chronic, you cannot hope to get better, you must accept it.'

Yet that patient recovered through refusing to accept it and determining to find some way through.

Elsie Salmon and Harry Edwards, Dorothy Kerin and of course many more, open the door to hope, and fresh resources can sometimes come into play that have been blocked by the fatalism of a doctor. It does not of course always happen; but our urgent need today is to pool all resources for healing or making whole, which is as much a religious concern as a medical one.

Doctor Arthur Guirdham, in *A Theory of Disease,* points out that some doctors have healing qualities or capacities which are integrally related to their personality, independently of their technical knowledge and skill. This is, I think, true, and it applies to many who are not doctors or nurses but who seem to have the knack of this deep inter-action with those who seek their help, which does bring into play their own resources to fight against disease due to an invasion by microbe, or to face up to their personal conflicts and difficulties creatively. This openness to deeper resources from within the human psyche which brings it into relation to resources from beyond the indivi-dual, is probably innate. Where it is present, training into the right use of it can follow, but it is not likely to be pos-sible to train it in some in whom it is too undeveloped to be a practical way of utilising their life and energies and mak-ing their contribution to society. We all realise the difference between creative musicians who may be able to produce symphony after symphony that others can play, and those who may not only be unable to play but unable even to appreciate it. These differences in capacity, while they may be modified by training, for better or for worse, are inherent in the differentiation of types within humanity. Other things being equal, a person is likely to be most efficient, most effective and happiest in some occupa-tion which allows expression to inherent capacities that are essentially a part of his own make up, and correspondingly the frustration of deep-seated capacities is likely to lead to very disgruntled and dissatisfied lives. If we can see this, we may be able to utilise more adequately the scientific knowledge that results from accurate diagnosis of types of disease and the application of these principles and practices by those who also can reach the human being in whom some disturbance has been too much for the total integrity of the body, mind and spirit unity and more or less completely incapacitating illness has followed.

We will later on consider the part played by stress diseases in modern life, but for the moment the point I wish to make is that medical science itself can only advance by exploring fresh avenues and not by closing doors on potentialities beyond the range of its immediate comprehension. The keynote here, as has been said before, is that we are not 'diseases' but *people*. Man cannot live by bread alone; nor by medicine alone. Life itself is primary, and we have by no means exhausted its potentialities, either physically, psychologically, psychically or spiritually. In all outstanding healers we have glimpses at times of the break-through of a divine compassion that reminds us of Christ's own healing ministry. We need to seek how to correlate these with the steady persistent work of the medical profession, which is pushing back the boundaries of disease every day. As 'allies and not enemies' much more might be done to enable those concerned to know to which kind of help a particular patient is most likely to respond.

Some bridges of understanding in the overlapping fields of medical, psychological and religious healing were outlined in my book *New Concepts of Healing*[1] as well as in *Bridges of Understanding* which followed it.

Studies in Spiritual Healing[2] followed this up in a rather different way. The outstanding work of a few people

[1] Hodder and Stoughton.
[2] The World Fellowship Press.

35

whose impact has been such as to win a world wide recognition was outlined. *This is something that cannot be ignored.* Such capacities are as outstanding as that of creative genius in music or art, but they must be comparable in kind with the lesser-developed capacities of others which may through training and experience in time develop a more comprehensive though less spectacular service through the general utilisation of whatever principles we find to be involved in these outstanding activities. This would then be comparable to the way in which a doctor, who has to have a certain degree of intelligence to be able to master the various subjects involved in the medical curriculum, can actually be trained to become a doctor and practise as such with the whole body of medical knowledge behind him and the whole resources of the medical world available to him to call upon for specialised work when at some point he realises the need for this as a supplement to his own.

It is very understandable that doctors who have qualified in this way, who have realised that their results are subject to criticism and comment by colleagues of similar capacity, who have to justify their treatment to those who understand what is involved, do hesitate to allow the non-medically trained person to enter into their sphere of work. It is not only understandable, it is desirable that they should be hesitant to accept at first innovations that come from outside. What is not either desirable or compatible with their expressed aim of meeting the needs of patients first, is to reject out of hand contributions from other sources when today it is obvious that no one man and no one kind of training can include all the knowledge that is pouring into our modern world through so many channels of research which cannot be assimilated by any one mind. The great call to-day is to be flexible enough to be prepared to investigate the new with an open mindedness that can enable it to function and at the same time a sufficiently critical attitude to be able to disentangle naïve assumptions as to what is at work through a perhaps lesser or differently trained mind from that which is actually producing its results. We are being bombarded from many sides with claims for all sorts of spectacular results, which may in the long run do harm to the true spiritual healing which brings insight and maturity to the individual. As I have said elsewhere, any doctor in his surgery in an evening might be hard put to it to justify his activities for so many patients by the results; yet every doctor realises that what he does within his surgery is playing a small but vital part within the health of the community. Even though he may not cure, in the real sense of the word, a single patient within that session, he is helping many to respond or go in the direction towards health and checking their downgrade tendencies.

So with healers, an atmosphere of hope, a hope that does not close the door and yet at the same time does not make exorbitant demands for spectacular results, may do very much to help towards overcoming the apathy, despair and disillusionment that is issuing in so much melancholia, and so many split minds, today. The doctor is associated in the public mind with disease, the appeal of the healer is that he is associated with the idea of life, of healing, of cure. I am not saying that either of these are deliberately thought out by the public but it is obvious that the difference is there. It is also there on the religious side amongst the vast majority who think that if a priest is called in the person must be dying, and who do not realise that prayer is not just something to be brought into play at death or in a crisis but an attitude of mind and spirit that may make all the difference to the quality of living every day through whatever exigencies, mishaps or misfortunes may arise.

We have here therefore a two-fold problem. One is a measure of communication which it is essential to build between members of different professions who all have some part to play in the health of the community. This applies to educationalists as well as the healers and doctors. A common approach would make a very great difference to the effect of their work instead of so frequently neutralising that of each other. Healing and education cannot be wholly separated, as every doctor realises, in the growth of children. A child has to acquire certain skills, both physical and intellectual, in order to be able to live as a human being and move about actively; his growth towards his own physical and spiritual potential depends upon being adequately trained to utilise whatever functions are available at each state of growth. The mother here can develop healthy capacities by right training, or can lay the foundations for much ill-health subsequently through faulty education. So here again we see that there is an overlapping of functions in human life, and that health is not the concern of doctors only. They are concerned with some aspects of it and must be more prepared in future, I think, to co-operate with other resources, other associations which are also involved in the quality of human living.

The second problem of communication is that between those who are in a position to lead, either as doctors, as clergy, as teachers, as healers, or as writers who write from an educational rather than a inspirational or fictional point of view, and those for whom their specialisation exists. The doctor must be able to communicate to his patient enough to enable the patient, not to become a doctor, *but to become more fully himself*. The teacher must bring out the capacities of a child and train him so that that child may be free from internal inhibitions to express and develop his capacities within some sphere of the world in which he can earn a living by skills that he has acquired. The minister of religion, whether priest or minister, must similarly be able to impart to his congregation or to those who come to him for counsel sufficient to enable such individuals or congregations to fulfil their own function in the whole and not to usurp his. Here, I think, there is a very real problem involved. The idea of the religious vocation has been too narrowly conceived, and in many cases it is assumed that the official minister is more holy an individual than those who are expressing their vocation in other fields. This is not necessarily true. There are vocations in other directions which are as fully expressive of the spirit as that of the minister, but they are different vocations, and each man or woman is judged not by that which is not their own real sphere of living, but by what they are able to effect within that which is their sphere. We need, as I showed in *Bridges of Understanding,* the sanctification of secular life, the recognition that all that contributes towards the wholeness and the harmony of living has its rightful part in the Kingdom of God. This brings the technical knowledge of the doctor within the same universe of discourse as the earning of a living in any other way which can be dedicated to God, and through which some function within the human community is carried on more effectively by those who are whole, who are integrated, than by those who are at loggerheads within themselves with emotional conflict that saps their energies and makes of them disruptive forces within society. It is to deal with the latter, the emotionally immature or the emotionally disorganised, that psychiatry has developed. It is also probable that healers may be able to reorient such a personality, without the technical knowledge of a psychiatrist, through the integrity of their own personality. It is recognised that in the home the mother who is herself happily married, finding real sexual satisfaction and fulfilment through her husband, and who is emotionally mature in her attitude towards the children, can give them a balance and an atmosphere within which to grow up, which is of far more value than any amount of technical knowledge through a Psychiatric Social Worker which has to be imparted through some mother who is unsatisfied sexually and who is incapable of that intuitive rapport which enables her to sense its real needs and respond to them spontaneously.

I am sure we are only on the fringe of the recognition of the importance of the quality of personality and the necessity for its maturing if we are ever to win a peace in the world that can enable people at different stages of development and different degrees of culture to participate within the commonwealth of the world which sooner or later must be achieved. We have reached the point at which major conflicts between millions grouped in nationalistic camps in opposition, are not only nationally but racially suicidal. The next step is not just the British Commonwealth of Nations, but a World Commonwealth of Nations and within this Commonwealth there must be a common faith in the ultimate values of spirit, which can be expressed in very different forms, but *which has its roots in the very nature of the reality within which we find ourselves*. The crucial issue of our times hinges on this recognition of spiritual values which are *inherent in reality*, not values that we have to create, but to which we can respond, values which we find express in the long run something deep within us which is baffled and bewildered so long as it is in antagonism to others. On the level of multiplicity there can be no harmony; every kind of life fights for its own maintenance; on the level of the unity of life there can be harmony amongst competing interests, each of which has something to give and something to receive from others. The health of the world is not just a matter of individuals in isolation. It involves a co-operation between many at different ages and stages of development, and both the science and the art of healing in medicine include this attitude towards increasing health and maturity of personality through social and cultural activities as well as through medical or surgical techniques. This may be one of the lessons that we can learn from the outstanding healer who is as yet unable to build the bridge between the scientific approach to the problem of life and health, and his own more intuitive one. We may get guidance through these as to the way in which we can prepare the environment in which health is more likely to occur, and minimise and eliminate some of the factors which make for frustration and illness.

It is again important in assessing any new or unusual form of approach to be able to distinguish between the sincerity of the person who is inevitably bound to express it in terms of his own experience, and the possibility of retranslating his interpretations into other forms without impugning his own integrity or the reality of his achievements in the lives of others. The real bugbear of the conflict between both medicine and religion and various forms of healing work lies in the fact that any criticism that does not allow for the reality of something that cannot be doubted by the person is taken for granted as uninformed; it is just as true from the side of medicine as it is for religion. If it can be recognised more widely that all our forms of communication have different meanings to people of a different background, and can be re-translated without impugning the reality behind the symbol, our modern Tower of Babel could be greatly reduced. It is, as I discovered many years ago when working with doctors and clergy, a primary need not to convert each other, but to *understand* each other. The need for bridges of understanding on every level of life is one of the most urgent if the peace of the world and the harmony of nations are ever to be achieved.

A very simple illustration of this was given once, when an American and a Frenchman saw a dog. The Frenchman referred to it as *chien* and the American as *dog*. One of them said to the other, 'Well, to think that after all that is *chien*'; the other retaliated, 'It is not *chien*, it is a *dog*', and the reality of the animal which these different words described and meant to the individual was ignored. We must reach behind our symbols to the reality involved if understanding is to be achieved. Language is more important than is commonly realised; every tribe that has developed culture at all, on even primitive levels, develops an insight into certain aspects of experience for which it coins words. Tribes with a different experience in different parts of the world without that experience, coin words that cover different associations on some level that matters to them. If these two meet they may use words, even if they once learn each other's language, in such different senses that confusion arises. A very great deal of the misunderstanding of the present world situation is due to that fact that different nations use words, even when translated into a language which is understood by both, in different senses because behind their interpretation of the word there is *a different level of experience*. This, as I have shown before, is at the root of many of the misunderstandings and the mutual distrust of doctors and those who seek to help or heal from another angle.

We need to realise more fully than the human race has yet done, that our symbols are only partial representations of a reality that is greater than we have as yet apprehended. One of the big differences in specialised technical education is the development of a 'jargon' which conveys a great deal more to those who have mastered it than it can possibly do to others. But it also raises barriers that need not perhaps be so great between those who have developed an equally complicated but dissimilar jargon. It is not perhaps always realised that an electron, for example, doesn't actually exist. No one can understand what an electron is without sufficient understanding of mathematics to be able to realise it as a probability of something happening in a certain way at a certain place at a certain time. Yet by understanding it in this way, abstraction though it is from our experience, the probabilities on a statistical scale are such that we can rely upon the whole development of electronics in modern life through those people who are able to translate their mathematical insights and terminology back into a world that includes the activities of what for *their* purpose they call electrons. If we can in this way realise that neither atoms nor electrons exist in isolation, that they are cross sections of reality symbolised by the human mind, and that the symbols have to be checked again and again experimentally, within the context of nature, we might be much more able to understand how people like Harry Edwards or Elsie Salmon or other healers for example, may be unable to translate their symbolism of the particular forces with which they seem to be in touch into language that can be understood by others without that kind of experience. It is helpful to realise that this difficulty applies both from the side of science and from that of religion.

Bertrand Russell complained at one stage that the mystic vision wasn't something that everybody could see, and that what he failed to see he distrusted and therefore disbelieved in it. What he failed to realise was, that there is as much skill in acquiring the capacity to perceive within the invisible world of realities that are at least as relevant to our experience as electrons, through the discipline of the mind that so seeks to apprehend them. The mystic vision has occurred in so many ages, races and times independently, with certain features sufficiently in common, for us to recognise that there is some *common* experience, although every such mystic must translate his experience into symbols relevant to the culture within which he is living, since he has no other language available. So the language of the healer who is in a half-way house so to speak, or half-way condition, between the individual patient he seeks to help and whatever forces within the universe come into the range of his perception and response, may use symbols that are very inadequate to describe the realities that actually show in the results that follow. I am trying as far as possible in this to indicate that here are forces that come into play, or influences that are brought to bear, when spirit with spirit meets, when some level of the psyche is open to the impact of other minds, which are not available to those who are not prepared to develop the necessary skill to perceive and the steady persistent training to act on such perception reliably. I am not staking a claim for any particular interpretation of these as yet; there is not only too much divergence of opinion even as to what actually happens, but also too much divergence of interpretation. But the very something which is, so to speak, knocking at our door in this generation is, I think, shown by the prevalence of such activities independently in many parts of the world with people of different religions, different cultures, and different nationalities. There is some awakening of the human psyche to another range of experience, and it is essential that we should learn how to correlate this with our everyday activities. It is shown, as indicated in *Bridges of Understanding*, in the development of para-psychology, psychical research and spiritualism as well as in psychiatry and psychotherapy within medicine. Here our great need is to be humble learners until we discover the laws of behaviour which are expressed within this realm of human activity, which goes beyond the mechanical cause and effect which have already been shown to be inadequate on the physical level itself. As I said a long time ago, the answers to some of the problems in physics at its boundary situation may come through para-psychology and the spiritual healer, but they will only come if, instead of deprecating the crudity of expression which may jar against the meticulous detail of the scientist, we seek to realise what is behind and beyond the symbols the healer uses to express *something which does affect our mundane world*.

I was criticised for using an example of a case quoted by Dr Rebecca Beard in which a cancer disappeared within a night—a cancer of 38 pounds with no discharge of material. It was vouched for by Dr Beard herself and by the doctor who was attending the case, and a medical friend of mine said he thought it would be wiser not to include that kind of example, there was obviously no way in which this could have happened. Later I discovered that one of the examples given at Lourdes, which was vouched for by the very stringent medical examinations there, included a similar case with a tumour of 23 pounds disappearing. This linked on in my own mind to the phenomena of materialisation and de-materialisation, which have been explored within psychical research. There is a link here somewhere and we must find it. Two examples of my own on a very much smaller scale, may perhaps be relevant. I was on one occasion joining in prayer with a priest who was developing a capacity for spiritual healing for another at a distance. At the time it so happened that I had an abscess under my arm which the doctor was going to lance the next day. I said nothing about this and was not thinking of it at the time of praying, but suddenly, as with the woman in the biblical story who touched the hem of Christ's garment and suddenly perceived that she was healed, I realised this was healed. I was not seeking healing for it, I was not asking for it nor had I mentioned it, yet next morning there was no trace of that abscess and there was no matter that had come from it; it had disappeared like the cancer. A second example where again there was no thought of seeking help for myself, came indirectly when I was praying for a child with a high temperature. I realised of course that within a few days her temperature would go down as it does in children, but it did rather matter, as it happened, that it should go down quickly, because it otherwise would interfere with the holiday arrangements for the whole family. The child was nearly two hundred miles away. The whole of my energy was focused upon being the channel that would get in touch with her, which would hold the line in contact with her, and whatever forces are available through prayer for healing in such cases. As I realised the contact was made and knew she had taken a turn for the better, I suddenly became aware of a cold current through my left ankle which as it happened was swollen and inflamed after a sprain. Again there was in my mind no thought whatever of seeking the help for myself, but that inflammation went down. The strained ligament is still slightly strained and the foot doesn't wholly go back into its position, but that inflammation went with that cold circulation at the moment when I was aware of having touched both the child for whom I was praying and forces that go beyond the range of my own vital organism. These two examples are perhaps small in comparison with some of the cases that are quoted in literature concerned with this, but they are I think significant as coming through a mind which has had scientific training and also a psychological one, and has spent so many years trying to build bridges of understanding between all forms of life, health and wholeness that can bring peace and harmony into the world and health to the individuals within it.

It shows that it is still possible to retain one's critical intellect and use it to the full without blocking the way to creative forces that have first to be allowed to express themselves in whatever forms become possible, before criticism can evaluate their significance for the whole of our experience.

We have all so much to learn here, but we can only learn, as Professor Soal remarked some time ago in the *Hibbert Journal*, when people who have received the benefits or the privilege of an education also develop their own psychical capacities to the limit of their own make-up and so enable us to deal with the spontaneous occurrences that happen more frequently, possibly, among the less cultured elements, or less educated elements of the communities involved, because they have no articulated knowledge to put up as a barrier between their own experience and the unknown. It is more difficult for the fully trained doctor, for example, to hold in abeyance this critical faculty long enough *for new facts to register in ways that seem alien to his previous experience*; but until he can so stand aside to allow them to register, he will never get the full interpretation and integration of such experiences with the steadily growing body of knowledge through which the experiences of millions are pooled and focused within this particular profession which is primarily concerned with the healing of disease.

This does not mean asking any doctor to be credulous; nor does it ask him to suspend his judgement permanently; it does ask for every doctor to be capable of suspending that judgement until he has got at the facts. This, from his own disciplines of course, is very obvious. Of anything on his own medical line he will say, 'I cannot tell you what that is until I have taken certain tests and have got the results'; he bases his judgement not upon a naïve apprehension, but upon the results of ascertainable variations which he has been trained to obtain and assimilate. But he does not always realise that in the same way he must be prepared to allow facts of another order of experience to impinge upon his technical knowledge, in such a way that he can eventually relate them to what he himself knows. There must be, as I pointed out from another angle in *Bridges of Understanding,* a suspension of judgement until he is aware of what his judgement is to be exercised upon, and then an assessing of that both in the light of what this had brought into focus and of his own experience. If we could get doctors who genuinely would work with either spiritual healers or clergy who are working on this line, not as at present each specialising on his own, but genuinely trying to see how to correlate the different activities of the other, we might begin to see how to educate the public in such a way that so many of our diseases, both social and individual, could be eliminated. The keynote for the future obviously lies in some form of re-education of the human race. It has reached the climax of dissociation with hydrogen bombs produced by Christian nations, which shows there has been a split in the human mind, which has gone on two separate lines. The bridging of this is essential if we are to use our technical knowledge in such a way as to help humanity in its growth towards maturity and not reduce it to either robots in a totalitarian state or robots under a scientific dictatorship, instead of a fellowship of human beings, each of whom has mastered some speciality in order to be able to make his contribution reliably to the community through that. This is going to include a very much wider range of specialisation than has at present been recognised.

In *Studies in Spiritual Healing* I described as nearly as possible in the terms of the people who are practitioners or exponents of some particular point of view, some complementary ways of cutting into and evoking capacities that apart from those ways, go over our heads without our realising their existence, just as for so many hundreds of years electricity, though it could be realised as being present in lightning and rubbing amber, could not be utilised by man. When we realise the next ranges of force that are coming into play through human personality, we may in time be able to call upon the resources of a spiritual background to human life as reliably as we now can use a telephone to ring up somebody here. There is enough evidence to justify opening our minds to seeing how to paint a picture of the universe which includes such resources in harmony with our everyday realities through which our human lives have to be lived. It is not a question of superseding the natural by something that is supernatural, it is a question of finding the place of the natural within a universe which has produced people like ourselves, capable of asking questions such as 'What does it all mean? Where are we all going? What part do we play in a universe in which we are beginning to discover things that were happening millions and millions of years ago in distant stars, which we can recognise now?' The stage is set for a very much more comprehensive viewpoint of reality and everyone who is at all awake in spirit can play some part in building bridges of understanding between their own kind of experience and that of others, in so far as they respect the integrity of others and do not seek to impose their own view on anyone else. It takes all the viewpoints in the world to make up the world. It is probable that there is ahead of humanity a very great extension of harmony to be achieved within the next two or three generations, now that the barriers on the physical level have been transcended by radio-communication, television, air travel, and so on, so that we are bound to mix with each other, instead of each developing in isolation.

Though at first this brings conflict, in the long run we have to learn how to live together in some measure of harmony, if we are to survive on earth at all.

The sphere of healing is one that affects and concerns everyone. It is therefore of fundamental importance to seek to bring harmony within it as a step towards achieving effective co-operation on an international scale.

D

3

SOME ASPECTS OF LIFE, HEALTH AND CULTURE

Much work from many quarters is showing the need for a radical overhaul of our conceptions of the nature of health and the value or dis-value of varying 'patterns' of life, of health and of disease. Special emphasis will be given to some such approaches which are not as yet very widely known. From very different starting points and specialised training, they reach conclusions and insights which may throw light on the present situation, with its wide range of contrasts and insecurities, in the midst of great advances of knowledge in some directions.

Arthur Guirdham is a psychiatrist who in his book *A Theory of Disease* has shown that this depends not only on the quality of the individual, but on the degree of importance attached to personality and to a large extent on the religious and philosophic outlook of the community in which he finds himself. He considers that contagious fevers and terminal illnesses are more natural forms of disease. Whereas psychosomatic and neurotic forms of illness are the result of the excessive development of the cult of personality.

Hans Selye has been working on the nature of stress disease from the physical and endocrinological side. These are brought together in this chapter because, though they start from opposite ends of the scale, so to speak, they have reached conclusions which tend to confirm and support each other. This seems very desirable in view of the great increase in our knowledge in the fields of psychiatry and psychosomatic medicine. These show how widespread such troubles are. Moreover the various spiritual adjuncts to healing are also showing that another dimension of our experience is involved in the problem of life and health.

No one can master the detail of any one of these approaches. But all doctors and those concerned with healing in its various forms should have sufficient knowledge of the outline or 'grade of significance' of such detailed studies to recognise when the need is on either primarily psychiatric, endocrinological or spiritual levels, and perhaps in due course on a psychical level.

To adumbrate the latter, some references will be made later to the work of Dr L. Bendit, a psychiatrist, and his wife, Phoebe Payne, who has well-developed psychic gifts.

They have written several books together, combining medical, psychiatric and psychic knowledge. This may make it easier to appraise the work of others who have specialised in psychical or religious methods of healing, with perhaps little knowledge of the psychiatric or medical approach. We may learn from these if we can see their 'pattern processes' as part of a still wider 'Process Pattern' that is gradually taking shape as fresh reaches of experience are included within it.

There is a widespread urge today to seek non-medical and non-physical methods of treatment. People are finding that we can mechanise life too much. We may have excellent hygiene and yet find children suffer from disease. We may have poor hygiene and yet children may be healthier because they are given an understanding love which is not being finicky and giving rise to actual anxiety. There are many examples of this; but the important thing at the moment is to recognise that from the medical and psychiatric side some doctors are realising that there can actually be forces of personality that are making for healing independently of technical qualifications.

From various angles it can be seen that there is this wider

background of help that is available through personality and not just through drugs or test tubes. But at the same time it is also true that very much knowledge has come through the steady research of doctors into different kinds of disease and disorder. On certain levels the quickest and most effective method may be the giving of a particular drug. Thyroid for example, in the case of a cretin, makes all the difference. Penicillin can make a great difference in acute infections, and insulin for diabetes turns an otherwise fatal condition into a reasonably active and still worthwhile life.

There is work being done on both levels, but diseases do not exist in isolation. It is always a person – or of course, an animal – an existent being, who suffers from the particular disease, and today we need very much more to study the nature of the personality and the kind of personality that is vulnerable in certain directions if we are to develop a truly healing ministry both within the church and within the medical profession itself. As one doctor once said, 'We can only patch,' and another in a mental hospital said, 'People come to us too late.'

We need something of a wider field in which we can see health as being primary and stimulate that level of the psyche which can utilise the constructive elements that a good doctor, a good psychiatrist, a good psychologist or a good priest can bring to bear upon the level concerned. *No one can supply this from outside.* One may give exactly the same drug to two patients suffering from a similar disease – one will respond because he wants to live, has something to live for, and his whole personality is behind the effort to get better. The other treated physically in exactly the same way may die because he has no will to live; because the conditions to which he would have to return are something it is beyond him to face. This does seem to me to show the importance of a fundamental attitude to life which matters probably more than specific details.

Hans Selye, working from the endocrinological side, has also been studying what it is to feel ill, apart from the specific symptoms that go with different illnesses. He, too, is coming upon a general factor. He had a hard fight for a long time to get this accepted because the general medical tendency has been to specialise on the specific syndromes. It seems interesting that from two completely opposite standpoints in the medical world itself both Guirdham and Selye place an emphasis on a *general central* factor.

It may also connect up with some psychological work that is not on the line of psychiatry at all, but in connection with the nature of intelligence. Here, there has been recognised what is called 'G', a central factor, a central quality of intelligence or level of intelligence, in each individual, which is capable of being applied in a wide range of different spheres according to specific gifts, qualities or capacities, whichever they are called. Some people may have a very highly-developed 'G' as Professor Thorndyke called it, and wherever they have an actual technical capacity or specific capacity, whether it is for music, for mathematics or whatever it may be, they will reach a high level in that because of their general level of intelligence. On the other hand somebody with a low level of intelligence—a low 'G'—might inherit a specific capacity that was greater than that for somebody with more general intelligence. He would probably excel in that particular sphere if life gave him the opportunity for it. But he would probably not be as effective in living because his low level in other directions would prevent him making the most of the capacity that was actually there. We so often blame our misfits without full understanding of the very mixed bag of tricks that we inherit.

The more understanding we can get, both of ourselves and of others, the less we are likely to blame the failure who had not the capacity, and the more we are likely to be able to recognise when someone who had it has misused it, through ignorance.

These various lines of thought are all coming together from different workers in so many different fields, many of whom know nothing of the work of the other.

Here, in this recognition of a central factor which has a particular *quality* in each individual, is something which, while it has a physical aspect in the sense that it is rooted in our biological organism, is also related to something which is non-physical. This is able to express itself in and through the particular assets and limitations of any specific organism. No human personality has all the qualifications that humanity as a whole can present. We all have our blind spots. We all have some gifts and also some very real limitations. But we can see in this general factor which we are beginning to recognise from many sides that there is the possibility of stimulating it in such a way that any specific gifts that there may be can be exercised on what one might call the optimum level.

An example on a rather different level perhaps is the necessity for testing drivers for colour blindness because they must be able to see and distinguish colours. It seems to me that we are all spiritually colour blind in many directions, and do not realise it because we can only see as we do see. But if we can distinguish the general level of intelligence which is able to use whatever information comes our way through our senses with either enhanced or diminished sensitivity, we can learn to train people for the kind of life in which they can be effective as people. At present many are treated merely as functions, and they then break down under the strain of perpetually trying to do something for which their equipment is inadequate.

The fact that stress diseases have so developed in these last few generations with the increased mechanisation of life seems to show we are over-taxing this general central element in human nature. The very rapid change of social strata and social inter-action is greater than many individuals can respond to. The psycho-neuroses and social misfits (at all ages) are our indication that the pace is too much for all to rise to it or find fulfilment within it. Preventive medicine by better hygiene is eliminating some of the major plagues. But our need now is to see how to combine technical efficiency with personal responsibility, and then how to combine this with the spiritual expression of a deeper level of being than it is possible to spread out under the microscope, so to speak, for actual analysis.

We are all differentiated in innumerable ways. We are a diverse association of tremendous complexity. Yet also we are each of us in some sense a *unity of all that complexity*. How far was the healing power of Christ the expression of his complete unification of all the diversity within him? This seemed to be such that he could also reach that *centre of wholeness* in those to whom he ministered in such a way that they too could hold together all the discordant forces within themselves so as to issue in a harmony. Apart from that contact with One in Whom it had been achieved, they had previously been unable to manage this. This would allow for His capacity to deal with the possessed in terms of 'Legion', with those whose complexes or those whose association with other levels of being alien to themselves had disrupted their personality, and thus to cure what we would call the insane. It would also enable Him to reach the physical manifestations in people in whom disease was expressed physically. Examples here are the woman who could not straighten herself, which presumably was the poker-back of rheumatoid-arthritis, or the man with the withered arm, paralysed from whatever cause. Some of the implications of these will be considered further, later in this book.

Both the physical and the psychological or spiritual effects of disintegration can be to some extent counteracted if that central factor in personality is rightly related to the source in God from whom the unity actually comes which makes each of us an 'I' who has no plural. Those whose religion is real can find help through prayer, their own or those of others who are sufficiently concerned about their need to bring them within the 'field' that extends through their own deep centre to that in others. But it must be real in its own right, independently of whether its fruits are manifested in temporal betterment or not, for any effective betterment to follow. The fundamental conception of our organic solidarity, or social community, and our spiritual heritage in common, makes it so important to bring together both the medical and the religious aspects life and health. True healing may involve a making whole of the individual in his relation to that which is below him, around him, within him and above him. Right relatedness is far more fundamental than willed actions in isolation; these are so often self-defeating. Nevertheless, the idea of original sin, or a certain inherent element of 'morbidity' within each of us *as human,* not just as our particular selves, needs to be seen to fall within a wider community of 'wholeness'. This is also shared in common, and can transcend the individual expressions of morbidity, when accepted as Good in itself, and not confined to the welfare of the ego. This is worked out in more detail in the chapter on 'Sin, Psychology and God' in *Bridges of Understanding*.

What Guirdham calls the 'You which is not You' is obviously what St Paul described as 'I live, yet not I, but Christ who liveth in me'. In the whole question of modern neurosis, individual and corporate, with emphasis on the aggressive, striving, conflicting nature of personality, we are tending to put up an absolute barrier between this and the deeper underlying self, which in the long run must produce harmony and fellowship amongst *all* for its own existence. The ego can swell for the time being, when it takes from another and aggrandises itself at the expense of the other. The spirit can only grow in its true nature by fostering the full development and welfare of others, so enriching and enhancing *both* whenever 'spirit with spirit' meets.

The curious fact that the nations which are supposedly Christian and are aiming at welfare for individuals, are also producing the most destructive weapons that have ever marred the history of the human race, does need some explanation. I think the over-emphasis on the separative aspects of personality is very largely responsible. This throws the total responsibility on the individual, instead of the individual coming to maturity as a member of a community with a fully shared life. We need to come to terms with, and into relation with, different levels of the self, as we have seen and not merely concentrate upon that which makes its most effective contact with the superficial and material aspects of life. From many sides we see there is coming this awareness of a depth of *guidance from within which is related to happenings in other lives and not merely something in one's own life.* This can only have its source in a life of the Spirit, which transcends the individuals through whom it is expressed. This is another way of recognising a 'Divine spark' in us, which is related to the fundamental ground of all Being; and yet which also becomes differentiated in the process of living on earth, as our complex personalities develop in relation to it and to the external world.

Those are most healthy spiritually who have found the supreme value of living from the deep centre and as a result are able to face the cost of adhering to it, as an athlete faces the rigours of training. There is a very great difference between emphasis on the desired result, whatever the cost, and *real enjoyment of the process* involved in it, even when in part this includes the overcoming of obstacles and enduring some pain. The spiritual way of life is demanding and exacting, as is that of the athlete in comparison with the demands of daily routine. But it involves a sense of 'worthwhileness' that carries us through difficulties that can never be surmounted by the merely ascetic. There are many casualties in life through ignoring this.

Health, life and disease all involve universal patterns modified to a greater or lesser extent by the individual and the society within which he lives. Such morbidity as is present, will fall within the most relevant pattern that is available.

Every type of progress brings with it fresh dangers to be overcome. If we assume that all change must be for the better we actually prevent the kind of constructive change that could bring a balanced development at a slower rate. Such a real growth would eliminate many of the disadvantages that have come as the result of speeding up progress too rapidly for individuals to assimilate the rate of change. The very consequence of this lack of assimilation and the enormous increase of neuroses, as well as the various psychoses or insanities in our generation, is one of the results of this. In itself this produces a whole fresh series of consequences. It involves many more people living an unrealistic life. They then throw their spanner right into the works of those who are more mature or disinterested, and who are living from that deeper level of the 'You which is not You' and 'I that is not I' but the Spirit living in and through them.

The complications and conflicts amongst the many who are striving to develop the temporary aspects of personality instead of the fundamental ones, is at the root of a great deal of the trouble in the modern world—as it was in the days of Christ, when it led to His crucifixion.

This brings us to the recognition of a distortion of Christianity which has profoundly affected its historical development. Christ Himself did not offer easy ways of living. He referred to living with a halter round our necks, the taking up of a cross. This was no figure of speech, but a very obvious reality in His own life and experience, and which he foresaw was coming His way. He promised a joy that nothing could take away, to those who were able to let go the lesser level goals and accept the suffering involved in creative living, rather than, by trying to escape that suffering, losing the very capacity for the joy from the deeper level of the self which has its roots in God. *This when so rooted, plays back into the life on earth, so to speak, and raises it to a higher level of being.* It raises the man or woman so responsive to the Eternal on to that higher plane which Christ called the Kingdom of God.

This brings out another important distinction. So many tendencies today are emphasising the separation, the differences, the minor deviations, instead of recognising the unity of a going concern which may carry within itself quite a lot of disabilities and yet make it possible for the individual to live a full and satisfying life in spite of them. It is almost as if one tried to make a car run better by merely cleaning the outside, forgetting that if the engine is good quite a lot of splashes are not very serious. The ability of the blind and deaf Helen Keller to travel round the world as a lecturer, is a most striking example of the spirit triumphing over what might be thought to be an impossible handicap. The attempt to learn how to speak when both blind and deaf, involved great skill on the part of her teacher. To become a lecturer was perhaps a still greater one on her own part.

It seems at the present time as if two conflicting conceptions of medical work are involved. The old clinicians, with a measure of real personal insight into the nature of the life the child or the patient was living, were able to relate the symptoms that occurred to their environmental situation. They were often able to do much more with less resources than those who are so specialised that very accurate tests have to be taken before they can be at all certain of what they are dealing with. This is not to decry the value of accurate diagnosis, but it is never possible to diagnose the full capacity either for illness or health by merely distinguishing the separate symptomatic disturbances. The background of the individual must be taken into account, if health and efficiency are to be restored.

Signs of mental and spiritual health also differ among Christian bodies. Some are teetotal; yet Benedictine liqueurs were the speciality of monks. Some consider celibacy essential to the spiritual life. Some think this involves a distortion of human nature. Some think it wrong to eat flesh; some think it right. Local customs and religious cults in this way influence the behaviour and way of life of individuals for both good and ill. This shows the need to re-centre our religion in Christ again. It is obvious that the development of hydrogen bombs among Christian nations reveals something wrong with Christianity itself — though not, of course, with Christ; but it involves a distortion of the very trend of life He came to show us how to live. I do feel very strongly that there is a big element of distortion in Christianity as it has often been preached and practised. This was shown very markedly in the days of the Inquisition in which Christ Himself would probably have been burned as a heretic by His own Church.

Something has gone astray. Fundamental moral, spiritual and social influences play a part in the pattern of disease in different cultures. This brings to the fore a very much needed corrective of the over-stress upon separately diagnosed individual items in an individual. When once taken to pieces in this particular way, he cannot always be put together in terms of a living human being again. It was said a little while ago, though I am unable to verify the quotation, that the Mayo Clinic in America was the most up to date in the world, but that by the time a patient had gone through all the investigations available *there was nobody left who could put together the findings from so many different levels.*

This illustrates the point I have in mind. We need sufficient diagnosis for our purpose in helping an individual to live as fully as possible within the limits of his own make up, his own constitution, his own family circumstances and environment. By so doing he can be helped to achieve the *balance between inner nature and outer environment that in itself is involved in health.* Health is never something which is merely self-contained. This is true whether it is physical, mental or spiritual health. It always involves a relationship between the individual and his immediate environment as well as his more distant background. The latter goes back not only into the racial past of humanity, but also includes the very background within which humanity itself has come into being. The ultimate background is on a cosmic scale. For full health and 'wholeness' the balance of a mature personality must include that cosmic background and its fundamental nature. All our attempts to tinker on the surface without taking that central factor into account, end in throwing out the baby with the bath water. It is rather like a comment once made by a surgeon who carried out a very intricate operation and was very pleased at having managed it. Somebody then enquired, 'Well, what happened to the patient?' 'Oh, the patient died' he replied!

Patients do not die only under operations. They can die as individuals if they are too closely inspected for the living reality within themselves to keep its touch with the whole organism within which either infectious diseases or reactions to stress or strain, are impeding activity. *There is a central factor within every human being which needs to be taken into account if medical work is to produce its best results.* This of course brings us at once into connection with the work of both psychiatry and pastoral psychology, and those concerned with the various forms of spiritual healing — using that term in the very widest sense of non-physical methods of dealing with disease on whatever level it occurs.

There is a paradox in the situation in which a Welfare State attempts to cushion the individual at every turn, and labour-saving devices cut the expenditure of physical energy to a minimum, while athletes are showing how much more effort the individual is capable of when he is aiming at making and breaking records. Many stress diseases arise through the impact of comparatively minor strains in those conditioned to expect life to run smoothly without any real effort on their part. This again brings in the fundamental attitude both of the individual and of the society within which he lives, for releasing the fullest powers of any one of us. We all have many more unsuspected reserves and resources than we ever draw upon. We live out only a fraction of the life that is open to us, and a great many of the inhibitions that prevent this have come, not from individuals themselves, but from the particular belief that this is impossible. People today are doing many things that a previous generation thought were impossible. Every generation must find for itself the optimum balance between capacity and expression on the level appropriate to the culture within which the individual lives. This inter-relation between health and culture is very important, as we are seeing on many levels and in many ways. It also shows the importance of a sound attitude to religious and spiritual values, through which the deeper resources of the individual can be expressed. Without this the lowest and least desirable elements may be fostered, at the expense of both the individual and the community.

4

SENSE, NONSENSE AND THE SPIRIT
—A CHALLENGE TODAY

The late Archbishop William Temple drew attention to a distinction between sense and nonsense which throws light on many of our dilemmas in re-thinking the significance of religion in daily life.[1]

'In the Nineteenth Century', he said, 'theologians could undertake the task of showing that Christianity enables us to "make sense" of the world with the meaning "show that it is sense". And those of us who were trained under those influences went on talking like that. I was still talking like that when Hitler became Chancellor of the German Reich.

'All that seems remote today. We must still claim that Christianity enables us to make sense of the world, not meaning that we can show it is sense, but with the more literal and radical meaning of *making into sense what, till it is transformed, is largely nonsense*—a disordered chaos waiting to be reduced to order as the Spirit of God gives it shape.'

The implication of Dr Temple saying he had been thinking like that up to the time of Hitler coming into power is that that kind of thinking had left the way open for the forces of disorder to manifest themselves as they so tragically did. This outbreak necessitated a re-thinking of the significance and relevance of Christianity in a world in

[1] Supplement to *The Christian Newsletter*, No. 198, 29th December 1943. This is quoted in full with the permission of the Frontier Council, as an appendix to *Bridges of Understanding*.

which many destructive forces seek to destroy the values of life, wholeness or holiness, beauty and happiness. This re-thinking is going on apace today, amongst many in whom the Spirit is ushering in 'the winds of change'—sometimes at almost gale force!

The change from 'making sense of' intellectually to 'making into sense' dynamically, is the challenge to us all today. 'Making into sense' is making an ordered whole, a going concern, from what apart from the spirit of God is a chaos of conflicting and competing influences.

We can no longer see the death of a child and say 'It is the will of God'. We must be up and doing to find *why* the child died then, and to use any knowledge or insight that can be gained to prevent the deaths of other children from similar causes. The almost complete disappearance of diphtheria in this country through the use of antitoxins is an example of the validity of this dynamic approach.

Within the sphere of religion the difference is shown by those entrenched in maintaining dogma or custom uncritically — those who seek to hold correct beliefs *about* God, *about* life, *about* religion, *about* science, but never make any attempt to *know* God, to live life fully and freely from their own true centre, or to respond to the Holy Spirit of Truth creatively in their own lives and circumstances. This also applies to those who give lip service to science, without any understanding of the way the mind of a true scientist works in his exploration of any of the forces of nature he can discover.

This is the difference between the old static idea of a rigid perfection, and the dynamic idea of creative will, bringing harmony out of chaos.

The rise of so many groups today concerned with healing is an expression of a dynamism which will not attribute disease—or the *status quo*—as God's last word. All such realise there *is* a power that can transform the consequences of the 'sins, negligences and ignorances' of mankind, if we seek to align ourselves with the true formative influences involved in *creation, evolution* and *revelation*.

The widespread revival of meditation and contemplation today—which at one time was largely confined to monasteries and convents—is another corrective of the over-intellectualised conceptual world which was shattered by the impact of two world wars in one generation—and is paralysed by the threat of a third. The Spirit is seeking to bring order into a disorderly world.

This is not to undervalue intellect in its own place. It has led to much knowledge that can be turned to good account: but it has not brought the wisdom to use it aright. But it is to destroy the idolising of intellect over the actual processes of living—and of living in fellowship with God and our neighbour.

The results of psychological depth analysis show how much of our thinking is adulterated and distorted by negative emotions centred in or on our primitive egos. The rationalisations we tend to throw up to disguise our real motives from ourselves—which may be all too blatant to our friends—act as distorting lenses to both thinking and seeing truly in Reality. The projection of our undesirable qualities on to those around us, leads us to blame them for what we cannot accept in ourselves. This is another great barrier to 'the Truth that can make us free'.

The fixations on some infantile emotional possessiveness prevent our growing up into the freedom that longs to share all that is worthwhile. This is another enemy of the soul, which plays so large a part in quarrels between individuals, classes and nations.

We hear much of the need for 'right thinking' but do not realise the need for right *thinkers* with the blinkers of self-love, conceit and arrogance truly discarded. Nor do we always realise the need for the purification of desire that is essential for the vision of God—for a realisation of that which in its very essence is good, and is therefore concerned

E 65

with the good of *all* and not a few selected favourites. 'Truth in the inward parts' involves a real humility, without which our own self-engendered opinions masquerade as truth—so that the Truth is not in us.

It is here that meditation and contemplation can resolve our egoistic desires and transmute our very natures into a higher level of being and open the way for the Kingdom of Heaven to come on earth. There is a tremendous change and challenge in our ideas of meditation today. To 'wait on the Lord' is no longer a passive resignation to whatever His will may be. It is a triumphant gathering together of all our forces to become open to, and receptive of, the Power of the Spirit. It involves a dedication of the whole self—wheat and tares together—to be 'baptized into Christ' so that we may become true vehicles for the will of God to be expressed in and through us, just where and as we are.

In the long run we can only make sense of the past, in our own lives or on the wider scale of the history of many lives, in so far as we are 'making into sense' the heritage entrusted to us within which the true grain of the spirit can grow to maturity, and the self deception of the many tares that blind our vision can be left behind. These are no longer operative when once we have seen through them.

The spirit is indeed stirring and the door to the future is wide open, with prospects ahead of a greater good than the human race has as yet envisaged, *if* we have the courage to venture forth in hope, in faith, and in trust. The great formative powers of the Universe are behind this challenge to 'leave our nets' and follow Christ, the Cosmic Christ in whom we find the Way, the Truth and the Life revealed progressively in our own experience as we actually follow Him.

5

MAN THROUGH THE AGES

We live in an age of revolutionary thought. Since the close of the nineteenth and the dawn of the twentieth century a change has come over the world, the meaning and direction of which, even yet, are hidden from us. New ideas, new conceptions of life are sweeping over the face of the earth. The image of God as well as the image of man is changing. Every day the habits and thoughts of mankind are changing under the influence of new discoveries.

In *The Phenomenon of Man* Teilhard de Chardin postulates the reality of what he calls the 'noosphere', the sphere of mind circulating round the globe, a world-wide continuum of the thoughts of mankind as they interact with each other. This for him is a *human* layer superposed on the biological layer which is called the biosphere, within which the inter-relatedness of all forms of terrestial life occur. He traces the ramifications of this through his studies in palaeontology researching into the relics of the distant past as shown in fossil remains.

He stresses the solidarity of mankind, with all its divergencies, with an intermingling of thought, conceptual, imaginative, analytical and intuitive. Within this he sees humanity ultimately converging upon the 'Omega point' of its spiritual fulfilment.

From another angle this supports the value of Professor Jung's concepts of a collective as well as a personal unconscious, a residue of the mental life of the whole race and a matrix for its potentialities for the future. Man does not exist as a series of independent isolated units. That image of man has gone the way of the indivisible isolated atom. Always man is found within a framework of family, tribe or nation. Always he is found trying to extend the boundaries of his little kingdom. Always, too, he is found trying to relate the episodes of daily life to a wider framework that gives them more than subsistence value—always too, in some form he has tried to relate life this side of death to life beyond it. He has sensed even in primitive days a measure of continuity of life that is greater than the physical body left behind at death. His symbols, his images, as we have seen, change as human experience extends. The application of the psychological clue to the riddle of humanity has become the fashion of today. 'Man, know thyself' is being urged on many sides. Sometimes this is used to depreciate higher values, to try to reduce the higher to the lower, to level down instead of to raise up. But this is only a temporary phase and the greatest minds realise more fully the potentialities still hidden, but capable of development in the less mature.

The attempt to explore these hidden potentialities is coming from both the East and the West. Studies in psychical research and para-psychology are being carried out in Europe, in many countries, in America and in our own land. They are also now being studied in Russia, and though their present aim seems to be utilitarian, it is likely, if carried through, to bring them to a realisation that their fundamental materialism will founder on the rock of man's innate powers of response to a psychological, psychical and spiritual environment.

The present urge to explore man's inherent capacities is thus world-wide. It follows the discovery of the importance of mind, of mental and spiritual elements in the very course of evolution. It is shown in the attempt to outgrow or debunk primitive aspects of religion. It is shown in the search for a religion that can lead mankind into a fuller life for all. It is shown in the many attempts today to reconcile the work of scientists with religious experience, as we have seen.

It is behind the upsurging nationalisms which threaten the peace of the world, until they find their true niches within mankind as a whole—within a unity of mankind within some form of a commonwealth of nations.

About 2500 years ago there was a similarly world-wide expansion of the human spirit. It took different forms in different races and communities. Yet the influence of that period of rapid development is still felt in the world today, and much of our civilisation is founded upon it.

Between about 760 and 530 B.C. there arose the Hebrew prophets, who reacted violently against the mechanical or ritual observance of the law, and who preached a God of all the earth, who was righteous and demanded righteousness of man. Amos, Hosea, Micah, each had his distinctive message. Isaiah, Jeremiah, and Ezekiel followed on, and the culmination of prophetic insight was reached by Deutero-Isaiah about 530 B.C.

The spiritualising of religion began then, and its divergence from magic and ritual has been one of the factors making for progress in the human race.

About the same time Gautama Buddha (born some time between 550 and 450 B.C.) protested against the formalism of the Hindu religion in North India, and Buddhism developed on the basis of the enlightenment he felt he had achieved. Here, too, when stripped of the pessimistic Indian philosophy of Maya (which makes all historical or temporal existence unreal), Buddha carried ethical theory a long way towards the view then developing amongst the Hebrews.

His noble eightfold path, 'Right Belief, Feeling, Speech, Action, Living, Effort, Memory, and Meditation', speaks for itself in comparison with primitive, even debased religious practices. He too separated moral rules from prescriptions of ritual observance, making the *motive* their criterion of moral action. Moreover, his ethical teaching concerning non-injury, forgiveness of enemies, and friendliness to all, was a revelation of ethical ideals we still need to remember, as Germany's attitude to Jews, and the European attitude to Germany, illustrated during the war. The conflict between Communism, Fascism, and Democracy expresses the difference between attempts to dominate and exploit others, and the recognition of the rights (as well as duties) of *all* men.

The last of the most fundamental rules for the order of Buddhist monks is illuminating. The four rules forbid unchastity, theft, taking life or inciting to suicide, and *making a false claim to supernormal powers*.

The necessity for the last-mentioned rule is important as showing the tendency even then for such temptations to arise through dedication to the specifically religious life. But the recognition of it as a temptation and not a sign of sanctity is an amazing piece of insight, which we do well to remember even today.

Confucius, contemporary with the Buddha (the Buddha is a title like that of Christ) and Deutero-Isaiah, attempted to lead men to a better way of living, not by appealing for personal conversion and dealing with individuals, but by reforming governments. Yet he too reveals insight into the fundamentals of morality, and bases all on the five right relationships. These are the relationship between ruler and ruled, father and son, husband and wife, elder brother and younger brother, friend and friend. His humility is shown by his recognition that, fundamental though this was, he had not yet achieved the status of the 'Higher Man', though he held this to be open to all who would make the necessary effort and carry through the needful training.

'These marks of the Higher Man,' said he, 'I do not claim to possess. I have not fully learned to serve my father as I would like my son to serve me: to serve my elder brother as I would have my younger brother serve me: to behave to my friend as I would have him behave to me.'[1] Thus

[1] Quoted by E. E. Kellet, *A Short History of Religion*, p. 435.

several centuries before Christ we find the recognition of both 'Render unto Caesar the things which are Caesar's' and 'Do unto others as you would they should do unto you'.

Soon after this Socrates, Plato and Aristotle, in Greece, began the emancipation of the human mind in another direction. Socrates died a martyr in 399 B.C. as witness to the supreme importance of truth, and the search for it that throughout the ages has come into conflict with human prejudice and opinion. The influence of Plato and Aristotle, with their differing interpretations of the relation between the Universal and the Particular, still affects the development of thought today. They in their way were attacking the same problem as the Hebrew prophets, they too were considering the relation between the One Supreme Reality and all finite existence. And none of us today can say the problem is solved adequately. After 2500 years we too grope our way towards the real relationship between the human and the Divine, however differently we may postulate the problem.

About the same time Hippocrates was laying the foundation for medical science by accurate observation of symptoms, and especially those that tended to occur together in different individuals. So accurate were his descriptions that more than two thousand years later diagnoses can be made from them.

Simultaneously the genius of another race developed the great idea of law and justice as binding upon man; and our present legal system is based upon the old Roman Law. The tragedy of Pontius Pilate was his failure to be true to the principles which as governor he was appointed to administer; not that he failed to recognise in Christ what even His own nation and priesthood failed to see.

The Spirit seems to have been stirring throughout the world. Yet in no case was the insight gained permanently assimilated by the majority. The Jews could later crucify Christ, while about the same time Mahayana Buddhism developed to spiritualise the formalism that had crept into and submerged the Buddha's teaching. Later, too, the insight of the Greek philosophers lost its direct contact with contemporary life, and much idle speculation took its place, as it often does today.

Nevertheless, the period from the eighth to the fourth century B.C. has influenced the whole course of history. Its world-wide range does seem to imply a *definite stage in the development of man as he becomes able to respond in spirit, with genuine insight into the reality of moral values.* Cycles of spiritual expansion, followed by periods of crystallization and a return to formalism or mechanism and superstition, seem to alternate.

A similarly world-wide movement seems to be developing today. In Europe and America it is a reaction against the crude materialism of the early nineteenth century. It is not always realised that Christian Science, Spiritualism, psychical research, the Salvation Army, the Oxford Movement, the Oxford Groups, innumerable faith-healing organisations, so-called 'spiritual healing' and medical psychology, have all arisen within the last century.

This period includes the development of the sciences of biology and psychology as independent sciences, not necessarily bound to the mathematical basis of the physical sciences. It also includes greater spiritual freedom in the removal of barriers due to sectional religious differences and the growth of the Ecumenical movement, which in the long run must bring our real humanity into ever fuller harmony with our eternal environment, whether we call that God or not.

Nor is it always realized that this movement within the European and American culture is paralleled by an expansion in Asia, China, and India; much as the aforementioned creative centuries B.C., were world wide, though apparently independent, movements.

Buddhism today is reviving the Mahayana Buddhism of

the first century and many, even Europeans, are feeling its attraction. In Mohammedanism the Sufi movement, following the Christ-like martyr Hallaj, whose emphasis on interior religion, in spirit and in truth, led to his martyrdom in A.D. 922, illustrates the same attempt to spiritualise religion. Though the last adherents of the sect founded by Hallaj disappeared in the eleventh century, today the Hallaj question is being raised with keen vigour again amongst Moslems. It brings out the antinomy of personal inspiration and external law, which has never yet wholly been resolved. The Oxford Groups have revived it amongst ourselves today.

A more adequate understanding of the problem of inspiration, providence, and 'guidance' and its relation to other activities of the human mind in its attempt to grapple with Reality is urgently needed.[1] History is strewn with the wreckage of movements which, while begun in good faith, lose contact with reality, through over-emphasis on the importance of the human translation and interpretation of experiences taken to be Divine in origin.

In India the impact of Western thought led to the formation of the Brahma-Samaj, the 'Union of God,' about A.D. 1800, with emphasis on God as endowed with personality, moral attributes, and intelligence, but without incarnations such as earlier Hinduism had manifested. Following this the Arya-Samaj (1875) has had great influence, especially in the Punjab. It inculcates a pure monotheism, though it attacks both Christianity and Islam. More recently the influence of Mahatma Gandhi was very far-reaching. He seemed to focus a distrust of the materialism of the West (the element of 'mammon' which Christ condemned as incompatible with the service of God, with which our real contribution to the life of the Spirit through material means is unfortunately riddled) with a deep admiration for Jesus

[1] This has been considered by the present writer in *Victory over Suffering* and *The Dynamo of Prayer*.

Christ, and an attempt to combine the teaching of the Sermon on the Mount with the ethics of the Bhagavad-gita[1] (written about the same time as St John's Gospel. It should be noted that the development of Mahayana Buddhism, to which reference has been made, which has also been revived in this century, occurred within the first century, illustrating once again the world movements of spirit involved).

In China, too, the idealism of Sun Yat Sen became a great driving power; and in Japan the response Kagawa won illustrates the same reaching out after spiritual realities. Although the rise of Communism in China checked this, the search for freedom and autonomy goes on within the surge of nationalism throughout the world. An internationalism of co-operating nations, pledged to justice, freedom and compassion without resource to war and force would combine effectively the relative antinomies under the law of co-operation and harmony.

The varied activities of the United Nations are bringing hope of this, especially through Unesco, with its social, educational and cultural aims. The World Health Organisation is also playing a constructive part that is essential to raising the level of physical health through better hygiene, as well as the overcoming of infectious diseases, which ravage so many parts of the world and prevent men and women reaching their full stature mentally and spiritually. War on Want is making its contribution through seeking not only to supply minimum food needs, but by helping to educate primitive peoples to grow and develop a more balanced diet, and to eliminate some of the deficiency diseases.

As men of differing races, traditions and stages of development work together for common aims for the welfare

[1] It is not always realised that Gandhi gave up a law practice in South Africa that had been bringing in about three thousand pounds a year in order to dedicate himself to what he felt to be the real needs of his people in India.

of humanity, they needs must grow in mutual understanding. For 'Man Tomorrow' to succeed in maintaining human life on earth 'Man Today' must gather up all that has been of value in his past. He must sift the chaff from the wheat and focus his aims on releasing and harnessing the potentialities for the future in it constructively.

The days of a philosophy of materialism are numbered, by the very magnitude of the destructive powers of nuclear weapons, which mankind is so afraid to use that they are referred to as 'deterrents'. The mind of man is awakening to this as a threat to our *fundamental humanity*, and to the need to find some way of learning to live in harmony with others if we are to survive at all. Materialism is also dying, if not dead, through modern scientists who have discovered how to release so many fascinating and wonderful properties of the matter they have analysed into 'electrons', which are 'waves of probability' that something will happen according to expectation. The essential 'know how' is a mental and not a purely physical activity. The 'know why and when' which controls the use of this 'know how' involves a spiritual appraisement of the possibilities and probabilities of the situation. As man gains greater wisdom in this deeper knowledge of himself and his environment, so the mental and spiritual factors involved in living as human beings, and not just as animals, will increase. The heritage of the ages can be passed on in appropriate forms for the harmonising of the needs of each with the welfare of all. Until this is implemented in action the needs of all are imperilled by 'man's inhumanity to man' which breaks out whenever real needs are threatened and lives frustrated beyond a certain range.

The next stage of progress must be within the minds of men—the raising of the standard of living to include the standard of true fellowship. Science, as we have seen, must play a part: but only a true humanity which sees itself as one with all who have lived, are living and are yet to come, can utilise its gifts for the welfare of mankind and not as a monopoly for a few who wish to contract out of the greater whole in which their true significance can be found.

Although the man in the street may quote from some scientists who, like Laplace, may say they have no need for God, the leading scientists today, those at the real growing points of our knowledge and experience, realise that at best they can only record 'pointer readings' from a substratum that is beyond the range of their measurements, within which the realities of our existence subsist. This substratum, as Professor Jeans indicated in his book *Physics and Philosophy*,[1] involves mental activities or process patterns that play a part in the outcome of what might otherwise be expected. Through this, he suggests, our own mental—and I would add spiritual—activities can modify the future. The process patterns we discover in nature are not inviolate rigid structures. They are, as the name implies, patterns of change, which involve unlimited potentialities for future development. Man today is making the pattern for man tomorrow, whether he realises it or not. If we can become aware of this on a sufficiently wide scale we may be able to see to it that a better pattern than that which has been reached so far, can come into being in the future we ourselves are making now.

The Gifford lectures by Sir Alister Hardy, *The Living Stream* and *The Divine Flame* are so relevant to the theme of this book that some reference to them must be made, although all but one chapter of this book were written before these came my way. Sir Alister Hardy shows, in *The Living Stream*, that the discovered facts of evolution do not lead to materialism, but indicate a natural system in which there is a place for man's spiritual and religious feelings. In *The Divine Flame* he examines these feelings, the divine flame which so far as we know distinguishes man from other animals, as he says.

[1] Cambridge University Press.

It is encouraging to find an endorsement of the main theme of this book from a biologist who has built a real bridge between our biological inheritance and our spiritual potentialities, as Sir James Jeans had done in connection with physics—and as I, in my small way, am attempting to do from the side of psychology. Sir Alister Hardy shows that there are two streams of life flowing forward in time. One is the actual biological evolution prior to and including Man. The second is the stream that, as he says, Sir Julian Huxley and Teilhard de Chardin talk so much about. It is the stream of thoughts and ideas handed on by the spoken, written or printed word, and by works of art. This, as Sir Alister says 'grows, evolves and throws out branches like the organic stream to which it is related'. He also stresses the value and significance of psychical research, a research into a realm that goes beyond sensory perception. In addition he is convinced of the overwhelming importance of an experimental faith for the future of mankind. Sir Alister sees the need for testing and collating the results of prayer that seem to go beyond the range of our own unaided competence. He ends his book with a most striking comparison:

'As the making of physical fire was one of the great milestones in the rise of man, so I believe also was his discovery of prayer as a means of kindling and fanning a flame he found within him: a flame which like a spiritual engine, has brought him to higher and higher things. Let him not throw it away.'[1]

The idea of prayer as a spiritual engine was developed in my own book *The Dynamo of Prayer* published in 1961 before these books came out.

The convergence of so many lines of approach is significant. This shows how we may become 'at home' among the immensities of time and space which seem to dwarf us into

---

[1] Alister Hardy, *The Divine Flame* (Collins), p. 244.

insignificance, and at times may seem to paralyse our endeavours, by finding our true place within them. The flame of the spirit in one who has known God cannot ultimately be quenched.

6

THE NEW MORALITY

Much has been written and talked about the 'new morality' within the last few years. Yet strangely enough *nowhere* have I come across the realisation that true morality is *always* new.

Morality is not a code of behaviour: that is convention. Morality is not obedience to law, whether law of the land or the law of some secular or church organisation. Morality is the expression of our whole being in harmony with the reality of, and respect for, the true being of others. This is what is behind the much misunderstood statement by Professor Carstairs in his Reith Lectures. He asked: 'Is chastity the supreme moral virtue? In our religious tradition the essence of morality has sometimes appeared to consist of sexual restraint: but this was not emphasised in Christ's own teaching. For Him, the cardinal virtue was charity, that is consideration of and concern for other people.'[1]

In *Honest to God*, Bishop John Robinson said, 'Chastity is the expression of charity—of caring enough.'[2]

Christ Himself said 'But I say unto you that everyone that looketh on a woman to lust after her hath committed adultery with her already in his heart.'[3]

This seems on the surface to be a hard saying. Yet if charity is the supreme virtue, and compassion with a

[1] *The Listener*, 29th Nov., 1962, p. 893.
[2] John Robinson, *Honest to God* (S.C.M. Press), p. 119.
[3] Matthew 5, 28.

consideration for others the sign of maturity, then the lustful look, stripping a woman mentally of her defences, without the personal relationship entering in, is *more* unchaste than the actual contact which expresses mutual love. It is to fall below the level of human love, which includes sexual elements but transcends them in an achieved harmony. When a girl attracts a man as herself, then, though sexual desire may come in long before it can be consummated, it will not descend to lust—the man who really cares for a woman wants to win her response, not to rape, seduce or dominate her. So the real chastity, which includes respect and concern for others as having the right to give or withhold, is an expression of the 'charity', the caring which is the mark of humanity, of humaneness—real morality.

Morality cannot take advantage of the weakness of another. To do so is immorality. This is so whether this involves 'pulling a fast one' and making money out of the ignorance of another, or whether it involves taking advantage of a temporary attraction sexually without respect for the personality of the other. Any exploitation of human weakness or human need betrays the 'human pact', the human fellowship. It breaks the law of charity whether it steals a woman's chastity or robs an old widow with violence. This is the real immorality.

Society has always had to make laws to try to control primitive expressions of instinctive life and provide education up to standards of behaviour that can enable a reasonably orderly shared life to be open to the majority of its citizens. Although so far there have always been pockets of disorder and rebellion within even the best organised tribes or nations, as the number of prisons in our own land shows.

Morality in such settings is always *new*. Someone realises the need for a change which can make us freer to enjoy friendship, fellowship and the many wholesome forms of social life in which we can find fulfilment in work and in play. When Moses brought down the ten commandments

God was not repressive. He was enunciating laws of social living that were essential if everyone was to have a chance of living fully. We are discovering the consequences of ignoring them. When Christ summed up the two great commandments 'Thou shalt love the Lord thy God with all thy heart, all thy mind, all thy soul and all thy strength', and the second as 'Thou shalt love thy neighbour as thyself' He was not imposing an impossibly high standard. He was showing the only way in which mankind could find fulfilment. So much of the suffering in the world is due to a falling short of this in man's inhumanity to man. It is fundamental if the man–woman relationship is to reach its maturity.

Comments on the Kinsey report in America showed that a large number of both sexes were satisfied with adolescent sex behaviour and took it for granted that this was all that was possible. The higher reaches of experience that a mature relationship makes possible were beyond their capacity to achieve. There is a stage in sexual development which is primarily attracted to the opposite sex as such. The 'any man will do' stage. But as the sexual libido itself matures, it grows beyond this to focus on one man or one woman in particular. When this is reciprocal and a man and woman have found a fulfilment in marriage and parenthood, others do not attract. It is the unsuccessful in marriage who stray, not those who have fully grown into the unity that fulfils each and links the generations together through a family.

When I was lecturing to the A.T.S. during the war I told them that flirting was a natural stage through which they learnt to know more about the opposite sex as real individuals. But that it was a stage to go through and grow through, but not one to *stay* in. The many who fail to mature and carry on adolescent activities with promiscuous intercourse, are making trouble for themselves in the long run, as well as for others.

So many today fritter away their vital energies in superficial attachments, which sooner or later turn to dust and
ashes, as the high rate of suicide shows. The tragedy of
suicide is not only that someone is unhappy enough to
commit it: but that they have not been able to enter into a
sufficiently satisfying relationship with someone other than
themselves, to draw upon the courage and ability to live so
that others will not be hurt or left desolate by their action.
To love another more than oneself is the key to sanity. It is
written deep in our actual constitution. As we know, we
are born into families and families live in communities in
which every family plays a part. A happy family helps
the whole to live more freely. A broken home radiates
trouble.

Immorality, whatever its outward form, whether in sex,
violence, embezzlement, or the cashing in financially on
human weakness or ignorance like Rachman, betrays our
humanity. It curtails our potentialities for the living of a
full and satisfactory life. Then we tend to blame life for our
misuse of it.

In the Profumo case, at first the fact that Christine Keeler
was paid so much for her life story might look as if the level
of life she lived brought satisfaction—others might be
tempted to think it was an easy way to earn money. The
suicide of Mr Ward showed that if we break faith with the
fundamental decencies of human fellowship, we are broken
ourselves by the long-term consequences.

The old saying 'the wages of sin is death: the gift of God
is eternal life' is actually true. Every falling below the best
that is possible at any stage, lessens our potentialities for
living—the end result of this, if continued, makes enjoyment of all that can enrich and fulfil our lives out of our
reach. This is a dying of our higher potentialities—many of
which are stillborn—undeveloped in this life. To respond
to the best that it is in us to do at any stage is to keep the
channel open for further growth and development—it is a

'living into life Eternal'[1] not in a far distant heaven, but now.

Morality is not a narrow, puritanical avoidance of the joys of life. It is a fulfilment in harmony with the great creative forces in life—the forces that have brought us into being and which maintain us adequately so long as that harmony is maintained.

In *Honest to God*, which has been such a talking point recently, Bishop John Robinson shows that the winds of change sweeping over our world, upsetting old ideas of the nature of God, have tended to remove the incentive to right living that came from belief in God. This has led to a lowering of moral standards. Man's instinctive sexual energies can only be rightly controlled when the higher functions of human personality control them through love and respect for the partner. As we re-think our ideas of God we can no longer think of Him as a 'law-giver' whose commands must be obeyed—'or else!' Yet we are finding that there is a law and order in the very structure of the universe that we disregard at our peril. We are part of the universe. We come into it with potentialities relevant to life in it. The law of our inward being is a law we cannot break with impunity. We are made for life, fellowship, wholeness and harmony. Happiness is a by-product of right living. Negative emotions, resentment, bitterness, anger and hatred, all produce actual physical tensions in our bodies. If long continued they give rise to diseases which cripple our living still further. The healthy emotions that follow activity that combines our mental, physical and spiritual energies in harmony, bring renewed life to our very tissues. Life is on the side of wholeness, harmony and happiness if we co-operate with its true direction in us and in our fellows.

Roger Bannister broke the record by running a mile in

[1] See my book *Bay Windows into Eternity* (Allen & Unwin) for illustrations of this.

under four minutes, by a combination of a belief that it could be done, and a determined effort to train himself to become able to do it. And finally an ability to draw upon spiritual resources that eliminated the tension and anxiety that would have slowed him down. This set an example that has been followed by others since then.

Throughout the ages progress has come through those who raised their sights above the average and then concentrated on achieving their target. The 'relaxed' all-out running of Bannister increased the range of human capacity. This attitude expressed a genuinely new morality—not the kind so often called this which merely reinstates an old immorality. There was in it that creative element in which mankind finds he is not alone, but is in touch with a reality which transcends him—which is greater than unaided human response.

This is very relevant to the ferment and confusion going on at present in connection with a so-called new morality in connection with sex. Advice is sometimes given that teenagers should be equipped with contraceptives and then such precocious sex relations will not prejudice future marriage relationships.

This, however, I believe to be dangerous—not only because no contraceptive is fool-proof, as the number of illegitimate babies shows. To eliminate the desire for sharing in the production of children as a consequence of sharing life and sexual activity is to fix the personalities involved on a very immature level. And this does very frequently interfere with successful marriage later—as the very great rise in divorce indicates.

As we have seen, marriage is much more than the legalisation of sex relationships. It is not only the nucleus of the family and a primary group within the nations of the world. It is also a link between all ages and all races. From prehistoric times, all through the rise and fall of civilisations, marriage in whatever was the accepted form, has carried life itself forward. So many valuable human qualities can only emerge where the growing child is surrounded by evidences of past culture to emulate—and so create higher values in the present. Many years ago I heard Dr Julian Huxley speaking at the Fabian Society. He showed that innate differences in capacity gave rise to the variety of society: but that no amount of nurture could wholly replace the quality of the genes that are inherited. So that no attempt to raise everyone to an equal capacity could succeed. One of the Labour Party said, 'If what you say is true, then by trying to make everyone equal we are going against nature and trying to do the impossible.' Dr Huxley agreed. It made those present realise there were factors beyond our control. We need to develop the highest human potentials *wherever* they are to be found. And these must be allowed to pass as much as possible on to and through their families. Many men and women from humble homes have risen to high levels of service. Nature does not confine her gifts to the so-called privileged classes—and many with better opportunities fail to avail themselves of them. But it is disastrous to aim at levelling down instead of allowing those above the average in any field of human experience to give a lead to those less well endowed. Many with less innate equipment can do better than might be expected, if they are willing to learn from those who can do better still. I remember my father, who was a Director of Education, once saying, 'Some of these young teachers think they know everything. If only they knew how hard I am still trying to learn at my age, they would realise how much more there is to life than they think.'

The ability to play a part in the transmission of life from one generation to another, is a privilege and an opportunity. It is entrusted to every individual to nurture and transmit cleanly if the race is to go forward healthily and social life is to be harmonious and stable. Through marriage this transmission is obvious. There are new babies born, new lives to be fashioned into something worth while. But there is also another level of transmission that is equally important. Part of this comes through the maturity or otherwise of the parents. Part of it comes through all the forces making for education which no family alone can provide. Part of it comes through doctors, nurses and other social services which come to the rescue when something is amiss. Part of it comes through a religious attitude to life which sees us all as falling within a greater mind than our own powers if we seek Its help. Some call this the *Universal Mind*. Some call it the *Infinite*. Some call it *God*. But the reality is something beyond us that can raise us above the antagonisms and petty emotions that prevent real harmony or happiness. It opens vistas for a world of fellowship where we can learn how to get on with each other. Where those who can work with their hands can respect those who work with their heads and the latter can realise the equal value of both—the human heart may find itself 'at home in the universe' and life worth all the suffering that at times it brings.

Procreation through sexual activity is an expression of a life force that is greater than the individuals concerned. We cannot make a baby as we can make a doll. Life alone can do that. We can only start the process and then nurture the life that is born between man and woman. This partakes not only of something from both parents but also from the whole race, whose potentialities lie in a germ plasm that passes from generation to generation.

When the responsibility for this is consciously accepted, when a baby is desired to express the love of two human beings, and not a disastrous accident, another factor comes into play, which is also greater than either man or woman alone. In fulfilling their destiny they become aware of the greater plan for their lives and can rise above the merely physical heritage and enter into a full fellowship with others who also rejoice in parenthood, with all its joys and sorrows.

This enriches them personally and not only through the coming into being of a child.

To anticipate the fellowship in which a man and a woman find themselves co-creators with nature, and with the Supreme Mind beyond and within nature, is to throw away our human privilege. It is to sell our birthright for a mess of pottage in terms of short term pleasure, which may prevent the full creativity and maturity which comes when 'Spirit with Spirit meets', through the bodily relationship.

Professor William McDougall, amongst many other books, wrote one on *Body and Mind*. He said that on all the evidence he believed that heredity did not only come through the sperm and ova, but that in some way the unity of man and woman played a part in bringing into being the soul, or higher mind, of the child. I too, believe this to be true, and that God also imparts a Divine Spark which is destined in the long run to control and harmonise all lesser energies.

Real morality is an expression of this through which love and respect lift the physical relationship beyond the animal level, which is merely instinctive. Premature precocity prevents the maturity which can provide adequate nurture as well as nature for the growing child to realise and develop the immense potentialities inherent in each one of us— however few of them we develop into actual capacities.

Civilisations can be seen to have failed when promiscuity took the place of a stable and respected unity. This is not just a ' moralisation'. It is a fact of history. Where there is insufficient reverence for life, life withdraws and the outer structures of the world, the framework of societies, crumble for lack of mature men and women to maintain them with the law and order which civilised living entails.

About thirty years ago, when lecturing to a group of clergy, I predicted there would be a considerable increase in pre-marital relationships in the coming years. But that through this a higher morality would eventually emerge.

The double standard which divided women into two classes, the married respectable woman on the one hand, and the mistress or prostitute so frequently used and despised on the other, would have to go. Women were then, even before the war, breaking through their previous position on all sides. The fact that women were showing that they could compete on equal terms with men on so many levels meant that men had to become more mature to satisfy such women. Moreover, as they could increasingly earn a more adequate living, they could afford to refuse those who could not provide real companionship.

The great freedom of mixing with the opposite sex I foresaw would—as it has done—lead to women claiming the right to pre-marital intercourse if they wished, not for payment as a prostitute, but as a partner on more equal terms. Again this would mean that a man had to offer more of himself to the 'amateur' to win this as a privilege, than he would to a prostitute who took money from many men.

But I also pointed out that this would be an intermediate stage. In time the necessity for a stable background of family life was bound to re-assert itself. By then the double standard which made for so much hypocrisy would be realised as a falling short of true manhood. This respects womanhood because a man has learnt to love and cherish *one* woman in such a way as to find fulfilment in the family and in maintaining the civilisation and culture needed for their children.

What is commonly called the new morality today describes the interim period I forecast so long ago. The fact that teenagers themselves are beginning to revolt against the pressures brought to bear on them by a society which is titillating them and parading sexual appeals in advertisements, books and pictures, is an indication that nature—real human nature, not instinct—is breaking through to demand a greater wholeness and responsibility in living. The wonder today is not that some teenagers fall victims to a pressure imposed by an exploiting money-making appeal to rouse their desires, but that so many do win through to a higher standpoint and a satisfying and satisfactory marriage eventually. The immorality lies in the society which puts money and opportunity in the way without the examples and influence that enable sex to include modesty and reverence.

Sex is a great gift. It can torture or bless us. It can tear human lives to pieces for lack of its true creative and stabilising influences. It can bring happiness in spite of all the difficulties that occur from time to time in all lives.

To set before the young the possibility of a fuller life if they don't fritter away their energies before they find someone they want to be the mother or father of their children, is to help them to achieve it. Sexual energies are procreative, and can never be rightly divorced from a relationship in which this potentiality is accepted. Although, as has been shown earlier in this book, they are much more pervasive in the whole relationship and not just when procreation is consciously desired. Sexual activity between men and women who have found fulfilment in parenthood, is deeper and different from that which occurs before this. Broken homes do not inspire the younger generation to 'make a go' of it. Happy homes do. I remember hearing one man say he could never seduce a girl from a happy home! There are more of these than the headlines which stress the failures seem to indicate.

Nature is very strong. If we betray our heritage she has a way of coming back and leading us forward through the consequences of failure. We are *people*, not just sexual animals. We have minds that are capable of entering into the heritage of the ages through literature, drama, music and art. We can see human frailties and human successes in various cultures, and *need not repeat the failures indefinitely*. We can choose more effectively than before the 'image' of marriage which can harness creative energies so as to raise the quality of fellowship within the family and the community. We can see where excesses in different cultures bring unwanted results. We can see that too rigid control in childhood is self-defeating and prevents the growth of initiative and independence that are needed for a fully personal and social life. If we can help the next generation to find an inner harmony in which their varied aims and aspirations can express themselves without guilt or shame, this will reflect itself in a more peaceful world.

The winds of change are blowing on every level. Old norms are being overthrown. But at the heart of life is the same dynamic urge which has brought mankind from the stone age to the atomic age. As we gain the power to reduce poverty and overcrowding, not in one favoured part of the world, but in the whole of it, men and women will demand the freedom to live out their lives and rear their families without the threat of nuclear war hanging over their heads. When enough of us put first things first, we shall find there is a new morality which transcends the old 'Thou shall not' into 'Do this and live'.

Real morality is not written on tables of stone, but in human hearts and minds. To see life as a growing potential with the need to ensure that each stage is lived through rightly if the next is to develop, is to set a dynamic goal that can *control from within* the partial urges which at times clamour to take the centre of the stage. To express prematurely is to express immaturely.

The new morality will differ from the old in that, as has been shown, women have real sexual needs of their own. Sex pleasure is not a male prerogative. A man who marries should make himself responsible for seeing that his wife is sexually satisfied, as well as happy in the home. If he does this the nagging and bickering that go on in so many homes would not arise. There is an art in marriage that only love can develop, so that as both partners mature they can face each stage, each change, as the family grows up, with deeper affection and understanding. And this can last right on into old age when the children have gone out into the world and they are alone together with a life-time of shared experience between them.

But for this there must be respect for the real nature of the other, not an attempt by either to dominate the other. Neither the hen-pecked husband nor the clinging vine wife expresses the true man–woman relationship. In this the equal importance of their difference in function is essential to ultimate harmony.

The present generation is growing up in some respects. It is maturing earlier. Nor is it possible simply to say that pre-marital or extra-marital relationships are wrong or sinful. The new morality rightly asks why such intimate personal activity concerns anyone other than the individuals concerned.

Yet no man or woman lives to himself alone. What we are as well as what we do affects others in our environment. We may enable the younger generation to steer through the pitfalls of developing sex desires by setting them in the wider background of the whole of life. If they can be helped to realise how greatly mature sex development can enhance and enrich all other truly human capacities, they can see the need for a self control that expresses a more fully *human* activity than a spontaneous instinctive one, akin to the animal.

It is possible to help the younger generation to realise that if they care about someone they will be able to forgo much that they would not otherwise give up. The positive goal is more inspiring than prohibition—though it always entails discipline—whether training to run a mile in four minutes or training to win through to a happy and satisfying marriage with a clean record.

To let physical intimacy without respect or caring have free play, means that intimacy within marriage has lost its freshness. Something of the furtiveness or guilt that so often accompanies bravado about sex creeps in and colours something that can be holy in the real sense in a full and mutual self-giving act. This sense of guilt in sexual relationships has a long history—as the allegory of Adam and Eve illustrates. Yet it is not inherent in sex as such. Here some elements in the new morality are a healthy reaction against the hypocrisy that pretended nice people had no such desires. Nevertheless respect and modesty and an element of a fundamental worthwhileness in fulfilling the real nature of man and woman as made 'one flesh' by God is essential to real morality.

Our problems today are enhanced by the upheavals of two world wars, and the break up of family life which resulted. This brings the need to help such broken personalities, or warped ones, to such fullness of life as is still possible. We are not in a position to plan as if all young people today had had a fair start. We know some of them have not. This is why we must give understanding help and not just condemnation to those who have fallen by the way, not chiefly through their own fault but through major failures in our culture—which pays pop stars more than prime ministers! The younger generation is not getting the right example from its elders. I am told that strip tease shows appeal chiefly to the over-fifties. What can the youngsters who can earn big money that way realise of the true values of sex in fully personal relationships?

The new morality must lift sex up to the mature human level if it is to bring the fullness of life which is our human birthright to the many who get caught in a glamorous net, which leads to disillusionment and despair in the long run. Remember the suicide of Marylin Monroe.

To recognise that we can—if we will—co-operate with God in bringing a fresh life into the world is to bring another dimension into our being. Bishop John Robinson quoted Tillich as saying that there was a need to go beyond naturalism and supra-naturalism to a third position, that in which the transcendent is not 'out there' but is encountered in, with and under the 'Thou' of all finite relationships as their ultimate depth and ground and meaning.

The new morality—with all the immorality it is including —is an attempt to bridge the gulf between naturalism and super-naturalism, which leaves instinct and spirit in opposition. The reality of Christ's Incarnation, of His living a fully human life on earth, shows they can be united in a creative harmony when each has its true place in nature and in grace. God as well as man is involved in the course of evolution. Professor L. L. Whyte, as we have seen, said that the next development in man must be 'the child of Christianity and exact science'.

New morality, real morality will express this, when it is realised that God is not dictating the way from outside and a way against which we can rebel, but that God is directing a process from within which must ultimately bring us into the 'life more abundant' that in our various ways we are all ultimately seeking. On this level the goal can control the means—and the means will no longer be mistaken for the goal.

7

A WAY TO MATURITY

Some Problems of Maturity

What kind of maturity is possible to mankind today? The level of maturity in a simple tribal life in which a boy of fourteen could carry out all the necessary sexual and social functions relevant to life in that tribe is very different from the kind of maturity essential in a highly complex civilisation. Social maturity may be postponed to the late twenties or early thirties while acquiring the specialised functions necessary for the medical services, teaching profession, the law and the various managerial and scientific occupations.

Sexual maturity precedes social maturity in such a setting, and gives rise to many problems. In the past, social attempts to control sexual activities prior to the social maturity needed to maintain a family within it, have been based on fear. But these, though successful up to a point until recently, also set up unfortunate attitudes that made happy marriages more difficult. Outward conformity was sometimes bought at too high a price. This has been realised by doctors and psychiatrists. Yet the problem remains.

How are sexual energies to be controlled and directed so as to ensure a responsible maturity, capable of reaching the higher standard demanded both by a more differentiated civilisation and the greater freedom of women within it? Fear and taboos are inadequate. There must be deeper insight into and intelligent recognition of the importance of sex, marriage and the family within the community, if positive incentives which can integrate and mature the individuals within it are to emerge. Recognition of the equality of importance of the difference of function in men and women opens up a new field of sex relationships.

Social and sexual maturity entails the capacity to earn a living and maintain a family in the particular way of life appropriate to the development of culture and civilisation of the community.

Spiritual maturity may need to go beyond this to give a lead to a community that is immature in some sections of its life.

Sexual, social and spiritual activities modify each other. Each stage of development in the individual or the race has its own particular problems, its own special difficulties and its own level of capacity. The paradox of the threat of destroying the very basis of civilised life by hydrogen bombs discovered and made by twentieth-century men, seems to indicate a one-sided development that must be counteracted by seeking to include ideas or disciplines capable of controlling destructive emotions, and the international tensions within mankind.

This age is perhaps more sex-conscious than any previous one, not because sex as a natural function was not expressed and even exploited before: but because we have become more self- as well as sex-conscious. Although there are greater possibilities of married happiness, less drudgery and sheer exhaustion through annual pregnancies amongst women, the divorce rate has risen considerably. A Marriage Guidance Council has come into existence in this country to cope with the many marriages in danger of breaking down. Something seems more fundamentally awry than we are willing to face. We find another paradox when surplus stores are destroyed while millions of underfed, underprivileged folk need them, but cannot pay for them. The money-token is given priority over the real goods the exchange of which it was originally designed to facilitate.

These are all problems that come into sight as we mature

today. Either within or without marriage, within the family or the unmarried, no one can escape the tensions between sexes, classes or races that are accentuated by personal insecurities and immaturities. The prevalence of mental and nervous breakdowns is another indication of the pressures beyond which an individual cannot carry his responsibilities in actual living.

Yet externally life is easier and more secure than it has ever been, except for a very favoured few, in other ages. Much is provided by way of amenities and entertainments. Help for the sick and unemployed is more adequate over a wider range of the public, at least in this country, than before. This is now taken for granted. Nevertheless, mankind is not happy. We sense the writing on the wall, but can see no way of averting disasters that arise out of faulty ways of living except by the slow and sometimes painful process of changing our ways.

There was a strange apparatus in a fun-fair called, if I remember rightly, a joy-wheel. As its speed increased, the people sitting on it were edged further and further from the centre until they were flung off on to the surrounding matting. As the tempo of modern life increases, more and more people get edged from the centre and lose their balance. The joy-wheel of life does not seem to produce joy or serenity and happiness that wells up from within.

The immediate success of Colin Wilson's *The Outsider* shows that many feel themselves in that predicament in the confusions of today. Although the problems of the Outsider, who cannot find his niche in society as it is, arose in the secular world, Colin Wilson showed that only a religious (not an ecclesiastical) solution could suffice or satisfy in the long run.

The anxiety involved is an 'existential' one, of which we are hearing from many quarters. His examples are culled from literature and psychological works. These raise a challenge to a quietist or quiescent Christianity: though the more heroic elements in Christian living endorse the need to 'live dangerously'. The contrast between the 'bedouin' and the 'settler' in human nature goes deep—the story of Cain and Abel in Genesis shows how far back this arose. It also reveals an existential aspect even then, since it was God's apparent approval of Abel which roused the jealousy of Cain, who needed to feel his own offering was acceptable as well.

The conflict persists into the present age. Neither the bedouin nor the settler has all the values. The collapse of civilisation after civilisation seems to indicate that decadence follows too much security. Yet some values can only flourish with some measure of external security and stability.

Today, the position may be more hopeful, in spite of, or perhaps because of, hydrogen bombs. More people in more countries are aware of the threat to a civilised life or even any life on earth at all—and so may be stirred to find ways and means to live in greater harmony with the various peoples of the world, who are at such different stages of development.

Conceptions of Maturity

Professor C. G. Jung, from another angle, shows that the 'existential' problem of relationship to reality is fundamental. He stated many years ago that in all people over the age of thirty-five coming to him for psychological help, the fundamental problem was religious. He said that none were cured without regaining their faith. This does not mean faith in a particular Church, but faith in the fundamental values of life which depend on the reality of God or Spirit. Neither the *economic* man of Marxism, nor the *superman* of Nietzsche, nor the *sexual* man of the early Freud does justice to the *whole* man in his living reality.

The key-note lies in the conception of maturity. A happy,

well-balanced person has matured on several levels simultaneously. An unhappy, frustrated person has matured on some level at the expense of the other qualities needed for success in it. This is also true for the aggressive nationalism of younger nations, out of relation to their capacity for functioning responsibly within the wider arena of a world forum within which we must achieve a 'comity of nations' or perish.

We are familiar with the idea of intelligence quotients, which indicate whether a child's intelligence is the average for his age, or below or above it, by which we can assess his mental age. We do not, however, always realise that emotional development may also be relevant to the age level, or below or ahead of it. We might speak of emotional age as well as mental age. Behaviour that is appropriate in a baby that can only cry to call attention to its needs, is referred to as ' being a cry baby' if it persists too long in the child. Each age has its appropriate emotional expression and responses. Neurotics and criminals have failed to reach emotional maturity. Although their bodies have matured and they may have married and had children, they have not grown up emotionally or socially. Many of the various types of welfare societies, probation officers and special schools have arisen to meet the needs of these emotionally undeveloped people—who may be intelligent, some even highly intelligent,[1] but unable to adapt adequately to the demands of life.

But there is another section of the community for whom a different set of problems arises. These cannot be handled externally. Such people are more mature than the average conventional human being. They cannot find ready-made solutions thrown up by present-day life. They cannot find peace in the ministrations of a church that seems to them to

---

[1] The linking together of the neurotic and the criminal is not to confuse them. The neurotic is involved in a civil war within himself: the criminal avoids this, but is at war with society.

miss the point of their real difficulty in finding and responding to a God they can *respect* as well as worship. Yet they cannot find peace or happiness without this—whether in marriage or outside it. It is for these, whether few or many, that this chapter is written. It is on these that so much depends for the future of the race. If we can see a way for the more mature to find fulfilment in actual living now, this may well point the way for the race.

Relative Maturities

Physical, social, mental and spiritual capacities do not all mature at the same rate. Education for wholeness, for a happy balanced maturity must be based on a recognition of this. When I was lecturing to the Forces on Sex and Morale, many men and women came to me with their personal problems privately after each lecture. It was possible to give more help in short interviews because those who came had responded to my approach in the lecture and my answering a barrage of questions publicly for nearly an hour as well.

If any practical help in dealing with the problems of the more mature, who cannot be satisfied with 'ready-made' solutions, is to be given in the rest of this essay, it is necessary to give a sufficient background first, for the specific applications to be made effectively.

Aristotle drew a distinction between the way in which a geometrician and a carpenter drew a straight line. He thought that the geometrician was concerned with the truth itself: while the carpenter was only concerned with the nature of a straight line in so far as it was necessary for his practical work. Aristotle and the Jesuits, who based so much on him, attempt to fit morality to the reality of everyday life.

Plato and the idealists, on the other hand, attempt to find the truth behind or beyond life and aim at bringing human nature into correspondence with it.

It is not always realised that the shortest distance between two points on the surface of the earth is not in a straight line plotted horizontally, but the curve that follows the curvature of the earth along what is called a great circle: this is a circle the centre of which is at the centre of the earth. For small distances this is a negligible and finicky distinction. The carpenter can safely use a plumb-line and one at right angles to it. But in sailing to America, for instance, the difference is appreciable, amounting to about forty-three miles.

So too, in psychological and moral matters there are many problems in which provisional solutions are sufficient for practice. But there are also many that can only be considered adequately in relation to the fundamental nature of reality, whatever that may turn out to be.

There is a great need today to reconcile the demands of the moral consciousness that it shall be grounded in reality and not in subjective desire alone, with the necessity for adapting its demands to the actual opportunities and capacities of individuals within the framework of the society in which alone their action can be effective.

In other words, the time is ripe for a synthesis on a higher level of the contributions made by Aristotle and Plato, whose divergence of viewpoint has persisted for so long in the history and development of thought because *each* contained an element vital to truth.

This is very relevant to problems that arise in connection with personal and social life, as well as to relations between the sexes, which link the generations together. A rule of thumb, a reckoning of average behaviour, can only be approximate. All the finer adjustments and requirements of personality slip through such a mesh. Generalities based on averages and statistics can be very misleading. They are an immature form of thinking which leads to mass movements that sooner or later founder on the rock of some aspect of reality that has been left out of account.

There is a body of opinion on sex relationships and the

function of marriage within society, and the status of the family, based on precedents and empirical experience. This is increasingly being found wanting today for lack of more adequate knowledge of the real nature of man and his place within a cosmos that includes all the forces of nature and all the potentialities of mind. Dr Alexis Carrel wrote *Man the Unknown*. If we are to get beyond the confusions caused by the unthinking perpetuation of false ideas and faulty emotional upbringing, those who are more mature, who have begun to see through the naïve assumptions of the past, have a real part to play in clarifying the issues and discovering what a satisfactory and satisfying marriage really is. It is more, much more, than the link between the two individuals concerned. It has behind it much history, and even pre-history. It has within it the potentialities for carrying the race forward towards a greater destiny, not bounded by past immaturities or failures, but outgrowing them in the strength of a love and wisdom which can give their children a better start in proportion to the emotional sincerity and spiritual integrity developed within their family.

We think of the last half-century as marred by two of the greatest wars of destruction ever carried out by man. We are uncertain and afraid of the powers we have set loose which recoil on those who use them as well as those at whose destruction they are aimed. This is obviously one of the most critical centuries in the history of mankind. Destructive passions there have always been. But this time the force that can be unleashed is so out of proportion to the limited wisdom of mankind, that we must grow up or destroy ourselves and the cultural values that have made human, and not merely biological, existence possible. Yet it may be that historians in a couple of hundred years may see this century, *taken as a whole*, as a turning point in human history on quite a different count. The change in the status of women may lead to a change in the structure of society into one based on co-operation instead of domination.

Cole[1] shows that masculine arrogance has vitiated much of the moral theology produced by a celibate priesthood, which has not always been as celibate in practice as in theory. He shows that it has played a part in sexual *mores* in practice over long periods. He also suggests that it is not even absent from the psychiatric guardians of mental health: though this is changing as more women participate responsibly, and, like Melanie Klein, Karen Horney, Susan Isaacs and others, make real contributions in this field. The tradition of 'spare the rod, spoil the child', of destructive criticism, of God the snooper, prohibiting activities that appeal to us with His 'Thou shalt not', are all examples of a patriarchal attitude to life, which has led to atomic and hydrogen bombs as 'deterrents' which maintain the hostilities, fears and suspicions which lead to war.

True manhood and womanhood only knows itself as such in relation to the other. We discover ourselves in distinction from others only to the degree that we recognise others as of real significance, in their own right; not as appendages to our self-esteem, which is fictitious as a guide to actual value. As men and women are increasingly sharing common burdens, the woman's point of view, which arises out of her nurturing the weak and finding real satisfaction in helping her children to grow up, must modify the more aggressive, trigger-ready male, who tends to sweep obstacles out of the way instead of coming to terms with them. To love one's enemies so that they become friends, as Christ bade us, is not just Utopian idealism. It is sober common sense in a world in which man can only wrest a living by co-operating with others. All nations are feeling the strain on their resources of piling up gigantic armaments for offence and defence. We are being bound together in a vicious circle by fears of each other. We angle for trade agreements on the one hand, with hydrogen bombs in the other. No wonder the man in the street is confused, and so many break down under the

[1] C. Cole, *Sex in Christianity and Psycho-Analysis* (O.U.P.).

tensions that a kingdom so divided against itself inevitably engenders. We are interdependent on so many levels. To change an enemy into a friend is creative, also on many levels. It can only be done by realising that he is as human as ourselves, neither more nor less. To treat anyone as an enemy is to be tied to him by antagonisms and all the negative emotions that disrupt our own lives, whereas our lives are enriched by loving and valuing those who differ from ourselves and being able to appreciate and enjoy not only their contribution to life, but themselves. The immature tend to bolster up a false sense of security by repudiating whatever differs from them. They maintain cohesion on a limited scale, at the expense of antagonisms with all who differ in colour, race, intelligence, culture or religion. The more mature welcome diversity. They respect and appreciate differences and extend the range of co-operation ever more widely. The most mature, the Christ who still forces us to ask the question 'What think ye of Christ?' anew in every generation, was friend to publicans and sinners, which the more respectable folk found shocking. The surprising thing was that this friendship was deep enough to win the response and loyalty of fisherman, tax-gatherer, prostitute and artisan, as well as the cultured man of the world (St Paul, an educated Roman citizen as well as a strict Pharisee, a Jew of the Jews). Each found something akin to himself, as all true friendship must, as well as something that was infinitely beyond himself, in relation with which he could grow into a new, a better self. We can only be loved into lovability. We may be browbeaten or literally beaten into external conformity. We can never be beaten or bludgeoned into the Kingdom of God. Christ's greatness appeals to each individually; yet so wide is the range of His understanding of what is in man, and what it is in him yet to become, that no one is beyond the range of His fellowship. To belong to it, is also to belong to the human race and not just a label, British, German, Japanese or Jewish. The distinctions are not abolished in this; but humanity is enriched instead of divided by them.

This is the ultimate goal of maturity, however far ahead of our practice and capacity it may be today.

Sex, self and society are too closely inter-related to be separated, though they are distinguishable aspects of a life that in each one of us includes all. The cycle of life goes through the stages of infancy, childhood, adolescence, maturity and senescence: but it need not include senility or degeneration if the earlier stages have been lived through rightly. Each stage holds within it the potentiality for unfolding and developing into the next. This is true even for the period of senescence, of ageing, after maturity, both for individuals and for cultures.

The preparation for a creative old age must be laid during middle age. We can slip back into a lessened consciousness, and lose touch with our contemporaries, living more in the past than the present. Or we can grow towards another kind of maturity. Consciousness then covers a wider and deeper range. Although physical activities gradually lessen, there can be an ascent of the soul that extends the range of insight and understanding. This can play a constructive part in the welfare of the community. Society as well as the individual is enriched. Moreoever family life fulfils its function as a link between the generations in harmony instead of in conflict, when the older members rise to their own level of maturity and offer an example of the fullness of living to the younger ones, instead of antagonising or repressing them.

According to Jung the values of the second half of life are cultural. True culture differs from civilised equipment, which can be used by many who would be incapable of understanding or devising it, e.g. a child can switch on electric light or a radio set and bring into play forces far beyond its comprehension. The level of culture decides what comes over the radio or on television; though the technical knowledge for such transmission had to be acquired before this medium of communication could be utilised.

Culture is something won by *individuals* out of their heritage and then given back to the *community* through them, enriched by the inner vitality and reality engendered in the process of creating and communicating their insights into the more permanent elements in that heritage. Artists, sculptors, poets, dramatists, architects and prophets all play a part in this. Culture involves a carry over of the best of the past into forms relevant in the present and formative of the future. Although expressed in temporal forms it in some sense transcends these, fusing past, present and future into a continuity that stabilises as well as enlightens each age.

Two different types of thinking are significant in this connection. One, as with the carpenter referred to by Aristotle, consists in knowing what others have thought or discovered, and applying this knowledge in concrete situations. A doctor, or a lawyer, for example, have behind their judgement, not just their own opinion, but a knowledge of the decisions, discoveries and precedents of others working in the same field. They may make mistakes, either through misapplying such knowledge or by ignorance of some relevant element in it. But they are blamed not according to whether a patient dies or a barrister loses a case, but according to whether they had treated the patient correctly in accordance with modern knowledge, on the one hand, or had not made the best use of the evidence available on the other. This kind of knowledge can be acquired by anyone with sufficient intelligence and application to undergo the discipline essential to this.

The second kind of thinking arises out of the assimilation of our own experience, in a more direct response to the situation. For example, someone may be asked what the weather is likely to be later in the day. He may quote the

B.B.C. forecasts, which may or may not be right in that particular locality. He will be quoting informed, but second-hand opinion, not his own. An old sailor, or farmer, on the other hand, may look to the various signs and conditions and make up his own mind as to what weather he expects to follow. He will often be right for his immediate locality. But even if he is mistaken, he has been thinking in the second way, directly and not in terms of other opinions or precedents. *His life experience is involved in his judgement.* This second kind of thinking is more mature than the first, at whatever level it occurs.

Christ was referred to as one 'speaking with authority and not as the scribes'. The scribes knew all the law and the precedents, but living issues cannot be confined within precedents from the past, either as excuses for failure, or as bondage to traditions that have outlived their relevance. When Christ asked Peter whom men said He was, He went on to say, 'But whom say *ye* that I am?' He wanted a man's *own* opinion, based on his own experience and insight. He brought this out also in another way when replying to Pilate. When Pilate asked, 'Art thou the King of the Jews?' Jesus answered, 'Sayest thou this of thyself, or did others tell it thee concerning me?'[1]

The need for this inner integrity in the face of mass movements that inhibit personal responsibility and initiative is more essential today than ever. *This is the kind of maturity at which we need to aim.* No one can drift into maturity by the mere passage of years. Some bodily organs may mature through the passage of time, though even here more than time is involved. But the use made of them depends on personal factors, mental, moral and spiritual: and this also affects their condition, for good or ill.

---

[1] John 18, 33–34.

Steps Towards Maturity

Each stage of marriage has its own blend of opportunities and difficulties. Life is not a problem to be solved like a mathematical equation. It is a privilege, with great prizes to be won and great penalties to be paid for failure to rise to its challenge and opportunities. Every stage holds within it, as has been indicated, potentialities for the future, which, if actualised, provide a foundation for further development. If these are not developed *at the right time in the life cycle,* future development is hampered and the potentialities they still hold are less than they would have been.

The phase in which the choice of a marriage partner is made, is obviously of great importance for the life to follow. If this choice is mature, in the sense of involving a total commitment, and not a temporary infatuation, any actual difficulties that may arise will more likely be met adequately. Each one overcome will increase the maturity of those concerned. A young man not long ago said that he and his wife would be much more mature by the time their first baby had arrived, as a result of their co-operation and planning for it during his wife's pregnancy.

In co-operating to bring up children the partnership between husband and wife grows, and their links with other families, teachers and doctors, extend the range of their social contacts. Their mutual concern for the well-being and maintenance of the children they have brought into the world extends the range of their responsibility. They learn to love each child with a distinctive love that is not just replaceable by any other. Each one counts. In the real interpersonal relationships within a family which link the generations together, the personalities of all can develop towards a maturity that outgrows primitive egoisms. One-child families lose much of this. Interaction between parents and children and among the children themselves develops a loyalty to a group and ability to work off the natural tensions within it which provide a firm basis for social co-operation with other groups. Where this is lacking, where selfish or self-centred parents either dominate or neglect the children, social co-operation is hampered and life is harder and less worth-while for all concerned. The sins of the fathers are visited on the children, who perpetuate the consequences in their turn. This is no vindictive action on the part of God, but an inevitable consequence of the real value of a happy home life, and the basic contribution it makes to the stability of society.

Dr Rashdall once said that if the state was to give everyone equal opportunities it must provide everyone with an equally good mother.[1] This he thought was beyond its capacity.

A happy marriage, however, is something to be achieved. The old ending to love stories, 'they married and lived happily ever after', was misleading. A happy marriage is one of the greatest prizes and privileges in life. But, like all other prizes and privileges, it has to be worked for and requires continuous adjustments and efforts to maintain it. It is, however, through love-inspired efforts, whether love of work or family, country or God, that personality matures, and finds increasing enjoyment through endurance and achievement. If hard times come, those who have so matured can stand up to storms before which the pleasure-seekers, the passive amusement fans, the slack or the lazy, break down. The real values of life come from within. Each must make them his own, if he is to survive the shocks and challenges of life.

Middle Age—What Next?

'Grow old along with me.
The best is yet to be.

[1] H. Rashdall, *Theories of Good and Evil* (O.U.P.).

The last of life for which the first was made.
Our times are in His hand
Who saith: 'A whole I planned,
Youth shows but half: trust God, see all, nor be
    afraid.'[1]

One of the advantages of living in a community that includes people of all ages is that we can foresee something of
what lies ahead. The child wants to grow up, to be able to
do what others can. The adolescent wants to grow up, to
share in adult life. But few want to grow old. Is there a way
of facing the climax of physical and mental maturity in
middle age, so that we can continue to grow up, rather than
grow old? I think there is: though not everyone as yet finds
it. Dread of old age is in part the outcome of seeing the
failures who have lost the elasticity and zest of youth without gaining the resilience and serenity of maturely elderly
folk, who still add their quota to the wisdom and culture of
the community. In some cultures old age is genuinely
honoured. The old China was an example of this. True community life involves the well being of people at all ages. The
attempt to ensure more adequate retirement pensions for
all workers is a step in the right direction. People who have
worked for the community as long as they had the opportunity should not have to drop to a very much lower
standard of living just when, with diminishing physical
strength, they need more, rather than less, comfort and the
amenities of life. Preparation for a *happy* old age, however,
must be undertaken by the middle-aged. To look backward
to the past is to lose the opportunities still within the womb
of the future. Many marriages come to grief at this stage.
They may or may not reach the stage of divorce or separation. But many an elderly couple have the memory of
temporary infidelities, of thought or act, which arose
through the real call of nature during middle age, which
mar the harmony of their later years. Some grow through

[1] Robert Browning, *Rabbi Ben Ezra*.

even this and acquire a measure of understanding that mellows and fulfils their later years in spite of it. A mutual forgiveness that is real sometimes provides a more secure foundation than a less close union that has never been so severely tested. Nevertheless, as St Paul said, 'where sin abounded, grace did abound more exceedingly. . . . What shall we say then? Shall we continue in sin, that grace may abound? God forbid'.[1]

So, though some marriages survive a storm and are more firmly knit as a result, others break down which might not have done so if the changes and challenges of middle age had been better understood.

The temporary infatuation with someone very much younger than a husband or wife is an indication of a dissatisfaction with the level of life reached together. This dissatisfaction in itself is neither reprehensible nor unintelligible. It is not a reflection on either partner as it so often seems to be. Nature is stirring and indicating that there is a change ahead. But to look backwards for it to someone who for the moment may seem to bring back an echo of the vigour or charm of twenty years ago, is to miss the opportunity to grow through this to a deeper maturity. The latter can enrich life: whereas the attempt to emulate the activities of two or three decades earlier, ends in dust and ashes sooner or later. A disillusioned and empty old age may be the sequel.

Anima and Animus

Professor C. G. Jung has postulated an archetypal image of man or woman which is within us, prior to our actual experience of male and female individuals. He thinks it is a composite image developed in the course of the history of the race, with all the variations of the drama of sexual relations involved. The *anima*, as this image is called in the

[1] Romans 5, 20 and 6, 1.

man, represents the alluring siren, the mysterious opposite, as well as the devouring possessive aspect of an exploited and exploiting womanhood. It also includes the witchery of intuitive responsiveness, and the wisdom of age-long motherhood and creativity. All the history of mankind is embodied in this unconscious image of woman, which no individual woman can ever embody in its fullness and contrariness.

The *animus* in woman, is a comparable racial image of Man. Man includes the boy child—the *puer aeternus*—as well as the dominant and dominating male. Man symbolises the intellectual conquest of nature and its subordination to his aims. Man spans the ages with his mind, as woman spans them in her heart or her children. Man symbolises brute force on the one hand: and yet like Samson, yields to a woman's wiles. Man is the protector, as well as the aggressor. Man is the supplicant, the hero and the villain in turn.

In these archetypal images all the differing types of humanity, both male and female, are condensed.

When boy meets girl, when man meets woman, when father begets his children and mother gives birth to them, some aspects of these hidden characteristics are stirred into activity and are attached to or projected upon the individual. They colour the relationship with elements that go beyond the real character of the other. They bring a sense both of mystery and intimacy into everyday life, transforming its humdrum routine into adventures of exploration, of an awareness of the 'other' that deepens and eludes as more and more of the hidden aspects of the images arising within are stirred by interaction with a living partner.

In Genesis it is said 'Male and female created He them'.[1] Throughout the ages interactions between these inseparable sexes, without both of which *neither can exist*, has set up patterns of relationship which influence us all, whether

[1] Genesis I, 27.

married or single. Neither sex is complete in itself. It is, by its very nature, impelled to seek its fulfilment in and through the other, in some role. This is true for the celibate as well as the married, for the prostitute as well as the honoured wife.

During courtship and within marriage the relevance of such aspects of these deep-seated images as have been evoked to the actual men and women concerned, is tested by experience. If the discrepancy is too great the relationship will break down in practice. If the reality testing in *life* brings out the real qualities of both parties to their mutual appreciation and satisfaction, the relationship deepens and becomes stronger than the projected 'haloes' or 'hates' of the racial past. Real love can then mature.

But even in the happiest and most mature marriages some echoes of desires for *other* aspects of manhood or womanhood than those embodied in the partner persist below the surface of consciousness. If any special strain arises, these may break through the cordon of love and loyalty and stimulate desires for some other man or woman who calls them out. If this process is understood, much trouble can be avoided.

It is only in the concrete living together responsibly, with the recognition by, and approval of, the social environment, that the unreal elements which can never satisfy permanently, are sifted out. The less mature relationships, while temporarily satisfying some aspects of the *animus* or *anima*, in time tend to provoke some of the less benign aspects of these primordial attitudes. Sex antagonisms, sadism, masochism and more broken hearts follow. The bewildering changes from desire to fury, which sometimes occur, make the partners seem alien to each other. They are, for the time being, possessed by some aspect of *animus* or *anima*, instead of being in full relationship with the living partner or in control of their own lives. Possession and alienation are real facts, when archetypal or collective elements in our make-up swamp reason, self-control and reality relationships with others. There is no need to postulate evil spirits to account for such conditions.[1]

With some measure of insight, however, a deep love that has developed through family life to the age at which the younger members are themselves married or at least grown up and self-supporting, can steer through the temporary restlessness and dissatisfaction that comes in some measure to all during the transitional period of the menopause and the corresponding, though later change in men. If man and wife can talk over any temporary attraction to someone younger, *without jealousy and without blame*, they can sometimes see just what element has been lacking in their own relationship, which could have made it even fuller. To see this, and to attempt to develop it between them instead of seeking it outside, can stimulate their marriage, and open up unexpected avenues for the sharing of fresh interests. Marriage *can* be rejuvenated in middle age, and if so, growing older together means going on growing up, through all the experiences of life. It is still looking forward. I remember an old couple who found real happiness in just being able to be together. They treasured any opportunities for this (in the midst of their social responsibility) as much as any courting couple, and on a much deeper level. Marriage for them had become such a real unity that it was not 'till death us do part' but a relationship capable of surviving the death of ageing bodies.

Literature and Drama

Many years ago I saw Margaret Rawlings acting in *Black Limelight*. She played the parts both of the wife and of the mistress. In a most poignant scene as the wife, she was asking herself where she had failed her husband, for him to

---

[1] This is not to deny the existence of evil beings on other planes of existence.

have sought satisfaction with someone so different, so much less mature. Many a man might perhaps ask himself where he had failed his wife, not to have awakened in her the response to his many-sided demands, instead of seeking someone else whose glamour was more superficial and whose sharing of intimacy brought deception into the relation with his own wife.

Literature and drama portray so many of the fidelities and infidelities of men and women. Both tend to think their life, their problems, their hopes, joys and despairs, are somewhat different. Yet the permutations and combinations of attitudes and relationships that have been lived out and lived through by millions of others throughout the ages, cover and convey more than any one man or woman can experience. To enter sympathetically into the great stories that portray these is another way of deepening the relationship between man and wife, purging, purifying and maturing them.

Narcissus

Mrs Grace Stuart has made a real contribution to the nature of maturity in her study of the legend of Narcissus.[1] In her foreword she says she set off with the question in her mind as to what psychologists, psycho-analysts and others meant by normality, mental health or maturity. She found three desirable capacities; to love, to work and to enjoy were all involved. But she found that the attempt to understand these apparently very simple things led to a voyage of discovery into the nature of self-love, of Narcissism, which prevented one from loving. She follows this thread through myth and legend, through the work of analysts, as well as through the great literature which reveals our conflicts, our loves and our hates. This study will help those who wish to

[1] Grace Stuart, *Narcissus* (Allen & Unwin).

mature through insight and understanding, but who are often baffled by what seems to be an 'internal saboteur' who intervenes to their discomfort, throwing a spanner, so to speak, into all their good works.

The most important contention in this book for our present purpose is that the right kind of love of self and genuine love of others are closely linked together, and not in conflict.

This endorses from another angle Christ's command to 'love our neighbour as ourself' (not instead of ourself, as it is often misconstrued). Narcissistic self-love, Mrs Stuart shows, is more like self-hate, a love rejected and turned back to go sour in the self instead of in its relationships. We are rightly warned against this, since it prevents the interpersonal reality of mutual love. Real love enriches both parties to it, and extends its benign influence in ever-widening circles. The Narcissist, in love with himself, is only gazing at a mirage, a reflection, a substitute for the self he has never known, because he has never truly loved or been loved into secure existence.

Mrs Stuart's treatment of Othello and Desdemona is very relevant to the problem we have been discussing, where fancies tend to fly to those outside the marriage relationship. She writes: 'Othello was in the unhappy position of too urgently needing Desdemona's love.' It is made clear that his dark skin has been the cause of what he felt to be a 'narcissistic wound'. In Desdemona's listening to the tales of his prowess we sense the healing he was finding— or was trying to find, for he remained an essentially unhealed person. But she was for the moment a mirror in which he saw himself restored. That it was she in her personal reality whom he saw, is at least doubtful, or surely, later, he would have known better what kind of woman she was. So when the wound was touched again by Iago, when Desdemona seemed to him no longer to reflect the exalted self-portrait, he had to destroy both her and himself. He needed even his over-hasty belief in her *complete* guilt to save him from a relationship *in any way* precarious.

'The tragedy is manifold. If Othello had been able to love Desdemona as she was, in and for herself, he might have found healing in her love. But that he was so hurt, that he so much needed healing, meant he could not love.'[1]

'So long as he sought for *an imaginary picture of himself*, a perfect reflection (i.e. a person seen unrealistically according to his own needs), *the real self* could not be healed ... assurance comes only in reality.'

Karen Horney points out that a person who can be genuinely fond of others, will have no doubt that others can be fond of him.[2] This too confirms the close relation of a right love of self, a true self-respect, as an essential factor in the ability to love rather than self-centred desire to gain an enhanced reflection of a half-made self of whose value the Narcissist is too unsure to trust to any realistic appraisal or relationship.

As Mrs Stuart points out: 'The inter-relationship of mature persons, able to give much and to receive much, is wholly different from the dependence which is no more than the demand of the "baby" in the grown body, for what should have been given in infancy ... the Narcissist, wandering and lost, is driven from one "friend" to another finding each abandoned one unsatisfactory or unable to understand him.'[3]

A similar principle is involved in the man or woman who flits from mate to mate, discarding each as the reality appears through the halo projected on to them through their evasion of their own inner reality. A comment on the Kinsey report on sexual behaviour in America as we have seen, pointed out that it showed the prevalence of a large number of immature people, who mistook the standard of their immaturity for the norm of maturity. This, however, brings us

[1] *Narcissus*, pp. 79–80. (Quoted by permission.)
[2] Karen Horney *The Neurotic Personality of our Time* (Routledge) p. 43
[3] *Narcissus*, p. 75.

to the recognition of the importance of inner as well as outer reality.

Inner and Outer Reality

For sanity, fulfilment and maturity, inner and outer reality must meet. Every stage of life has within it the potentiality for developing, maturing and maintaining the life style and cycle appropriate to its nature. But throughout this unfolding and developing also depends upon inter-action with an external environment. Failure may arise from within, from some inability to appropriate or respond to the environment. But it may also arise from the lack of something essential in the environment. Rickets are due to lack of calcium in the food of the growing child. Narcissism is due to lack of love —of genuine object love—in infancy or early childhood. This twists all subsequent development, as has been indicated. When the real need for affection, significance and security has been met in childhood, a sound foundation for subsequent maturity has been laid. Love and trust are evoked by the loving and the trustworthy. In turn, those who have been loved *wisely* and not emotionally crippled by spoiling nor crushed by excessive demands on them, carry the light of love further through their own relationships as they extend beyond the range of the family.

Life sets us a twofold task. We have to adjust to the nature of the physical environment on which we depend for food and from which we need some form of shelter. If we fail to adjust to it, or to obtain from it whatever is essential for life on earth, we die, whether slowly by starvation or rapidly if crushed by a falling tree or an avalanche.

This is the I–It world, which includes scientific, clinical and industrial aids to mastering and mustering the forces of nature in the interests of our survival on earth.

The other side of the twofold task is that with which we are concerned in this essay, namely the quality of and relationship between persons and the societies they form. This is the I–Thou world. But as Martin Buber says, one must *be* an I to meet a Thou. As we have seen, many relationships fall short of this mutuality; Narcissism and the exploitation of others to serve our own ends, treating persons as if they were interchangeable *things,* devalues human nature. The inner reality of each human being is unique. It is an aspect of the life of the universe which is irreplaceable by any other—God has invested something of His own reality in our existence, which He can no longer manipulate purely externally. This is a modern way of saying the same thing as the writer of Genesis: 'God breathed into men's nostrils the breath of life, and man became a living soul.'

We find freedom and fulfilment only when this common basis of our lives in God carries with it the recognition and respect for every man as in some sense brother. When inner and outer reality meet in real 'incarnation', a real person with roots in both the physical and the spiritual levels of existence, at home on earth as in heaven, we glimpse maturity and see the direction in which we must go and grow to attain it.

Work and enjoyment play as real a part as affection in maturity. We can tell much of the character of a man or woman by the kind of things they enjoy, *when they are free to follow their own bent.* The inner life is then manifesting itself in the outer world.

Middle Age Again

This brings us once more to the possibilities inherent in middle age. For the majority of people, circumstances and the demands on them by way of earning a living and bringing up a family, may have prevented them from developing some talent. Work has probably had to take precedence over hobbies. Passive amusements, cinema, television, watching

cricket and football matches, may have been for many the
only 'escape' from the work that has to be done whether
they like it or not: whether they feel like doing it or not. But
as middle age sees them established, with any children there
may have been out in the world, there is a real opportunity
to try to develop some talents that will bring increasing
satisfaction as they grow older. The field here is very wide.
All can, if they will, find an escape from futility and boredom in some craft or hobby. It is never too late to learn,
as my little book *Live and Learn*[1] showed.

Tuition in drawing, painting, sculpting, pottery, wood-
work, and dressmaking, for example, is available through
various agencies and often in local classes. The gaining of a
'skill' for one's own enjoyment in the doing, is an important
contribution to married happiness. The discovery of an
unsuspected bent in one or other of these directions can
bring a thrill in middle age that may be deeper than a possibly more expert performance in earlier years could have
brought. Husband and wife can bring fresh interests into
their relationship in this way. It is not necessary for them
to choose the same hobby. What is important is that each
should develop some latent talent that is a genuinely satisfying activity. Their satisfaction in this makes them more
satisfying to each other than if outlets for real capacities are
blocked. They discover unsuspected qualities in the
partner they have perhaps previously come to take for
granted as 'known through and through'. We all have more
capacities than can be expressed at any one time or age. To
look for some of them in middle age, and to develop them,
is to prepare for a happy old age.

Membership of various societies, and participation in
social and public work, also extends the range of interest
and prevents drifting into an empty disillusioned old age.
But these must not become substitutes for deepening the
personal lives of married people themselves. To be effective,

[1] Epworth Press.

such activities should express real interests, or they will not truly serve the community.

The trinity of love, work and enjoyment must be balanced. All three are essential. The hedonist in his search for pleasure loses the deep satisfaction that comes with the ability to do and hold down a job in spite of difficulties.

Enjoyment and endurance are closely linked and go much deeper than pleasure. All who have climbed a mountain that has taxed their endurance realise the contribution this makes to their enjoyment of the views for which they have so exerted themselves. Endurance and enjoyment in overcoming difficulties are an essential part of healthy living. We draw on deeper resources as demands on us increase, and we are richer, more mature and happier folk as a result. We are bound in a fellowship of those who say 'Yes' to life; or those who can see its worst elements and still say, 'Life is good'. No fair-weather partner can stand the pace when tensions from within or from without threaten the security of the home. There is a deep wisdom in the commitment 'for better, for worse, in sickness or health, till death us do part'. Some may fail to make the grade. Some breakdown of loyalty, of sanity, or nervous illness may actually be beyond the capacity of a partner to endure or cure. Separation or divorce may have to be accepted as a failure to be able to keep that promise. The roots of such a failure may go back to childhood. We do not all start with equal equipment, nor with equal opportunities, and no State can turn a one-talent individual into a ten-talent one. It can only give each the opportunity to make the most of such talents as he has. Much heartbreak and many breakdowns could be avoided if this were more fully and widely realised. We are judged, in the long run, not by the number of our talents, but by the use we have made of them. Those with fewest may rank much higher than some with many, because they have well and truly tilled the field of their opportunities as far as was within their capacity. Those with more capacity may have achieved less in the realms of reality. The widow's mite was a greater gift than the surplus wealth of others. So, in this matter of full commitment in marriage, some last reserve of spiritual effort may renew the springs of joy within some crisis which threatens it, that can never be tapped by those who enter into marriage with a proviso in their minds that if they can't make a go of it, they can get a divorce. The recognition that even with such a total commitment some situations are beyond the capacity of those concerned to endure, is a very different thing from entering into a marriage with the idea of escape from it there from the start. The latter are rating themselves too low to win the prize of a fully satisfying marriage. They are asking for trouble, and usually get it.

The principle of maturing through growing up together through the ups and downs of life which come to all, however, is sound. But it needs skill, information, intelligence and goodwill, as well as affection. Sometimes a marriage needs outside help to counteract the effects of neurotic or infantile reactions which had prevented emotional maturity from being reached, and so made the demands of an adult relationship a strain instead of a bracing challenge. The attitude of society plays its part, for good or ill. Marriage is a social as well as a family concern. It has also been a religious one. But this needs a section to itself.

Religious Aspects of Maturity

Sex and religion involve man's emotional nature, as well as his intellectual and physical make-up. There has been much conflict and confusion in religious approaches to sexual morality: but it is still true that there is no real peace or harmony if sexual behaviour violates religious convictions. The kingdom divided against itself cannot stand.

Morality is a concern of the tribe or community, whether primitive or civilised. Anthropologists report that no completely unregulated sex life is known. Some ways are permitted: some are forbidden, under severe penalties for the breaking of any such taboo. Practices vary however. What is forbidden in one culture may be socially acceptable in another. Polygamy, for example, is legal and normal in some cultures and condemned as immoral in others. Premarital intercourse is taken for granted in some tribes, and in some sections of the community in civilised countries. In others it is severely prohibited.

Since religion, as well as morality, is also a communal concern—however much individuals may vary in their loyalty to it— the regulation of sexual activities for the welfare of the community involves religious aspects. Tribal laws were maintained to satisfy religious demands in order to avoid the vengeance of the gods falling on the tribe. Offenders were sacrificed to save the rest. Loop-holes for evasion, however, have always existed. Human nature has never found it easy to combine the immediacy of sexual pleasure with the long term control needed to stabilise the group and protect children, whether the group is large or small, primitive or civilised.

A serious element in the cleavage between secular life and religion is the result of a conflict about the very nature of sex. World-denying religions have thought of sex and physical life as evil. They have exalted celibacy and virginity as more pleasing to God, and tried to beat down, eliminate or sublimate their passions. God and nature, however, both seem to be against them. Passions so battered down tend to break out of control. They may also lead to reaction formations to avoid or minimise the tensions which deform and cripple the personality that prides itself on being superior to the kind of life God has equipped us for on earth. It involves a very strange idea of the nature of deity to set a value on celibates who can only be brought into existence on earth through the sexual activities of their parents.

World-affirming religions, on the other hand, have sometimes thought of fertility as a proof of rightness with God, and have thought being barren was due to a curse from God, which is just as misleading. Any God there is must be concerned with and about the whole universe and all the inter-relations within it. If we affect the fertility of subsequent generations by the radiations from atomic or hydrogen bombs, it is not logical to think of God as singling out those yet unborn to suffer the consequences of our inability to handle the raw materials of life that are entrusted to us.

Mankind has never found it easy to combine the actualities of temporal life with the eternal background in which he finds his true significance. Thinking people today are reacting from forms of religion which deny the validity of any elements in human nature which are essential to human survival and life on earth. Consciously or unconsciously, in spite of deeper awareness of the evils and perversions, the crimes and the cruelties which humanity has expressed, there is a tendency to say with the writers of Genesis, 'God saw that it was good'. The germ, the potentiality, the nature was good. However infected by evil—and with concentration camps and hydrogen bombs in Christian nations, none can deny the reality of the infection—it is infection, not an inherently corrupt and depraved nature. The structural framework, so to speak, can carry real values. The sins and immaturities can be outgrown *as the true nature of man in relation to his Creator develops its full potentialities.*

Sex has a pre-human history, prior to and independent of personal relationships as we know them on the human level. The serpent in mythologies and dreams, as we have seen, often symbolises this pre-human element in sex. It has a dynamic of its own, something that can become a demoniac possession, a frenzy of desire, irrespective of social custom or personal choice of partner!

This pre-human element is often felt to defile a spiritual or personal relationship. But it is not the physical aspect of it that defiles or makes sex relations unclean. It is the failure to lift it on to the fully human level, wherein affection and responsibility are joined together. The power of untamed primitive libido is then held in leash by the mutual love and respect which is the basis of a happy home life. The family, in turn, needs to feel that it is accepted by the other families. Society gains in stability and quality through every happy family. It loses something, and is less in capacity, prestige and maturity through every family that breaks down.

Religious institutions vary in their sexual morality, and it is important that there should be a measure of harmony between marriage partners in this matter. Divided loyalties involve strains. Mixed marriages, even between Protestants and Roman Catholics, raise real difficulties.

The problem as it arises in middle age may take several forms, according to the religious life and experience prior to it. We may gain insight through considering some of the alternatives which may occur, if we bear in mind what Jung has said about neurosis after the age of thirty-five involving religious problems. He stated that none were truly healed without gaining—or regaining—a religious attitude to life. This involves a real relationship between the temporal and eternal aspects of experience.

The Secular Family

There are many families today growing up without any church allegiance. (Church here, is used in the sense of some form of organised religion.)

Such families cannot see the relevance of Christianity or any other religion to everyday life as they know it. Some have never wakened to the issues involved. But others, those for whom this is being written, have come up against anomalies they cannot honestly reconcile with belief in a good God—the only kind of God who can evoke worship. The problem of evil seems too great. Bertrand Russell could say that we can only build on the basis of unyielding despair. But if it is possible to build on that, then our roots in a spiritual reality must go deeper than conscious despair. The issue raised by suffering is considered fully in *Victory over Suffering*[1] by the present writer.

If religion has either been crowded out, undeveloped or honestly rejected in the forms known to the couple who have reached the watershed of life, some stirring of the issues involved is likely to occur. People ask themselves 'What is life for, what is it all about?' Though they may not realise it, this is a religious question.

The spate of books on occultism, yoga, spiritualism, and psychological Utopias that no responsible psychologist could endorse, appeals to the middle-aged who have not found their own spiritual centre, nor the kind of help they feel they need in orthodox religion. Those who are members of a church which gives them a real sense of 'belonging', are, for the most part, unaware of the extent of this literature, and the demand for it which this reveals.[2]

The Outsider, described by Colin Wilson, wants somewhere to come in, to become an Insider: but he cannot find a niche without betraying some inner integrity that gives him his assurance of existence. Sartre and the Existentialists are a response to this need to feel rooted in reality—good or evil as it may be. This is a reaction against the 'pie in the sky when you die' *parody* of real religion.

Questioners on these lines will not have an easy passage to convictions which will be strong enough to maintain an ascending curve in the inner personal life which can compensate for and give value to the descending curve of physical life. There are no short cuts to maturity and integrity. Moreover, there are alternative routes to it,

[1] Published by Arthur James.
[2] This was considered in my *New Concepts of Healing*.

according to the starting-point and level of life and culture within which the search for a personally satisfying and socially useful spiritual life makes itself felt.

The Family within the Church

For present purposes this is meant to include any and all branches of the Christian Church, and spiritual offshoots from them. Reference to non-Christian religions will be made later.

The situation differs greatly from the secular family with no affiliation to organised religions. The Earl of Halifax, in an article in the *Sunday Times*, showed how deep the influence of his father's religious faith had been on him. He looked forward to his confirmation and admission to Holy Communion as a tremendous privilege. Prayer and worship were an integral part of life from the start for him.

A family in which the reality of God, of a Creative Mind responsible for their very existence and for that of the universe in which they live, is realised, sees every detail of life in a different perspective from the secular materialist who takes his stand on the seen and not the unseen aspects of life. Material elements enter both; but a faith in the unseen yet *experienced* aspects of life opens up another dimension of being. For materialists, ageing is tragedy, a loss of vitality, with no recompense. For the Christian—and for the spiritually mature in other religions—ageing involves letting go some of the lesser goals of life, as an opportunity to awaken ever more profoundly to the spiritual realities that are 'the same yesterday, today and forever'. Death, the final shedding of the material body when it has served its purpose, is for him not an end, but a transition to another chapter of life. For the materialist, death seems to have the last word. For the Christian, Life Eternal, Aeonian Life, has the last word because he realises it also had the first.

With this faith within them, based on much experience,

a middle-aged couple can look forward with some eagerness to opportunities of deepening their knowledge and love of God *within the context of the events of their circumstances and daily life*. They will have found in the past that God has been 'a very present help in trouble'. So, though they cannot know in detail what further troubles may come their way, one deep source of fear and anxiety is removed. They know that whatever the trouble may be or however real some suffering or sorrow may be, God's grace, i.e. His loving concern, will provide a way through that will deepen their awareness of Him. Their treasure is not in what can be lost in the temporal sphere, but in what can be gained when temporal and eternal aspects of life are in harmony. As I have said elsewhere:

'Each of us is a focus of growth and development on the natural level, with a part to play in the historical continuity of all mankind. But each of us is also a locus through which the eternal significance of the temporal and contingent is distilled and taken up into God, through the Christ who so lived on earth that He took the fullness of His manhood into God as only God could do.'[1]

Because we are members of a humanity that is still young, still immature, still by and large unawakened to its spiritual environment and heritage, there is no primrose path to maturity and all the real values it holds for those who attain it. We bear within us, as well as around us, the consequences of the 'sins, negligences and ignorances' of others, as they must bear ours. This means that suffering in some form is inescapable. We suffer in one way if we try to evade life's demands, losing our capacity to respond creatively to them. We suffer in another way as we try to rise to this in such a way as to break the entail of evil and bring the best out of adverse circumstances. But this kind of suffering develops, matures and integrates us. We find increasing value in life, fighting, as St Paul said, 'not uncertainly as one that

[1] *Victory over Suffering.*

beateth the air'. No one can mature or save his own soul by contracting out of personal or social responsibilities. We mature through responsibilities accepted and shouldered: through skills acquired with diligence and persistence. We grow wiser through knowledge gained as a result of a real grappling with the intricacies of its subject matter until insight and a measure of understanding control is gained in some particular field of human endeavour.

These principles also hold good for the second half of life. With the achievement of physical, moral and social maturity, gained in the rough and tumble of life, there is no halt in life's inner dialectic. The goal of spiritual maturity still lies *ahead* of us. The zest of overcoming on a deeper, more interior plane of being, can enrich us right into old age.

It will also ensure that we do not hinder the necessary independence of children, grandchildren, nephews and nieces, or any other of the younger members of society by seeking to perpetuate ourselves by *dominating* them instead of living our own lives happily *amongst* them.

The spiritually mature, or maturing, do influence others, but this comes indirectly, not through seeking to assert their influence. The way of the spirit is a way of harmony and peace, not of aggressive domination or masochistic submission. It involves the fullest respect for the integrity of others.

East and West

There is an increasing recognition today that East and West have need of each other. Each has something of value which it is not prepared to surrender. In conflict, both may be destroyed in a global war. In harmony, a new era of humanity could be achieved.

As the East reaches out for the technical and scientific products and the ways of life that go with them, the West is realising the need for a deeper spirituality if its very successes are not to destroy the civilisation and cultures of both East and West.

Professor L. L. Whyte, in *The Next Development of Man*,[1] shows the need for what he calls the *Unitary Age*. This he says must be the 'child of Christianity and exact science'.

Alan Watts in *Behold the Spirit* stresses the need for a deepening and interiorising of a Christianity based on the Incarnation—on the reality and value of both flesh and spirit in harmony. Geraldine Coster in *Yoga and Western Psychology* indicates much that we can learn from some Eastern explorers and adventurers into the depths of the psyche. Dr Leslie Weatherhead has also pointed out the importance of yoga for a deeper understanding of the body–mind relationship which is so close and yet so baffling when we *think* about a unity which we all bring into play with every action and emotion.

Professor C. G. Jung describes the common matrix in a collective unconscious for which primordial images are thrown up in the differing concrete settings of life in both East and West. Buddhism is gaining recruits from Western sources through a spiritual awakening to the need to get beyond an aggressive distortion of Christianity. Not all that goes by the name or under the cloak of Christianity is truly Christian.

Insight into this from within Christianity could open fresh springs of life bringing it nearer to the character of its Founder.

The Ecumenical movement is Christianity and the World Council of Churches is a step towards this. It brings members of all races and colours together. East and West are mingling in spiritual conflicts and co-operation, as well as in economic and political fields. The Spirit is stirring

[1] The Cresset Press.

on a world-wide scale and many treasured idols are likely to be swept away.

This is the background within which those who are more mature can play a part right up to the end of earthly life. With the aim of fostering growth towards spiritual maturity disillusion, senility and degeneration can be averted.

All ways to increasing maturity, with the balance, poise, wisdom and serenity this brings, have one thing in common. There is no hope of growing into spiritual maturity for those who are self-centred. That is the way of increasing frustration, boredom and ultimate breakdown. To be 'cribbed, cabined and confined' *within* the ego, leads to increasing isolation, spiritual loneliness and depression. *Beyond* the ego, there are deep resources on which we can draw for a life that is *shared* not only within the confines of the family, but within mankind, which spans the ages and links us to the eternal background of all existence.

Possibilities Ahead

One way of developing after middle age, open to those who are happily married or have won through the shoals of a marriage that nearly came to shipwreck, is to train as Marriage Guidance Counsellors. The National Marriage Guidance Council provides training and has a panel of competent counsellors to help those in need. This is a very well worth while work which can provide rich satisfactions in helping others to find their way to the happiness they were in danger of losing or had actually lost.

Another way of opening up fresh interests comes to some through deep analysis. It is not necessary to be 'ill' to undertake an analysis, to deepen one's own insight into the hidden depths of our minds. Doctors undergo training analyses if they wish to practise as either Freudian or Jungian analysts. Some clergy and lay folk do the same to help them in their work with others. A well-known headmaster was analysed to enable him to understand his boys better. Others undertake it to clarify issues in their domestic life. Some, though not all, marriage tangles can be cleared in this way by tackling the forces making for disruption on a deeper level with the help of an analyst.

P. W. Martin's *Experiment in Depth* is valuable in this connection. He brings together the findings of C. G. Jung the psychologist, T. S. Eliot the poet and A. N. Toynbee the historian. Each of these has explored the range of creative and destructive forces latent in man. As Martin sees it, depth psychology and religion are complementary approaches to the same central reality. Like myself, he sees the need to reconcile the findings of modern depth analysis with the age-old insights of religion, if we are to control the destructive energies which, with greater material power at their disposal than ever before, now threaten to destroy the civilisation which produced them.

There is a need, as Jung puts it, to 'Christianise the unconscious'. This is predominantly a task for the middle-aged, who have made good in the ordinary ways of life, within their own family and society. The process is comparable to the mystical training within religious orders. Levels of experience that transcend the ego are drawn upon. The danger of being swamped by the irrational elements, instead of integrating the underworld with the outer levels of personality, is as real in depth analysis as in mystical introversions in religious orders. There need be no conflict between these two methods of getting into touch with deeper inner resources if we can see that something of the inner integrity essential to success in either is due to our being rooted in a spiritual world to which we are only partially acclimatised or open.

The symbols used will inevitably differ according to the nationality, the culture and the age within which such explorers of the inner world are living. If we quarrel about the symbols we lose the reality within them that transcends the formulations of the discursive intellect. If our eyes are open we can see a great developmental process going on in many forms.

Another way of deepening and enriching life which many are taking today, is, as we have seen, that of meditation and contemplation. Here too, unexpected depths of personality are opened up. This is no other-world escapism. Many of those who are giving time, thought and prayer to the reviving of the healing ministry within the Churches, are finding that their own spiritual life deepens as they set apart regular times for meditation. It is also found in experience that the mental control gained through such concentration makes for greater efficiency in other spheres which demand concentration; not only in opening up an intuitive response to a wider spiritual environment, which leads on to or into the sense of the Presence of God.[1]

[1] The description of a cosmic vision in which this wider spiritual environment was manifested dynamically, with great vividness is given in *The Great Awakening*.

8

THE UNITARY AGE

We have had man in the Stone Age, the Iron Age, the Bronze Age, the Atomic Age. We must go on to man in the Unitary Age, in which all lesser values will be conserved and harmonised and the costly and destructive wars which mar our history will be left behind.

In the creation of such a unitary world, some of the traditional elements in both science and religion will drop out as no longer relevant—they are scaffoldings no longer necessary. But the reality embodied in both the scientific and religious aspects of unitary experience will be shaped, or will shape itself, into a viable form with unlimited potentialities for the further development of mankind.

As has been said, Professor L. L. Whyte thinks 'the next development of man' must be 'the child of Christianity and exact science'. This rings true to the modern situation. So many partial expressions of truth have shown themselves incapable of solving the many national and international problems. They still bring us to wars that we cannot be sure will not spread into a suicidal global war.

Professor Whyte suggests that European and Western man has suffered from a prolonged dissociation for nearly two thousand years. Christianity repudiated the flesh instead of sanctifying it—and eventually the lower 'distorted man' broke out in the two world wars in this century.

This breakdown of the dissociation, tragic as it has been, nevertheless clears the way for a fuller, more holistic type of man. This type he calls 'unitary man', the precursor of a unitary age. This transcends and does not challenge the more primitive attitudes of the less mature as the self righteousness of the dissociated European and Western man does.

Its aim is the full development of man through a recognition that the formative processes in nature foster development. This is supremely so in man when he recognises the supremacy of process. This is a stage beyond the older emphasis on the static elements which were supposed to be more permanent than the flux of reality.

Change is universal: yet it is not arbitrary. There is a continuity of development. Process has a self-developing tendency: it facilitates its own development. Some of Professor Whyte's conceptions are very relevant today, twenty years after they were published. We are realising that there must be a unitary world if there is to be a world within which humanity may come to maturity and carry the torch of life on into the future.

This unitary approach can provide the framework within which the more primitive and less mature groupings of mankind can grow up to a social and spiritual maturity without the antagonisms that have been engendered in the past. The more mature will have outgrown the self-righteous superiority which is so galling to those who through no fault of their own have been unable to rise to their standard of living. When we realise we are *all* part of this developing process in nature, then we realise that *all* have a part to play in it. All the differentiations and diversities of skills can then be harmonised. Neither head, heart nor hands will look down on the other, when all are playing their real part in the service of a world community. This will not be the classless society envisaged in a communism that sought to make one class, the working class, the sole one. Yet neither will it be the class-ridden society in which richer or more educated sections despise those who have not had their advantages. There will be groupings of skill and occupation in which the affinity of common interests will draw people together. No one and no group can fulfil the functions of the whole. The actual acquiring of some skills prevents the acquiring of others. A skilled bricklayer has to have work-hardened hands to enable him to work without distress. A surgeon or a violinist has to have sensitive fingers that would bleed with contacts a manual worker would not feel. A brain worker has to be able to concentrate with a minimum amount of exercise, for long hours that a manual worker could not rise to. Yet the latter can carry on for long hours with arduous physical work without undue fatigue. I remember during the war one of the men in the Royal Signals coming to me after one of my lectures to H.M. Forces. He had been a bricklayer and was being trained to use Morse. He could not get the requisite speed and said that if only they had put him to bricklaying, or any work demanding the skill to handle heavier materials, he would be much more use. He just could not rise to the concentration for transmitting or receiving messages in the Morse code.

When every kind of worker can recognise and appreciate competence, real competence, in any other kind of worker, then the sources of antagonisms between classes and nations will be eliminated.

This will not happen in a day, nor even in a century. But the trend that is essential to avoid a global suicidal nuclear war, is on these lines. Every individual helped to wholeness and harmony plays a part in healing and harmonising others. To create a unitary age, unitary men, as Professor Whyte called them are necessary.

The contributions of science to our understanding of the amazing harmonisation of details on so many levels involved in everyday experience show the interdependence of the infinitely great and the infinitely small.

We see this not only in the realm of nature, but in human

history. At its root, religion is a search for unity; so also is science. Both contribute to the unity amidst diversity for which we are groping. A chapter on 'Spiritual Healing and the New Physics' in my book *New Concepts of Healing* indicated how the discoveries in the new quantum physics opened the way from the side of science itself to the realisation that the inanimate world was not a closed system impervious to mind. It showed that there was a substratum below space and time in which the springs of action are concealed and the future determined. Professor Jeans wrote, in *Physics and Philosophy*,[1] 'It may then be that the springs of events in this substratum include our mental activities, so that the future course of events may depend in part on these mental activities.'

Prayer would be one of the mental or spiritual activities which in this way would play a real part in determining the future. Healers who rely on prayer or non-physical treatment may in this way influence the very structure of the one in need, through being able to 'tune in' to this substratum which controls the phenomena which can subsequently be measured scientifically, but which elude scientific measurement or prediction in advance.

Healers feel they are only links between greater energies beyond and some specific need on earth. Such energies need a human focus to play into our world. We are only on the fringe of realising all the possibilities that lie ahead of us when the scientific and religious aspects of our total experience can be harmonised creatively in the Unitary Age.

Individuals will achieve this harmony before the race as a whole. Many today are rising above the old dissociation and finding that new creative and formative tendencies are shaping themselves within them—the results of this will be taken up into the heritage of the race and the cumulative effect will influence some who were not surely enough

[1] Cambridge University Press.

rooted to have pioneered for themselves: but who are capable of responding to the more inclusive way of life when it can be actually seen to be operative within the community. Professor Sir Julian Huxley, from the side of biology, as we have also seen, shows the influence of biological and psychological processes within the evolutionary unfolding of the potentialities of life. He suggests that we have a crucial role to play in the further evolution of life on earth, which cannot take place without us. As we have seen the new physics shows that the world of the atom is an abstraction from a fundamental pattern or substratum which includes mental activities. Now modern biology has also had to bring in fresh concepts to account for the actual processes of evolution. The Darwinian emphasis on natural selection is found to be inadequate alone. Professor Huxley stresses an ever-increasing mental and spiritual activity that cannot be mechanically engendered from lower elements. Process patterns, Sir Julian indicates, can be shown to control the harmonisation and integration of the actual material embodiments which are progressively taken up into higher and more complex 'wholes' until man himself appears and he becomes conscious of the process. Process patterns presuppose intelligence and insight into potentialities as fundamental. Biology in its later developments thus also points the way to a new Theism, which not only transcends space and time and all the phenomenal world, but which is also immanent within every structure that plays its part in the great drama of existence.

From the side of religion we see the same need. Christ referred to 'being born again' to see the kingdom of God, the Kingdom of the Real. St Paul referred to travailing until Christ was formed in his converts. The new man in Christ *is* a unitary man. The great dissociation in Christendom which led to the outbreak in this century of the most devastating world wars and the greatest cruelty ever perpetrated by man expressed the failure of Christianity to rise to or be true to the demands of Christ. Christ's call to recognise as primary the Fatherhood of God, as the Father of *all*, is the blueprint for the brotherhood of man, overriding all family and national parenthood. This was lost when the Church sought temporal power instead of spiritual influence.

Christ came to take fear out of our conception of God—and a supposedly Christian Church at one time persecuted and tortured all who disagreed with its conception of religion. It thus brought fear back into the centre, instead of the love which Christ had revealed as fundamental. It is this dissociation within Christendom in which good was identified with the repression instead of the sublimation of the instincts, that has led to such a breakthrough of perversions in sexual life, and bestialities in concentration camps. It has also led to totalitarian attempts to stifle the freedom of the spirit which alone can enable man to withstand tyranny from others. The very development of nuclear weapons on so large a scale in 'opposing power blocks' is a sign of this dissociation. But now that it can be seen as a division within a wider unity, there is hope for a real 'healing of the nations'. In the attempt to limit conflicts through using the threat of hydrogen bombs as deterrents, those on *both* sides of any conflict are being forced to try to find some way of averting the threat which must recoil on friend and foe alike. So a new attitude must in time emerge in which common humanity is seen to be a greater value than *any* one sided development at the expense of the less mature.

Only on the basis of our common humanity, a privilege of living humanly and humanely, can mankind continue to live on this earth, now that all barriers of distance are overcome. It must become one world, or all the amenities of cultural exchange that are made possible by modern transport and means of communication, will be destroyed in a holocaust beyond our power to imagine. If power is unleashed by distorted, dissociated men, who are ruthless —deliberately against all personal and cultural values, destructive, not creative—then the use of the stock pile of nuclear weapons will destroy our very humanity, and with it any possibility of the kind of co-operation which scientific advances have made inevitable if we are to survive at all.

The world situation is critical. The Chinese word for crisis means 'danger plus opportunity'. Now that we can see the danger, we may be able to rise to the opportunity to avert it. Everyone counts in this. If we shrug our shoulders and say, 'What can I do? I've not made the bomb,' then someone will explode one and we cannot foresee the repercussions it will produce. If, on the other hand, we realise that we are all in this together, then our influence can spread to strengthen all the forces of spirit that are making for harmony and understanding. In this way, even the most obscure of us can support those who are in positions of responsibility, who, without such support, may be unable to make the right decisions.

Le Noüy, the physicist, says, 'The moral and spiritual evolution of man is only at the beginning. In the future it is destined to dominate his activities.'[1] All these converge to encourage us to recognise ourselves as able to play a part, for good or ill, within a context that is wider than our immediate social environment—a context that includes all ages as interconnected. Some psychologists seek to explain away man's higher activities, his religion, as illusory, as merely projections from lower levels. The more mature psychologists, however, have found that spiritual activities interpenetrate the whole of man's being. Professor C. G. Jung, who was a pupil of Freud, broke away from him and started his own school of analytical psychology. Whereas Freud had written on religion as 'the future of an illusion',

[1] Vicomte Le Noüy, *Human Destiny* (Longmans).

Jung's most frequently quoted statement, as has already been quoted here, runs: 'Out of many hundred of patients coming to him from all parts of the civilised world, there was not one amongst them over thirty-five years of age whose problem was not in the last resort that of finding a religious outlook on life.' Still more significantly, he adds, 'None of them has been really healed who did not regain his religious outlook'.[1]

Jung based this supremacy of the spirit not on creeds or dogmas, but on the results of analysing the thousands of cases who came to him for help whom neither orthodox religion nor orthodox medicine had been able to heal. In *Modern Man in Search of a Soul* Jung outlined the world-wide search of the need for the spiritual values that alone make life on earth worth living.

This threefold contribution from physics, biology and psychology points the way to the fundamental part which mental and spiritual activities play in the nature of the Whole. This leads on to the validity of a study of the higher mental and spiritual qualities which have so far developed in art, philosophy and religion. These in turn will point to the future that will be created as 'a child of Christianity and exact science' when each makes its positive contribution to the culture and function of humanity.

Civilisations have failed before. But the whole world will be involved if we fail to keep the lamp of the spirit alive in the midst of both dangers and opportunities on an unprecedented scale. Never before has mankind held in its power such devastating forces: and never before has mankind been so blind to the fact that these monstrous weapons are the outward and visible signs of the hates and fears, the prides and prejudices of millions of people like ourselves. Nuclear force can be used for peaceful purposes. It is not the discovery of the power that can be so made available for our use that is the danger. It is that it has come while so

[1] *Modern Man in Search of a Soul.*

many are living in tribal and national rivalries, competing for prestige and place. The antagonisms and fears so engendered have led to the crippling effect of turning so much human effort, skill and co-operation into trying to maintain a false superiority over and against fellow human beings—who also seek to be 'superior' to others. When each can be content to be his real self, without camouflage and without the need to put on a 'false front' to hide the emptiness within, sure of the ultimate value of that real self within the whole of which it is a creative part, then, and then only, will the energy going into the making of deterrents be available for making the world fit for humanity—and not one priviledged section of it.

The disharmonies we project on to our environment can only be resolved in individuals, who then influence the community within which we live. Every positive contribution can be taken up into a wider fellowship which makes still further harmony possible.

Only those who, as Professor Jung says, have come to terms with their own shadow side, can play the role of peace makers. And we can only come to terms with the shadow that is in us—in *all* of us as a heritage from the chequered past of mankind—in the strength of the spirit which transcends our human differences.[1]

When we seek 'truth in the inward parts' with our whole being, we find the formative processes of nature are with us, and are calling us to rise to the opportunities of playing a more responsible part in human destiny.

Novelty comes through individuals who break out of the ruts of old ways of thinking in response to new situations. As Professor Whyte says, 'The individual forms the new and enriches tradition: the tradition moulds and matures the individual and enables him to carry the process further.'

[1] A practical outline of a way in which this can be achieved is given in my book *An Honest Way to God*.

So, if we can realise that the next development in man must be the child of Christianity and exact science, we can play some part in bridging the dissociation that has bedevilled our heritage.

Support will come from the side of science and of religion alike, each extending the range of real responsibility and feeding the results back into the world community which in the long run must emerge. Professor Whyte refers to the 'formatory processes in nature'. These have produced man as an agent capable of conscious co-operation with a law that is beyond caprice, which has no prestige favourites—and which can only be called upon in the service of the fullest life possible for all. The negative emotions that tear individuals and communities apart, have no part in the 'unitary man' that is to be. The New Man in Christ is the precursor of the Kingdom of God on earth—to be reborn into this Kingdom is to enter into our heritage as sons of God—and His agent for the bringing in of His Kingdom on earth, the final stage of human evolution. In addition to the three great creative leaps in evolution with the emergence of life, mind and spirit, Christ seems to have inaugurated a fresh level of evolution which is destined to take man as far beyond present day man as the sophisticated civilised man is beyond his stone age ancestors. It is this new quality of life that is breaking down the dissociation between the flesh and the spirit. Many today are participating dynamically as precursors of the Unitary Age, which will gradually emerge from and transcend the achievements of the preceding ages, which have prepared the way for it. There are many signs of this 'newness of life' breaking through the crusts of tradition and opening the way to a fuller implementation of it as it carries us forward into the New Age—the new Aeon, the Unitary Age that must transcend all the old dichotomies that have bedevilled man's history throughout the ages. There is a new stirring of the spirit, to match the difficulties of such transitional periods with the power to rise above them through a heightening of awareness, a deeper insight and a truer consecration of all our energies than has previously been possible.

9

CULTURE OR CHAOS—
DOMINATION, SUBMISSION OR
PARTNERSHIP?

The desperate need today is for a real life of the Spirit that can be expressed in a true culture within which *all* nations and people can find their niche and real significance, which would make war literally 'unthinkable' because of the overriding loyalty to that which is beyond the petty purposes of egoistic man. People are needed who can go deeply enough to reach the healing and regenerating forces that are also hidden within the underworld from which arise insanity in the individual, or the 'mass psychoses' which can sweep a nation off its feet.

Even a single 'personal focus' that can *stand its ground* genuinely orientated towards these deeper forces of being, becomes a real centre for the rallying of those who are also beginning to take their stand on the reality of the Spirit and seeking to bring the Kingdom of God on earth.

We so rarely realise the wealth of significance in this phrase. The Kingdom *is* a Kingdom, a community not a person. It is the Kingdom of *God*—the author and creator of all its potentialities—and it is a kingdom of God on *earth*. Incarnate, not discarnate: using the raw materials of the whole physical universe, sacramental in the bread and wine of the Eucharist, which itself expresses the *fruits* of the labour of God and man in co-operation.

We are reaping the whirlwind today of the terrible split between man's secular and religious life. This is a split for which an 'other worldly religion', a false dualism between body and mind, between spirit and matter, which betrayed the sacramental principle involved in the reality of Christ's full Incarnation, is responsible. The physical and spiritual aspects of life that God *has* joined together are torn asunder. So man, divided within himself, swings from one extreme of an inadequate materialism to an unreal idealism—and finds no abiding city in either. His loss of a sense of direction ends in turning the whole resources of modern knowledge into the perfecting of instruments for the destruction of fellow human beings.

There is insanity in the picture of mankind using every possible scientific device to blow an enemy to bits, and then, if there is anything of him left, having to use every scientific resource to keep his maimed and tortured body alive.

How are we to get beyond destroying not only individual lives, but all that makes life worth living? How are we to raise the profession of healing in all its aspects, therapeutic and preventive, so as to bring the resources of modern knowledge in the service of life to the forefront? How are we to realise that the human type is higher in the physician, whether of souls, bodies, or both, than in the warrior who has so far claimed the prestige throughout history? How are we to re-organise social structure so that more people are whole enough and stable enough not to be touchy and aggressive and on the defensive? How can we minister to the needs of others less fortunate than ourselves without the patronage that expects deference in return? We need a wholeness and an integrity that respects the integrity of others and seeks to make them whole too.

Social changes are accelerating so much more rapidly than before that adjustments acquired in youth have to be unlearned and fresh ones made, if any relevant leadership, or even real and effective citizenship in the new social environments is to be achieved. This is in marked contrast with the changes that took generations to be effected, with time to consolidate what was sound and to sift out gradually what was unsound. This made for a patriarchal framework which threw up leaders who *had* assimilated sufficient elements in the various cultures to guide that process still further. This was a framework within which it was possible to show the way to others without presumption, because it had been followed and lived before by the leaders concerned.

This whole framework is breaking down—nay, has broken down. New attitudes are essential if leaders capable of harmonising the many conflicting trends and tendencies today are to be thrown up to meet the needs of a wider range of social skills and inter-relationships than have ever before challenged the human race.

'Crisis' is really a relevant word today. We have not unlimited time for progress. A fundamental change is *actually occurring*. We must rise to the opportunities of a wider world fellowship into which the discoveries of science have precipitated us: or by our failure to adjust ourselves to the demands of this, spell the real end of Western civilisation, instead of conserving what has been of value in it within the new framework of the whole world.

Changes are going on which are much greater than any of us have really taken in and the outcome of which can not be foreseen. Yet in these *every one of us* has some small part to play, towards the issue of a fresh phase in closer touch with realities than our rather blind and dissociated separation of the religious and secular aspects of life has made possible. If we fail, a wide scale of destructive inter-national conflicts will occur, in which both our relatively sterile spiritual activities and our technical achievements in *separation* will be unable to prevent the destruction of the societies that could not hold them in balance. The issue is not decided yet: but the time in which the balance of forces will settle down for a new configuration *beyond the power of any one of us to modify*, is shorter than most of us can realise.

This note is being sounded in many quarters from those who have been able to detach themselves sufficiently from the framework of the past to recognise that the framework is separable from the actual spiritual life that man lived within it, so that the spirit which broke down the framework when it could no longer hold it, need not be destroyed with it. It *can* find a new form of expression, a new life, in whatever new framework actually emerges from the interactions of the many individuals and cultures which must form it.

D. W. Harding in *The Impulse to Dominate* shows how war inevitably arises between communities where the general pattern of life is that of domination and submission. He shows the need to develop a technique for dealing with differences on what he calls an integrative level. In this there is no question of just putting one's views across and over-riding objections. They are put with a view to being thoroughly tested out to the full extent of the capacity of and information of *both* parties, and agreement when it is reached is valued as a sign that the convictions eventually expressed have been found satisfactory in a real human context.

The attempt to argue about differences with a real willingness for the modification of one's own views in the process, is a much more mature process than either laying down the law autocratically, or accepting authority uncritically. But it is not possible where strong unconscious impulses leave us too insecure internally to dare to change. Hence the difficulty of getting a culture based on dominance and submission to risk letting go the idea of a final reference to force, rather than to justice or reality, and to be prepared instead to find the most practicable way of dealing with whatever divergencies of opinion arise. *It is our own inner insecurity from which spring the forces that break out in war.*

L. L. Whyte in *The Next Development of Man*, as we

have seen, shows a dissociation running through 2,000 years of European and Western history, and the need for what he calls 'unitary man' able to live in a unitary age. The unitary man must transcend the dissociation, which is not due to human nature as such, since it does not occur in all human races, but which is a cultural product of the European tradition, which was not mature enough to hold the tension creatively.

Demant, in *The Theology of Society* emphasises the false *structure* of society and the need for Christians to live in it under protest. 'The Christian,' he says, 'must learn to do his moral best even in his place in a disordered activity, and to keep his mind and conscience aware that the order of social activities is false.'[1]

Nieburgh prefaces his *Discerning the Signs of the Times* by saying: 'An age confronted with so many possibilities of realising God's will in *new* dimensions of historic existence, but also confronting so many historic frustrations, is in particular need of the Christian Gospel: and requires both the relative-historical and the final and absolute facets of the Christian hope to maintain its sanity and its sense of the meaning of existence.'

Nicodemus, with his emphasis on 'Renascence' or a need to build a bridge between the 'hither' and the 'nether' world, which is essential for the sanity of the individual and the cultural health of the community, goes deep into the heart of the problem. 'Salvation and civilisation,' he says, 'depend upon the re-building of the bridge between these two worlds and modes of consciousness: the nature of the "nether" world, which thus, like an Ark, survives the deluge of destruction, its apprehensions and its relations to the "hither" world of action, becomes of prime importance.'[2] As we have seen, this bridge must be built by and in persons in effective community.

[1] V. A. Demant, *The Theology of Society* (Faber), p. 174.
[2] Nicodemus, *Renascence* (Faber), p. 51.

Rilke, with his 'deeply kneeling man' feels, like Nicodemus, that the agonies of soul through which he has gone are in some sense a coming to consciousness of the forces of disruption in the whole social matrix, and that it is in some sense laid upon him to give voice to them. He was agonisedly aware both of the extreme necessity for such a rebirth of consciousness through 'dying into life' and of his own personal obligation to undergo it and extract a universal significance from his particular experience. He also stresses the 'tremendous obedience of spirit' necessary for this.[1]

T. S. Eliot, in 'the Waste Land' strikes a similar note. Graham Howe, in *The Present Question,* edited by him, shows how the way through to the new *can* only come from those who can be open to something so different that they cannot 'plan in advance', but can each in his own measure find 'the present question' in the heart of his own particular context and situation within the whole. The question as to whether the present chaos is caused by lack of scientific planning or by failure to recognise the reality of spirit, is, he says, a question to which there can be no answer except as it is born in time out of our own experience. We were looking, he said, for the growing point of new experience which would be emerging from the recent tragedy of the world's hardships and present confusions. Something was growing, if we could but find it and *be there as it grew.*

Planning, as Nicodemus, too, stressed, can only be effective *after* the pattern has emerged. He points out that it is rare for the kind of mind capable of planning and organising to be also capable of discerning the Divine pattern underlying the real structure, and the need to foster the conditions that would enable those capable of the closer touch with the 'nether' world to let the outline of a pattern in closer accord with the actual nature of reality emerge. 'At planning,' he says, 'modern man is an expert: at the process of pattern-formation he is still a tyro.'

[1] Quoted by Nicodemus in *Renascence*, p. 53.

Yet it seems to me that though this distinction is obviously valid and that it is impossible to expect the same amount of extraverted 'planning' from someone who needs to spend much time in introverted activities if the pattern is to be given time to *grow,* it is dangerous to divorce the pattern-seeking and the plan-making aspects of the mind too completely. The great need today is that both functions should be correlated adequately, and unless some 'perceivers of pattern' can go on to plan, planning is likely to remain unconnected with pattern and sooner or later come to grief for lack of accord with reality. To transcend the introvert and extravert tendencies in a creative altroversion is sorely needed today—as, of course, Nicodemus realises in the need to build the bridge between the 'nether' and 'hither' worlds.

The term 'altroversion', which expresses the building of such a bridge, was first coined and used by me in *A Study in Dissociation of Personality* published in the British Journal of Medical Psychology in 1924. It can be defined as being 'in reciprocal relation with others', 'turned towards others', 'the mature activity of an integrated personality in whom introversion and extraversion are so effectively synthesised that *psychic energy can be directed freely either inwards or outwards according to circumstances*'.

It involves the maturity of either introverts or extraverts through the development of whichever is the less developed or 'inferior' function (inferior in Jung's sense, applying to which of these is the opposite to the dominant function or attitude, not inferior in any absolutist sense, since *each* is capable of being matured eventually).

An altrovert is one in whom the dominant attitude towards experience is the expression of the balance between introvert and extravert tendencies. An altrovert is socialised, not egoistic. He neither dominates (nor seeks to dominate) the environment, nor is dominated by it. He is in *willing* reciprocal relation with it, whether the environment is physical or personal (i.e. social and spiritual). An altrovert is a personality who has assimilated the 'shadow' side of his nature and harmonised conscious and unconscious tendencies, through the activity of what Jung calls the 'transcendent function'. An altrovert is open to experience, not on the defensive either in relation to himself or to others.

Dr Graham Howe points out in all his many books the importance of this inter-play between the spirit with its timeless omnipotence and the other active aspects of the individual to be precisely expressed in 'time', limiting and confining the spirit, but only so incarnating it in the real world.[1]

Kierkegaard also stresses the need to become what he calls 'The Single One'. This is not an isolated individual, but the unity of the person who, as Rilke said, had won a universal significance from his own full participation in the chaos and confusions of the age. 'The Single One' has become 'one' through harmonising the 'many', and holds within *himself* something of the pattern needed to harmonise the world.

Buber writes as follows: 'If we begin with the Single One as a whole being, who wishes to recognise with his total being, we find that the force of his desire for truth can at decisive points burst the "ideological" bonds of his social being. The man who thinks "existentially", that is, who stakes his life in his thinking, brings into his real relation to the truth not merely his conditional qualities but also the unconditional nature, transcending them, of his quest, of his grasp, of his indomitable will for the truth, which also carries along with it the whole personal power of standing his test.

'We shall certainly be able to make no distinction, in what he has, time and again, discovered as truth, between what can and what cannot be derived from the social factor. But it is an ineluctable duty to accept what cannot be so derived as

[1] E. Graham Howe, *Invisible Anatomy* (Faber), p. 329.

a border concept and thus to point out as the unattainable horizon of the distinction made by the sociology of knowledge what *takes place between the underivable and the recognising person and the underivable in the object of his recognition.*[1] This duty has been neglected.

'This marks the beginning of a *disintegration of human faith*. True community and true commonwealth will be realised only to the extent to which the Single Ones become real out of whose responsible life the body politic is renewed.'[2]

In a chapter on 'Moral Disease, Sin and Responsibility' in *Education for Christian Marriage* the same note was struck by me before reading Buber. I wrote: 'We have to take into account that human beings with their own distinctive nature, transcend in their integrity any mere summation of their parts and inter-relations.

'We ourselves transcend in our essential being all that we can perceive, analyse or express as immanent within our bodies and the world of nature with which we act and interact through them. There is an element in the mystery of our own being in its point of contact with the Divine, that is to say, its relation to the Cosmical ground of all existence, which will always evade analysis, though we may always be aware of it as colouring all our empirical nature. In so far as this empirical nature is in harmony with this unseen yet fundamental aspect of our being, we get a unified personality, through which God can effect some particular fragment of his work in the world. We see this supremely in Christ where transcendence and immanence were united in perfect personality.'[3]

This is the ground of the 'underived' elements referred to by Kierkegaard, with its real participation not only *with-*

---

[1] This is the locus through which the genuinely new breaks through into actuality.

[2] Martin Buber, *Between Man and Man* (Collins), pp. 81–82.

[3] *Education for Christian Marriage*, a symposium (S.C.M.), p. 166.

in the Single One, but in the object of his recognition. The world really *has* another dimension as perceived through the eyes of a Single One, yet it is a dimension of the same world. There are not two worlds, but one where the hither and the nether really meet in true 'incarnation'. Differences are distinguishable but no longer separable.

Buber stresses this, too, when he says, 'It is enough to be there, *really there,* with those with whom we have to do.' He goes on to show that this new attitude is fundamental, no longer teaching or pointing the way, but really humble enough to make it possible for it to *emerge* when an I and a Thou really meet, with no risk of confusion or of being swamped. But as he said, it is necessary to *be* an I to meet a Thou. Most of us are too scared of losing our precious 'individuality' ever to reach the kind of relationship involved on an I and Thou level. We still tried to think in terms of being led, being in charge, being dominated or dominating—both of which satisfy instinctive tendencies, but which prevent the emergence of true spiritual activity which, as Buber says, is *between* persons. As Professor Macmurray said, 'All real life is meeting.'

Nicodemus said, 'We live by the ethic of the "strong man armed", we preach the ethic of the suffering servant.'[1]

It is this dissociation in our midst that paralyses all genuine effort which comes up against the frustrating realities of an inadequate and distorted framework. T. S. Eliot, in *The Idea of a Christian Society* points out that a non-Christian in a better balanced order would be more effective than a Christian working with the distorted order, which so often nullifies all his efforts.

The 'strong man armed' cannot go far enough ever to succeed on his own level through ignoring the inner needs of a humanity that must revolt against being held down indefinitely by brute force. The 'suffering servant' cannot redeem the mass because he is out of relation with

[1] *Renascence,* p. 81.

legitimate human needs which must be fulfilled and not destroyed.

In *Essays on Contemporary Events* (1947) Professor C. G. Jung wrote: 'For in reality the fight between light and darkness has broken out everywhere: the rent goes through the whole world and the very fire that burst into flames in Germany is smouldering and glowing everywhere. The fire that broke out in Germany is the outcome of certain psychic conditions which are universal. The real danger signal, however, is not the flame which leapt up from German soil, but the release of atomic energy which has handed man the means of destroying himself completely. The present situation is as though a little boy of six had been given a pound of dynamite among his birthday presents. We are not yet a hundred per cent sure that there will be no disaster. Will man be able to give up playing with the possibility of another war? . . . How can we save the child from the dynamite that nobody can take from him? The good spirit of humanity is challenged as never before and must come forward. For this fact can no longer be hushed up or painted *couleur de rose*. The realisation of such imminent danger might well act as an incentive to a great revival and lead to a higher and more mature consciousness and sense of responsibility. Dare we hope that it will?

'It is time, high time, that civilised man turned his mind to the fundamental things. It is now a question of existence or non-existence, and surely this should be submitted to a searching investigation and an exhaustive discussion. For the danger which now threatens is of such dimensions as to make the present European catastrophe a mere prologue.'[1]

In all this there is a note of urgency, of something new striving to come to birth through many from their various disciplines and different types of life. The Spirit *is* moving on the face of the waters, and though many will be swamped

[1] p. 90.

in the deluge, and many will fail to 'endure to the end,' many more can be helped to stand their ground and hold together some fragments of a new synthesis, a new context, through the help of spiritual directors, doctors, psycho-therapists and social leaders, and writers who have first to cast the beam out of their own eyes so as to be able to see the mote in those who come to them for help or whom they seek to lead to a fuller life.

The casualties in such an age of transition must be many: but everyone *really* salved, really made whole, is a fresh focusing point through which the Spirit can effect some fragment of the re-ordering and re-creating of cultural life which may carry humanity forward to the next stage of its pilgrimage.

Whether this *can* be done or whether the forces of des-truction will prevail, depends on how many real persons emerge throughout the world in *each* race and nation who can attract to them the sound elements in the 'masses' and really give a lead that makes their followers more and not less responsible. Otherwise the masses will respond to leaders who play upon the lower, distorted elements in human nature in an escape from the more arduous task of *really re-consecrating and transforming the evil in themselves,* part of which they have inherited, individually and socially, and part of which they contribute to by the renegade tendency which is in us all.

Religion and psychotherapy, mutually enriching and purifying each other, can do much to help the spirit of man to become mature enough to control the mechanical demons he has conjured up into the terrifying destructive force of atomic and hydrogen bombs, through failing to harness the destructive forces in *himself* in the only crucible in which they can be transmuted, the *real human being,* in his amaz-ing mixture of weakness and strength, blindness and in-sight, ignorance and knowledge.

Jung suggests that the very intensity of the danger *may*

evoke 'a sufficient uprising of the good spirit of humanity to break through and out of the vicious circle of a madness with which our whole culture is tainted, before the possession of atomic power leads man to destroy himself and his cultured.' He adds, 'Dare we hope that it will?'

Winning a real peace is a tougher job than winning a war, as we are discovering. Can Great Britain let 'power' go sufficiently to *give a lead* towards the new culture relevant to our age? The culture of Rome and Greece was based on slavery, and we took it over from them. The aristocrats and thinkers of their day were largely in ignorance of the contact and wrestling with recalcitrant material, and the humble but extensive manual labour by which their privilege was secured. This probably was the only way at first that the spirit could break through to an idea of something that could transfigure this world. Moreover, with slave labour there was not felt the same need for science to eke out the strength of a man's muscles, and what Professor Pear calls the 'intellectual respectability of muscular skill' was less realised.

Can we *now* begin to develop a culture from the *whole man*, unprivileged and defenceless, but alive as no mere 'thinker' entrenched in professional privilege can ever be? This would be a culture in which the 'common man' could find sufficient *inner security* to respect achievement in other realms of activities than his own, instead of resenting, despising or distrusting them as he does now. This would enable black-coated workers and manual workers to realise their complementary functions within a community in which neither *can* do without the other, so that co-operation in a friendly emulation and mutual respect can take the place of the aggressive self-assertion of the spiritually insecure. Such a community, sharing a common culture, would make it possible for each to *be* himself and thus to rejoice in *other* selves.

Such a community would then throw up real artists in

many mediums to express a glimpse of its own soul. This would be a healthier soul than that portrayed so faithfully by some modern work that is so akin to that produced by the insane. Such artists are sensing and responding to the underworld which made Hitler and the present widespread disorder possible. But we need more artists who can go deeper still and let the symbols appropriate to the healing, regenerating side emerge to focus and unify a direction that can illuminate the way for the many who cannot—and should not need to do so if they could—go into the depths. A Parsifal can find a Grail that is an inspiration and source of strength to many. These are directions in which 'the many owe much to the few'.

Buber points out that 'What the right is can be experienced by none of the groups of today except through men who belong to them *staking their own souls to experience it*, and then revealing it, however bitter it may be, to their companions—charitably if it may be, cruelly if it must be. . . . And if one still asks if one may be certain of finding what is right on this steep path, once again the answer is *No*: there is no certainty. There is only a chance; but there is no other. The risk does not ensure the truth for us; but it, and it alone leads us to where the breath of truth is to be felt.'[1]

We cannot be sure that the moral and spiritual resources of mankind will rise to the challenge *in time*. But I think we can hope that there may be enough of those who are really coming to grips with the forces *within* us, scattered about behind the scenes in the world, to at least *delay* the explosion until there may be a remnant capable of carrying on something vital through, and in spite of, the catastrophe of a third global war in a century; if it does come. More than that, I think, is beyond legitimate hope; though not beyond actual possibility. Creative forces are stronger in the long run; but at critical points, destructive ones cannot always be held in leash until they have found themselves defeated

[1] *Between Man and Man*, p. 70.

by the moral and spiritual forces they had despised, but could not destroy.

In the long run we have to choose between the love of power or the power of love. The fate of mankind depends on the choice.

STRANGERS IN
INDIA

STRANGERS IN
INDIA

by
PENDEREL MOON

GREENWOOD PRESS, PUBLISHERS
WESTPORT, CONNECTICUT

PREFACE

Facts and figures about India are easily obtainable. But these often tend to remain academic abstractions, unrelated to human life as it is actually led in that country. In this book an attempt is made to connect discussion of Indian problems with typical Indian incidents, illustrative of the way of life and the modes of thought and speech of the people.

In the course of the discussion there is a good deal of criticism of British actions and policies in India. To some people this may be distasteful. But it is time that Englishmen learnt to view their record in India more objectively than has been their habit in the past. Criticisms of the British Raj, though often ill-informed and ill-natured, are not on that account ill-founded. The critics may seem unreasonable; but psychologically, if not logically, they usually have some justification; and this ought to be recognized and understood. The customary idealizations of the British Raj are annoying to Indians, harmful to British interests, and quite unnecessary.

For the British achievement has been sufficiently remarkable to require no euphemism or exaggeration. It can stand on its own merits. It was no small thing for a tiny handful of Englishmen to conquer a distant and populous country, to administer it peacefully for over a century with tolerance and humanity, and to plant in its somewhat uncongenial soil the great liberal ideals and institutions of England. And no one intimate with India can doubt the admiration and gratitude which successive generations of Indians have felt for nameless Englishmen who have worked in their midst.

Indians are not unaware of what they owe to England. It is rather Englishmen who are apt to forget what they owe to India—not least how much of their own achievement in India has been dependent on Indian ability and co-operation. Neither the merits nor the defects of the British Raj are attributable solely to the British. Without Indian talent the

5

great fabric of ordered government could never have been built; nor could it have been sustained with such impressive stability without certain qualities—which are also defects—of Indian character—a respect for authority, a strong sense of personal loyalty, and a quick responsiveness to great ideas. The Indian Empire is the product of joint endeavours. Future ages will perhaps admire it.

Parts of this book will not be readily intelligible without some knowledge of (i) recent constitutional developments in India, and (ii) the system of district administration. Brief notes on both these subjects will be found at the end of the book.

Any official, e.g. judge, magistrate, or police officer, referred to in the course of the book may be presumed to be an Indian, unless the contrary is clearly indicated. The number of English officials in India is exceedingly small. In many districts there is only one; in many none at all. This is not always fully appreciated.

The Indian villagers and other persons of little or no education who appear in this book would have spoken in their own vernacular. What they would have actually said has been translated fairly literally into English. The English put into the mouths of more educated Indians represents the sort of English that they might have used.

P.M.

Aston Tirrold,
December 1943

CONTENTS

I

INTRODUCTION

'We must look at India with somewhat of an Indian eye.'
SIR CHARLES WOOD.

At the end of the 1914–18 War the Indian Empire presented to England a novel and disconcerting problem. India, it was not doubted, was still unfit to govern herself. 'The association of Indians in every branch of the administration and the development of self-governing institutions' could 'only be achieved by successive stages'. But meanwhile there was a singular lack of Englishmen willing to go and do the governing and administering for her. During the four years of war recruitment to the Services had been practically stopped; and this was followed by the resignation of some officers who felt that they could not adjust themselves to the new conditions created by the Montagu-Chelmsford Reforms. Thus in addition to filling ordinary vacancies there was a good deal of leeway to make up. But suitable recruits were hard to come by. The white man showed a disinclination to take up his burden.

The British Government attacked the problem energetically. In order to attract young men to the Indian Services they increased the material rewards; and they discreetly idealized the moral quality of the work. The conditions of service as regards pay, passages, leave and allowances were improved as a result of the Lee Commission (1923) so as to ensure a standard of living unsurpassed by any Civil Service in the world. The pay and security were certainly good. And the work was interesting, even inspiring. Retired civilians, public men, and the Secretary of State for India himself visited the Universities and urged young men to go to India where there awaited them a task, different indeed from that of preceding generations, but perhaps more enthralling, certainly more difficult and, success if fully accomplished, more redounding to the glory of the English name. It would be for them (so it was suggested) to see the

9

final accomplishment of England's mission in India—a mission foreseen a century earlier by Munro, Elphinstone, Henry Lawrence and others—namely, under her guidance and fostering care to bring India into the scale of free, independent nations.

To these siren appeals there was a gratifying response. A few early swallows in the middle twenties gave promise of more to come, and by 1930 *The Times* was able to congratulate itself and its readers on the number of English recruits passing into the Indian Civil Service with first-rate University records.

Some of these recruits, among whom was a sensible but rather earnest young man named Greenlane, were inclined to inquire why it had been necessary to wait right up till their lifetime to take any substantial step towards Indian self-government, said to have been the goal of English policy for nearly 100 years. They received no very satisfactory reply. For ever since the Mutiny, and increasingly in recent years, English writers on India had been discouraged from raising and discussing awkward questions. And this was one of the many questions which tended to be burked. It was, as Greenlane soon discovered, only one small example of a general defect which had made British Indian history 'the worst patch in current scholarship'. A century ago, when the East India Company still ruled in India, English historians' comment on the management of Indian affairs was often brutally frank and critical. For in those days there was no politically conscious India to be afraid of. Moreover the Company was not a national concern, and many who were jealous of its profits, political influence, and patronage felt no misgiving about showing (or learning) that its rule was corrupt and oppressive. But after the Mutiny and the final assumption of the Government of India by the Crown, India became unquestionably a national possession— 'the brightest jewel in Britain's Imperial Crown'—and incidentally the largest foreign market that any country has ever been able to control for its own advantage. Henceforward India was too manifestly mixed up with England's national pride and prosperity for English writers to be able to give a full, judicious, and unbiased account of British-Indian history. It became an acknowledged axiom that, barring a few painful episodes in the early stages, British rule had been for India as a whole an almost unmixed blessing. It was pleasant, it was natural for the English to believe this. And, in all classes, they did believe it.

'How do you like our rule in India?' inquired a cheerful bootblack of one of Greenlane's Indian friends as he shined his shoes in Piccadilly. 'I am afraid we are not at all fond of it,' came the obvious answer. It was puzzling and distressing to the bootblack who had confidently expected a bouquet.

But the confident assumption of the beneficence of British rule has not been confined to semi-educated bootblacks with a smattering of garbled history. A distinguished modern historian[1] has recited in stately periods the catalogue of British achievements in India:

'They have preserved India from foreign attack, and given it the blessing of unbroken internal peace and freedom of trade. There is not an acre of British India the title to which is not inscribed in the books of British administration and protected by the force of British law. Some forty million acres of desert have been reclaimed for cultivation by the art of British irrigation engineers. Though the number of Englishmen engaged on the administration has at no time exceeded five thousand, this alien people has so administered the country that the population has increased by more than 230 millions. Such measure of intellectual and political unity as may now be found in India is due to the English conquest and administration. The one common language which goes from end to end of the sub-continent, the one common medium of higher instruction . . . is the language of England.'

He goes on with evident sincerity to pay a remarkable tribute to the British official in India.

'The advantage to India of a Government exempt from irregularity, caprice, and corruption, and dealing out even-handed justice irrespective of caste and creed, has been generally acknowledged. The British members of the Indian Public Services have perhaps more nearly than any other ruling class realized the ideal of disinterested Government which Plato thought could only be secured if the guardians of the State were shielded from the temptations of ownership and family. Their task has been exacting: to suppress crime, to provide for the needs of a modern State out of the scanty resources of a

[1] H. A. L. Fisher in *A History of Europe*, ch xxii.

11

poor oriental community, to promote the unwelcome novelties of education and hygiene among a backward and superstitious peasantry, and to act as a buffer between hostile creeds and communities.'

These were the conclusions of a scholar and experienced man of affairs. And Greenlane, reading the standard histories of India, could hardly be expected to form a different opinion. Nevertheless, he had an uneasy feeling that important facts were being suppressed. He could not help observing that little was said of the economic factors affecting the history of India; and this was all the more significant in that Indian politicians were inclined to allege that the English had ruined India's prosperity, arrested her economic development and kept her in abject misery as one vast rural slum.

Of course, the early period of British rule in India had admittedly been very bad. After Plassey (1757), there was for thirty years a regular system of direct spoliation. The Company's servants plundered and oppressed the Company's Indian possessions without disguise or shame. The facts were notorious. They had been denounced in Parliament (with some rhetorical exaggeration); they had been more coolly reported by some of the Company's own servants. 'It must give pain to an Englishman', wrote one of them in 1769 'to have reason to think that since the accession of the Company to the Dewanee[1] the condition of the people of this country has been worse than it was before; and yet I am afraid the fact is undoubted. . . . This fine country, which flourished under the most despotic and arbitrary government, is verging towards its ruin while the English have really so great a share in the administration.'

Later, Macaulay had written of this period, 'Enormous fortunes were rapidly accumulated at Calcutta, while thirty millions of human beings were reduced to the last extremity of wretchedness. They had been accustomed to live under tyranny, but not under tyranny like this.'

But this disgraceful plunder was confined to the limited area of the Company's then existing dominions, viz. Bengal, Bihar, and Orissa. And measures were taken to stop it as soon as the facts became generally known in England. With the turn of the century the system of open

[1] The right to collect revenue; hence, Civil Administration.

spoliation was ended. And in 1833, when the Company's Charter was renewed, the grand principle was laid down that 'the interests of the native subjects are to be preferred to those of Europeans wherever the two come into conflict'.

And so all lived happily ever afterwards. Yes, according to English popular opinion, all save a small intelligentsia—a mere handful of the population. Yet it was disturbing to Greenlane to find that most of the Indian students, who, like him, were preparing themselves for service in India, belonged to this minority, and perversely carried the indictment far beyond 1800 or 1833. According to them, India's ancient village economy, based on the union of agriculture and domestic industry, was ruined during the nineteenth century by the flood of machine-made cotton goods from Lancashire. Unprotected by tariffs, millions of Indian spinners and weavers were thrown out of work and forced to crowd into the villages and thus begin the 'deadly over-pressure on agriculture'.

Not only, they alleged, were India's indigenous manufacturing industries ruined during this century; her wretched and impoverished people were saddled with the cost of their own conquest and subjection. The wars, whereby from 1800–50 England extended her dominion over the whole of India, and the military operations required to suppress the Mutiny of 1857 were charged to the Indian taxpayer. England, in fact, not only conquered India mainly with Indian rather than English troops, but actually made India pay for the privilege—a feat of ingenuity not often emulated. These payments laid the foundations of the famous 'Drain', 'Tribute' or 'Home Charges' whereby India annually hands to England large sums for services rendered.

Up to this point Greenlane could to some extent meet the indictment. The policy of *laisser-faire* free-trade which was applied to India in the nineteenth century in perfect good faith, may have led, he was ready to admit, quite unintentionally to some unfortunate results. But the error, if error it was, like the previous errors of the eighteenth century, was corrected as soon as fully realized. It was now recognized that India must be allowed to impose such protective duties as she considered necessary in order to foster her industrial development and that the manipulation of tariffs for the benefit of Lancashire

13

was a thing of the past. As for the so-called 'Drain', practically all the debt incurred in the nineteenth century had, by 1914, been repaid. The amount of unproductive debt then outstanding was only the modest sum of £13,000,000. The remaining debt represented loans for productive purposes, e.g. the construction of railways and canals. No one could reasonably complain of the payment of interest on such loans. The bulk of the other 'Home Charges' consisted of the pay and pensions of English civil and military officers. No doubt, English officers were somewhat expensive, but the labourer is worthy of his hire.

But if Greenlane gave this partial answer, it only provoked critical Indian students to a further indictment. The English, they would say, have a happy knack of representing that defects have been remedied, abuses and injustices corrected. The past may have been bad; but the present is always good; and the future is always going to be still better. In real fact however, as soon as one system of exploitation is denounced and ended, another covertly takes its place. The era when English manufacturing interests could freely control Indian trade for their own benefit passed away at the beginning of the present century. But long ere this a new method of sucking wealth from India had been devised. England, after plundering India for over a century, had been able from about 1860 onwards to use the proceeds to set up as a vast moneylender. At the time of the Mutiny English capital investments in India were negligible. By 1914 they had reached £500 million. By 1929 they had swollen to more than £700 million. With the profits from these ever-increasing investments steadily rising, England could afford to see her share in Indian trade declining and to grant Indians greater freedom in the management of their tariffs. By these investments she had secured for herself a first charge on the major productive resources and enterprises of the country. Provided internal peace was preserved, and provided English interests could control the banking system (where they were well entrenched) and influence Government's financial and exchange policy, there was no reason why the astute old moneylender should not comfortably rake in the interest on her investments for the rest of the century. As for the debtor—well he just had to pay. After all, if you are so poor that you cannot

14

develop your own resources without borrowing money, you must expect to pay for it. It matters not whether your borrowings are wise or unwise, voluntary or involuntary. A bond is a bond. The creditor must take his pound of flesh.

Here then, they contended, was England's new, respectable, yet diabolical system of exploiting India. Here was the twentieth-century model, smoother and more silent in its workings than its predecessors, but not a whit different in its purpose and effect, viz. to enrich England at the expense of the poor Indian peasant.

Greenlane, though a bit puzzled and distressed at this indictment, was more than a little sceptical of it. He could not perhaps satisfactorily answer all the charges and was vaguely aware that English writers tended to shirk these economic questions altogether. But this Indian criticism seemed to defeat itself by its own violence; and books about India by Indians usually bore such obvious marks of bias and rancour as to carry little conviction. In any case, he comforted himself, the critics were only a minute fraction of the population. This tiny over-clever minority might fail to appreciate the blessings of British rule, but the dumb millions of India, her 'backward and superstitious peasantry', were surely thankful to be saved from war, pestilence and famine, injustice and oppression by a just and powerful British Government. Surely there could be no doubt about this. Anyway, these dumb millions he and his brother officers were going to serve to the best of their ability, as so many British officers had done in the past, despite all difficulties caused by the increased Indianization of the Services and the growing power of Indian Ministers. To uphold the interest of the underdog and at the same time to facilitate the transition to Indian self-government—these were to be his guiding aims.

And so one autumn day in the early 'thirties he set sail for India, a trifle worried perhaps by Indian criticisms, but all the more eager to learn on the spot something of the realities of British rule.

But if he, as he sets forth, is a trifle puzzled and disconcerted, the officials of the India Office are not. They have everything cut and dried. Greenlane had met a few of them; for in those days certain India Office officials made a point of establishing contact with young English officers going out to India and encouraged an interchange of views. The conversation would range over current Indian problems; there would be speculation on the character and probable duration of British rule and on the real objects of British policy. The India Office officials were quite sure of their ground. Any misplaced idealism, any doubts regarding the continuance of British rule were quickly silenced with the curt remark, 'We have £1,000 million capital in India. We remain in India to safeguard it, not to teach them how to govern themselves.' These realists of the desk knew what they were about. Dealing at third hand with the affairs of a distant country which they had never visited, ignorant of its people and unwarmed by any personal affection for them, they could view the matter with cool detachment and flatter their sedentary selves that they were hard-headed. It was useful, no doubt, for Greenlane to meet such men, and to receive from them a refreshing douche of realist cold water. It was comforting, too, to be assured that the India Office would see him through—that his job would last his lifetime all right. With such men to protect his interests he could embark for India at the outset of his career with the feeling that his pension was already practically safe in his pocket.

We will follow him there in the next chapter.

II

THE PEASANT AND POVERTY

'No one can pass through various parts of India without being profoundly touched at the sad spectacles of malnutrition and semi-starvation that obtrude themselves upon the eye, or can doubt that many of the inhabitants of India never know what it is to have enough to eat.'—(Calcutta Correspondent—*The Times*, 1st February 1927.)

'An eye accustomed to flowery pastures and waving harvests is astonished and repelled by this wide extent of hopeless sterility.' With this observation Greenlane, as he travelled from Bombay to Delhi, most heartily concurred. He shared the feelings of many other people who on their first visit to India make this journey. For once you have traversed the narrow strip of coastal plain and begun to ascend the Ghats, you have before you a twenty-four hour train journey through country which appears uniformly depressing and infertile. Mile succeeds mile of stony, scrub-covered hills with only here and there a meagre patch of unpromising cultivation. For much of his journey the same prospect greets the traveller from Bombay to Calcutta. Nor do these journeys reveal the full extent of India's unfavoured regions. West of Delhi lies the semi-desert of Rajputana; beyond that the desert of Sind.

Yet despite these great barren stretches of country, Indian writers habitually harp on India's natural wealth and abundant resources. India is a rich country; but her people are poor. This is the grim paradox which the English have to answer for.

The people are certainly poor. But India's natural wealth has been much exaggerated. The impressions of the modern traveller, who in a single journey by road or rail can cover hundreds of miles of country and is not confined to the narrow limits of specially-favoured localities, are a safer guide than economists' glowing statistics about cultivable areas and mineral resources.

As an agricultural country, India is gravely handicapped by

17

the uncertainty of the rainfall. Even where the soil is good— and much of it is poor—large tracts cannot be cultivated at all without heavy preliminary expenditure on wells or canals. Still larger areas, in the absence of artificial irrigation, can only yield inferior crops and fail altogether in years of bad rainfall. The cultivator himself is debilitated by disease of which the most widespread, malaria, has not yet been mastered by modern science and is fostered by every extension of artificial irrigation. In many parts of India cow dung is the only con- venient form of fuel and what ought to enrich the land is required to boil the milk.

Industrially India suffers from a bad distribution of resources. The coal is awkwardly concentrated in Bengal and Bihar. Hence in order to run the north-western railway (covering the area Delhi–Peshawar–Karachi) 200 loaded coal trucks have to be hauled daily approximately 1,000 miles. It is as though Europe had to draw all its coal from the Balkans. The same problem of distance hampers the use of water power. If science could reveal how to transmit electric energy without wires (which the Brains Trust has said is now the most needed dis- covery), the whole of India might quickly be electrified. As it is, the high cost of transmission over long distances impedes progress.

Not all these facts could be known to Greenlane. Neverthe- less, as he travelled to Delhi he was struck by the barrenness of the scene and puzzled that so judicious an author as Sir Malcolm Darling[1] could write, 'The most arresting fact about India is that her soil is rich and her people poor.' Definitely wrong, he thought to himself. The people are poor—that is plain. But the richness of the soil is not apparent. 'De non existentibus et non apparentibus eadem est ratio.'

At Delhi he had an introduction to his father's old friend, Sir Digby Dinwiddy, a worthy gentleman of nearly sixty, who after twenty-five years of strenuous district life had found in the Government of India Secretariat a convenient resting-place before retirement. With little delicacy of perception Greenlane at once plunged him into a controversy, the very existence of which he preferred to ignore.

[1] Sir Malcolm Darling, K.C.I.E., author of the *Punjab Peasant in Prosperity and Debt*, *Rusticus Loquitur*, and *Wisdom and Waste*.

18

THE PEASANT AND POVERTY

'I hope you had a good journey up?'

'Thank you. Very comfortable in spite of the excessive noisiness of the train. But I was very much struck by the poverty of the country and of such of the people as I saw. Do you think, sir, Indians are poorer now than when we first came here?'

'God bless my soul, my good young man! Who put such ideas into your head? Do you imagine that all the railways and canals we've built in this country have not added to its wealth? Why, before we brought peace and order to India, the peasant had no security of tenure, no access to foreign markets, and no ambition to do more than scrape a meagre subsistence from the soil. If the rains failed, men and cattle simply died. There were no means of bringing in grain from surplus areas. But all that is changed now.'

'Then you don't agree with Moreland that India is to-day little, if at all, richer than she was at the death of Akbar?'

'I don't know anything about Moreland and his opinions, and if he has spent his time trying to compare the income per head of population to-day with the income per head in A.D. 1600 I don't want to.[1] It is obvious that he has been wasting his time. The material is not available on which to form a comparison. You may cook up figures to prove any absurdity, but whatever Moreland or anyone else may say, I can tell you that even in the thirty-five years that I have been in this country there has been a visible improvement in the general standard of living. Of course, owing to the slump, everyone is feeling the draught a bit at the moment. But that is only temporary. Prices will begin to go up again soon, we hope. Up to a year or two ago the people were really wonderfully prosperous.'

'But isn't it possible, sir, that the improvement which you say you've seen was also only temporary—I mean to say that temporarily owing to the high prices of agricultural produce during and after the war the peasant became for a few years more prosperous and this has given you the mistaken impres-

[1] In case the reader is more eager for enlightenment, it may be mentioned that W. H. Moreland, C.S.I., C.I.E., was a member of the Indian Civil Service and has made a study of the economics of Mogul times. He is author of *India at the death of Akbar* and *From Akbar to Aurangzeb* and *Jahangir's India*.

19

sion of a steady improvement during your service; whereas
fundamentally there has been no change?'

'Not at all, not at all. Even in 1914, before the beginning of
the war, people were ever so much better off than they were
in the 'nineties. I remember when I first came out and was put
on famine duty seeing cattle eating dung in the streets and
sinking down and dying. There has been nothing like that for
the last twenty-five years.'

'But the people still seem so poor that it is rather difficult
to conceive how they could be poorer and continue to live.
The Simon Commission, taking the most optimistic estimates,
concluded that the average Indian's income is barely £8 a year.
This was only an average. There must be many below it; and
since the depression and the fall in prices this average of £8
may, I suppose, have been halved.'

Sir Digby was by now becoming visibly restive. 'I'm blowed
if I know how you young fellows get stuffed up with all these
figures and nonsense nowadays. Here are we who have spent
our lives in India working for the peasants—devoting all our
energies to their welfare through the heat of the day—and then
you come out and tell us that they are worse off than when we
began. I don't know how they let you get these notions. It
must be due to that year you spend nowadays in England before
you come out, supposedly learning the language. I've always
said that they ought to get you out here quick and set you down
to learn your work, instead of leaving you to idle away a year
at one of the Universities, reading seditious literature and
studying phonetics.'

'I don't see why you should class the Simon Commission
Report as seditious literature,' said Greenlane, and immediately
repented of his rashness. For Sir Digby was now wrathful.

'Look here, young man, I haven't time to stop bandying
words with you. But I tell you again that in my time in India
I have seen a very marked change for the better in the condition
of the people, and the sooner you get that firmly into your head
the better. Well, I must be off.' He rose and with conscious
dignity and importance left the room.

His wife, who had listened to this unfortunate argument
with some embarrassment, felt that she should try to smooth
things over.

20

THE PEASANT AND POVERTY

'I am afraid my husband was a little annoyed at your remarks. But never mind; you needn't think any more of it.'

'I am very sorry if I was rude. I didn't realize that I was starting on such a dangerous topic.'

'Well, if you begin telling men who have worked most of their lives in India that their efforts have been wasted, and that over 100 years of English rule has merely resulted in the people getting poorer, you must expect them to get a bit nettled. However, never mind; you'll probably not have occasion to bring up the question again. You're going to my husband's old Province aren't you? Ah well, they always say that it is the granary of India and that no one there suffers from lack of food. I've sometimes heard my husband say that the prosperity of the peasant in the new canal-irrigated areas is unequalled anywhere in Asia. I don't think that when you're there you'll be quite so troubled by the question of poverty. Besides you'll be busy learning the language and your work.'

And to some extent she proved right. During the next two years Greenlane struggled with the language, his duties as a magistrate and the summer heat. It was not till 1934 that he again had occasion to discuss with a senior official the question of the poverty of the Indian masses; and this time it was not he who suggested the topic, but his own immediate superior, Mr. Lightfoot, the district officer of Sawanpur, to whom he had been posted as assistant.

Late one August afternoon in 1934, Mr. Lightfoot, after a heavy day's work in Court hearing appeals, was collecting his papers preparatory to going home. 'Sangat Rai' he said, addressing his Reader,[1] 'to-morrow is a holiday and I want to pay a visit to Gandiwind. It is your village, isn't it, and only about six miles off?'

'Less than six miles, your Honour. It is your Honour's kindness to pay us a visit. The people will be very pleased.'

'Well, as a matter of fact, it is not very kind of me, Sangat Rai, as I would like you to be present when I arrive, and I am afraid that may rather interfere with your holiday. I hope you haven't any important private business to attend to to-morrow morning?'

[1] A magistrate's Clerk of Court. Pay generally Rs.40–90 per mensem.

'If your Honour is coming to my village, what private business could I have? I have no business. I am absolutely at your Honour's disposal. May I tell the tahsildar[1] to be present?'

'No, I don't think we need bother the tahsildar. But I would like all the lumbadars[2] of the village to be present and, of course, anyone else who cares to turn up. Do you think you could be so kind as to inform them?'

'Your Honour's intended visit will be good news to all the people of the village. Your Honour's reputation for justice is so great that all will be longing to get a glimpse of you. What time shall I say that your Honour will arrive?'

'Oh, I should say about ten-thirty.'

'Your Honour works so hard that even on a holiday you don't take rest. I am amazed to see how your Honour works.'

'Why are you amazed? You have to work just as hard as I do. All the time I'm in Court you have to be here attending to what is going on. And you have to arrive before me and leave after me. In fact the more I work the more you have to.'

'We small humble clerks are expected to work hard. It is not expected of big officers like your Honour.'

'But I draw about twenty times as much pay as you, so I ought to do at least twice as much work.'

'It is your Honour's noble self that has these ideas. We humble clerks cannot say anything.'

'Oh, by the way, I would like the magistrate in whose area Gandiwind falls to be present to-morrow. It's Mr. Greenlane isn't it? Good, I can bring him along with me in the car. Good evening, Sangat Rai.'

Gandiwind was a large village with about 3,000 turbulent inhabitants. The land was fertile and, being near to the City of Sawanpur, well manured. In addition to the ordinary flat-roofed mud houses, there were several substantial brick buildings. These and a number of orchards instead of the usual fields of maize and millet testified to the comparative prosperity of the place. About half of the village was irrigated by a canal, and in the other half there were plenty of wells fitted with Persian wheels. In fact there was no land solely dependent on rainfall. Wells could be sunk easily; the sub-soil water,

[1] A revenue officer in charge of a part of a district.
[2] Headmen.

22

which was everywhere sweet, was only about twelve feet below the surface; and the strain on the well-cattle was therefore not great. Yet it was not a happy village. Owing to the increase in the population the land had become so subdivided that many of the peasants owned only half an acre. The struggle for existence—and for land—was keen. Fights and murders were the order of the day.

'The thanedar[1] tells me', said Greenlane to Mr. Lightfoot as they drove to the village, 'that since the establishment of British rule not a single murderer in Gandiwind has ever been hanged. The evidence always goes bad.'

'That's a pretty good record, considering that there seem to be three to four reported murders per year, let alone the unreported ones. At that rate the number of unhung murderers must now about equal the male population of the village. It is really rather appalling. However, now that *you're* magistrate in charge of this area, surely you can see that someone is hanged at last.'

'I think I've got one in the bag already—that young fellow Jarnail Singh who cracked open his uncle's head in order that he might inherit his land. It seems to be an absolutely cast-iron case. You'll remember I told you about it. I'm just going to commit it to Sessions.'

'Don't you be too confident. I think you said that the principal witness is an old woman. I bet she'll be got at by the relatives and when she comes to give evidence before the Sessions Judge she'll simply say, "I'm illiterate. I don't know anything about it," and no questioning will drag any more out of her. But really I don't know what to do with these people. I've got ready this proposal for punitive police[2] and we'll threaten them with that to-day, but I don't know that it will do much good. I feel we're just tinkering with symptoms and not really getting down to fundamentals. . . . Oh God, they've produced a band, I suppose that's Sangat Rai. Give me

---

[1] A sub-inspector of police in charge of a police station.

[2] This means the quartering of additional police on a village, group of villages, or town at the inhabitants' expense. The burden lies not so much in the actual cost of the police as in the unofficial trouble that the police can cause, and are often expected to cause, to the people.

23

a wink if you hear anything that might be considered to be "God Save the King"!'

A large crowd was collected at the side of the road on the outskirts of the village opposite what appeared to be a half-built temple. In front were lined up the six headmen all with garlands in their hands. Five were greybeards with gnarled faces and an impressive air of venerable wisdom. The sixth was a powerfully built man of about thirty, whose truculent demeanour indicated the sort of stormy past which might be concealed by the long grey beards of the other five. As Mr. Lightfoot alighted from his car, the band, with evident enjoyment, blared forth 'God Save the King' and the headmen, with a solemnity appropriate to the occasion, stepped forward one by one and put their garlands over his head.

Greenlane, a few paces away, viewed the scene with an expression of critical boredom. He could not understand how such a sensible man as Mr. Lightfoot could tolerate, much less enjoy, all this flap-doodle. And yet there he was apparently revelling in it. By this time, the headmen, having played their part in decent order, had retired and a throng of miscellaneous enthusiasts had surged excitedly forward and were heaping garlands round his neck pell-mell, while he, his face scarcely visible amidst the mass of flowers, appeared to be beaming with childish delight. 'Ah, there you are, Sangat Rai. Hooray!' he cried with obviously unaffected pleasure as a quiet, timorous, bespectacled little man wormed his way to the front and placed a garland over his head. 'How very kind of you to bring a garland!'

How ridiculous, thought Greenlane. Really, Lightfoot is a bit of an ass. Fancy being so pleased at having a garland put round his neck by his own Reader. These officers who have been some years in India have all, even the best of them, become so inured to sycophantic flattery and a display of exaggerated respect, that they positively enjoy it, and would miss its absence. What a corrupting atmosphere to live in!

But he hadn't time to pursue these reflections, for Mr. Lightfoot had already begun to disentangle himself again from the garlands and, handing the whole heap of flowers to his orderly, Khuda Baksh, to put in the car, called out, 'Come on, Greenlane; let's go round the village.'

There was nothing much to see in the village. After recent

rain it was a morass of mud and ordure and the surrounding fields were flooded with water. 'Why is there so much water standing about here?' inquired Mr. Lightfoot, and was answered by a tumultuous roar from the attendant crowd. 'We are ruined! We are dying of starvation! Our crops have been utterly destroyed!' In a few seconds they had worked themselves up into a passion of anger and excitement. Greenlane and Lightfoot looked at each other in amusement and shook their heads. There was nothing for it but to wait for the hubbub to subside. At last, during a momentary lull, Mr. Lightfoot said quietly, 'I am very sorry to hear that you are starving. Very sorry and very much astonished. For look at this man here,' and he pointed to a huge, burly, black-bearded fellow twice as big as himself standing near him in the crowd. 'If he is starving, I must be already dead.' The villagers smiled; in a second they had forgotten all their previous wrath and were quite happy again.

'Now, lumbadar,' said Mr. Lightfoot to one of the greybeards, 'what is the real trouble?'

'Sir, the water has been standing here for six days, and is damaging our crops. But if you will write to the canal officers to open the sluice-gate, it will all drain away into the big canal.'

'Haven't you been to see the canal officers about it yourselves?'

'Sir, we have sent so many telegrams and petitions but they take no notice of them. It is our good fortune that you have come here to-day and will be able to save us.'

'I will ring up the canal authorities as soon as I get back to Sawanpur. Sangat Rai, you had better let me know in Court to-morrow whether the water has begun to drain off; for if it hasn't, we'll have to agitate further. And now, I think, we'll go back to the car and have a talk.'

Chairs were brought for Greenlane and Mr. Lightfoot and they sat down in the roadway opposite the temple. The six headmen and Sangat Rai were allowed the privilege of sitting near them on charpoys.[1] The rest of the crowd stood or squatted on the ground.

'Lumbadars,' said Mr. Lightfoot turning to the headmen but addressing the whole assembled multitude. 'There have been

[1] Light wooden bedsteads with string webbing in place of springs.

25

six murders in this village since January. That is nearly one a month and it's far too many. What is more, several of them were committed in broad daylight right in the village itself before many witnesses. Yet the culprits haven't been caught and no one has turned up to give evidence. There was that poor old woman whose head was mercilessly battered to pieces right here in front of this very temple, I believe. There were several persons in the temple at the time, but they did nothing and will tell nothing. Then there was that young man who was mangled in the belly with a spear, managed to run away, and then was hounded through the crowded village streets and hacked to pieces outside the oil seller's shop. At least forty or fifty persons must have seen that murder and yet no one will give the police any information. Then there was Jarnail Singh who killed his uncle. We've got him—but he's the only one out of the whole lot that we *have* got. I can't remember all the rest, but it's a dreadful record. Why do you do these things? Or if you don't do them yourselves, why don't you help catch the ruffians who do?'

No one ventured to reply except Sangat Rai who said apologetically. 'Your Honour, they are illiterate, savage people without any understanding. It is ignorance which makes them do these things.'

'Recently I hear there has been another shocking episode,' continued Mr. Lightfoot. 'I'm told that one night last week a poor cobbler's wife was raped by no less than seven young Sikh zemindars[1] one after the other, and left unconscious. No report was made to the police and I don't know what redress has been given to the poor woman.'

There was silence for a few seconds. Then one of the headmen said, 'Sir, what can we say? We have been utterly disgraced by those misbegotten bastards. But one of them was the woman's paramour. While her husband was away, that rascal went to lie with her and then those other six also jumped in. What could we do? We only heard of it when it was over. We have ourselves fined them each Rs.30 and given Rs.50 to the woman. The rest of the money will go to the repair of this

[1] Zemindar=a landholder. In Northern India this is generally a peasant. In Bengal and parts of the United Provinces a big landed proprietor.

26

temple. I am ashamed that your Honour should have heard of this matter. But whatever your Honour may now order, we will obey.'

'Rs.50 seems to me to be rather inadequate redress for what the woman suffered.'

'Sir, she was fully satisfied. Your Reader, Sangat Rai, will confirm that she was fully satisfied. You may ask anyone. Her husband has returned and they have now both left the village. Why should your Honour worry about it further? But it is as your Honour pleases.'

'Well, as you seem to have settled up the affair in your own way I don't want to pursue it. But I can't overlook all these murders. And I'm therefore going to propose that punitive police should be quartered in this village for one year.'

There were some murmurings in the crowd and a middle-aged man with a bitter defiant expression shouted, 'It is injustice. We are dying of poverty already. We can't afford to pay for more police.'

But the headmen quickly silenced him, 'Take no notice of him, Sir,' they said, 'he is a bad character. It is he and others like him who disgrace us. What you propose is no doubt just. Though we wish that you could show mercy and forgive us, we must accept what you decide.'

'Bravo, Lumbadars,' said Mr. Lightfoot, 'I am pleased with you. You have spoken well. I will think the matter over.' He paused and scrutinized for a few minutes the crowd of villagers squatting before him, black-bearded, sullen-eyed, vaguely aggressive and defiant. Then he glanced at the meek, diminutive Sangat Rai, sitting squeezed between two large headmen like the Dormouse at the Mad Hatter's Tea Party. Speaking in English he said, 'Sangat Rai, how do you manage to survive amidst this gang of cut-throats?'

'It is through your Honour's kindness.'

'That is hardly an explanation.'

'Your Honour, they are all illiterate people, whereas I can read and write and have some knowledge of law. When they are in trouble they come to me for advice. I tell them true things, your Honour. I do not deceive them and make mischief. They have confidence in me. They have of course their own quarrels, especially about their land which has become sub-

27

divided into very small fragments. But they have no quarrel with me. So I am in no danger from them, although it is true that they are very violent and dangerous men.'

Greenlane meanwhile had also been surveying the crowd. He turned suddenly to Mr. Lightfoot. 'And these are what Congress call the oppressed and downtrodden Indian villager! Good God, did you ever see such a crowd of toughs? Each one of them is ready to stick you in the guts for two pins. Downtrodden and oppressed indeed! A bit of oppression is just about what they need. I'd like to get hold of one or two of them and give them a hammering. That is about all they understand. I wish we had Gandhi or Nehru or one of those chaps here and could just show them this lot. Downtrodden and oppressed! What bunkum it is!'

Mr. Lightfoot meditated for a few moments and then said, 'Yes, it does seem rather rubbish. But you must remember that not all Indian villagers are quite so violent and aggressive as the people of Gandiwind. And, I suppose, Gandhi and co. would say that they are what they are—little better than untamed savages—because they have been oppressed, or perhaps rather, depressed, economically. After all, in their present condition, they're not exactly a good advertisement for 100 years of British rule.'

'Then do you really think there is something in what Congress say about our having impoverished the Indian masses?'

'I should have to have notice of that question. It is a difficult subject. I'll try and give you a discourse about it this evening, if you like.'

'Oh, please do.'

'Well, we had better be getting back now.' Mr. Lightfoot rose. 'Good-bye, Sangat Rai,' he said. 'Thank you for collecting all the people. Good-bye, lumbadars. I'll consider further about the punitive police and I won't forget to ring up the canal authorities about that flood water. Good-bye, good-bye,' and Mr. Lightfoot and Greenlane had stepped into the car and started home before the people were well aware that they had risen to leave.

'We got away quickly enough,' said Mr. Lightfoot laughing. 'I was afraid we were going to be let in for another go of "God Save the King".'

'Oh, I thought you rather liked all that sort of stuff. You seemed very pleased with all the garlands.'

'If a child offers you a daisy-chain you generally try not to look too annoyed. I'm used to it; perhaps now I even positively like it. A state of semi-deification, though dangerous, is not wholly unpleasant. Khuda Baksh!' Mr. Lightfoot suddenly called to his orderly who was sitting in front with the driver. 'What do you think of those six Sikhs all raping that woman?'

Khuda Baksh gave a grunt of infinite disdain. 'The Sikhs are a race of swine,' he said.

That evening, after dinner, Mr. Lightfoot gave his promised discourse. He rather enjoyed holding forth. A bachelor of just over forty, he had spent almost all his service as a district officer. The loneliness of the life and the habit of deciding everything autocratically for himself had developed certain eccentricities of manner and thought. He had the air of one who knew his opinions to be valuable and assumed other people would wish to hear them. In point of fact they were sometimes rather boring. But Greenlane had discovered that Lightfoot combined with his eccentricities and queer philosophical detachment a remarkably strong common sense and a fund of well-digested experience. He was therefore quite happy to lead him on.

'When you spoke this morning about the Indian masses being economically depressed, I couldn't help recalling how much I upset Sir Digby Dinwiddy when I first came out by suggesting that the average Indian is poorer to-day than he was in the time of Akbar. I've never risked raising the question again.'

'You shouldn't tease elderly gentlemen, my dear Greenlane. In any case, such comparisons can have little value or exactitude. Indian nationalist writers are very fond of quoting Tavernier and other seventeenth-century travellers as evidence of the prodigious wealth of India in Mogul times. They contrast these travellers' tales of riches with India's present poverty, and blame us. This is hardly fair, as we are certainly not wholly responsible; but we ourselves invite criticism by our ludicrously glowing accounts of the effects of our rule.

'Travellers' tales will clearly lead us to no certain conclusion regarding India's *absolute* wealth in Mogul times; but they can give us an idea of her *relative* wealth. The seventeenth-century traveller from the West was impressed by India's riches. The modern traveller is impressed by her poverty. It is fair to conclude that relatively India has retrogressed economically since Mogul times, whereas Western Europe has advanced. This conforms with what we should expect on other grounds. The Mogul regime ended in eighteenth-century anarchy, which must have meant economic stagnation, if not actual retrogression. In Europe, on the other hand, the eighteenth century saw the first beginnings of the Industrial Revolution with all its potential additions to wealth.

'We English were not responsible for the Mogul breakdown. We were merely a few of the many vultures that fed on the carcass of the rotting empire. While it rotted, the Industrial Revolution in England began. For in England at that time there existed the necessary basis of peace, order, established government and accumulated capital. These did not exist in India. Peace and order were, in fact, only with difficulty achieved by about 1830—mainly through English efforts. But by 1830 England was already semi-industrialized and equipped to pour into India cheap machine-made cotton goods. And this she proceeded to do, dissolving what remained of the old Indian village system, based on the union of primitive agriculture with hand-spinning and hand-weaving, and driving millions of craftsmen to draw their livelihood solely from the land. Can you blame her? Or can you conceive how this result could have been avoided? As a matter of fact Indian domestic industry had already been much impaired by eighteenth-century anarchy. But leave that aside. Deal for a moment—though I admit it is a foolish pastime—in a little hypothetical history. Suppose the English hadn't conquered India; and suppose that in the early nineteenth century some Indian Government had managed to establish itself on the Mogul ruins; do you imagine that that Government would have been capable of preventing the decay of the old village system through contact with the industrial West? Surely the industrial West must have broken into and overwhelmed the old Indian economy and nothing could have stemmed its onrush.'

'I agree.'

'We ought, of course, to keep clear in our minds that the

impact of Lancashire did in fact accelerate the decline of Indian domestic industry. We should not forget this; for we gained by it very greatly. But I don't think we need blame ourselves over-much for that inevitable impact and its inevitable consequences. Actually I regard the first forty years of the last century, when this process was beginning, as the golden age of English rule. It was then that we laid the foundations of ordered life in India. A fine period. The age of Malcolm, Munro, Metcalfe, and Elphin-stone. A brief but glorious interregnum between eighteenth-century corruption and nineteenth-century complacency.

'I pass on to the next part of the story, which may be taken as covering roughly the period 1860-1900. The Mutiny had been quelled; the English were everywhere undisputedly dominant; peace and order were assured. The Government embarked on a programme of railway and, to a lesser extent, canal construction. This seems to me to have been a natural and, so far as it went, a sound policy. It had the effect of em-ploying some of the displaced craftsmen and labourers who were crowding on to the land; and as India is a great agricul-tural country, it was quite right to develop her agricultural resources by irrigation works and to open to her the markets of the world by railway construction. I doubt whether in that period any conceivable native government would or could have done very differently, if indeed it could have done as much. True, the Government did nothing to encourage any large-scale industrial development. But in view of the actual circumstances and prevalent economic theories of the time they cannot be seriously blamed. The people of India were back-ward and illiterate; and the doctrine of *laisser-faire* was still fashionable and appeared justified by results. The possibility or propriety of building up industries behind protective tariffs or with the help of subsidies or other government support was not so generally accepted sixty years ago as it is to-day. More-over canals and railways provided employment and certainly added to the wealth of the country. It must have seemed to the English officials of that time that they were undertaking quite enough in the way of economic development. Perhaps the most serious criticism that could be made is that the railway con-struction was carried out in an unduly extravagant manner.'

'Oh, you mean the old complaint that the English investor,

31

who provided the capital, was guaranteed 5 per cent by the Government of India; so he didn't care at what exorbitant cost the railways were built or whether they showed a loss or profit?'

'Yes, that's it. Whatever happened he got his 5 per cent. The loss, if any, was borne by Indian revenues, which meant ultimately the Indian peasant. And down till 1900 there was a loss. Of course, it may be argued that there was no cheaper way of raising the capital with which to push on rapidly with railway development. In any case, the total loss resulting from this extravagance must have been too small to have any appreciable effect on the general level of prosperity of the Indian masses. But I think we must take note of the criticism. As I shall explain in a moment, it is connected with one of the defects in our rule—or perhaps I should say in our relationship with India—which began to show themselves during this period.'

'What were those defects? I thought the period 1860–1900 was about the hey-day of our rule in India, when everybody recognized its beneficence, and felt grateful to the "benign British Government".'

'Very true; it *was* the hey-day of our rule, and the remarkable veneration still felt for Queen Victoria in many parts of the country indicates that during this period our rule really was appreciated. If ever you visit Amritsar, you'll find in the centre of the city a statue of Queen Victoria with the nose broken. During the 1919 disturbances a furious mob, which had already murdered several Englishmen, surrounded the statue intending to smash it to pieces. They got as far as breaking the nose; but then someone said, "She was a good old Queen. We had a happy time in her reign," and this so appealed to them that they desisted from further desecration. But you must remember that, if, in Victoria's reign, British government was really felt to be benign, this was not because it was British, but simply because it was government. After the preceding disorder and confusion any stable government which could ensure tranquillity was welcome. The fact that it was British and foreign was a disadvantage. Indeed the increasingly alien character of our rule was perhaps the chief of the defects of this period to which I have alluded. Everything Indian was despised and Indians were rigidly excluded from all the higher ranks of government service. This was now settled policy. Left entirely to our own counsels, we proceeded, with the best of intentions, to clamp down upon India a vast system of law and administration which was for the most part quite unsuited to the people. You see the results to-day. You don't imagine that if we had a system of criminal law and administration adapted to the needs of the country we should now have all these murders in Gandiwind going unpunished? I don't say that we should have hanged all the murderers, but I do say that in most cases we should have secured some sort of redress which society would have considered adequate. You and I might not consider it adequate, just as the settlement of that rape case at Gandiwind by the headmen did not seem adequate to us. But redress which satisfies society is what you want. The system we have introduced satisfies no one. Your short experience as a magistrate must already have shown you this. I need not dilate on it.

'Our foreign conceptions also led to the peasant being enslaved to the moneylender. In some parts of India we had, at an earlier stage, reduced the peasant cultivators to rack-rented tenants under a new class of landlord created by ourselves. In other parts, where independent peasants were preserved, the moneylender became their master. This took place right under our very noses; but we were too complacent to do anything about it, till in the seventies serious peasant rioting in the Deccan startled us into legislative activity. But in spite of volumes of special legislation, the evil is still with us. It is a curious paradox that while English officers have generally felt a genuine affection for the Indian peasant and a desire to protect him, the effect of English rule has been to enable the moneylender—the despicable, disloyal bania—to suck him dry. The simple peasant has been allowed to ruin himself by improvident borrowing at usurious rates. You see, by creating proprietary rights in land, which could be transferred and sold in settlement of money debts, we suddenly placed in his hands an amount of credit undreamed of previously; and he had no idea how to use it wisely. In pre-British times proprietary rights in land, as we understand them, hardly existed. A peasant, as a member of a village community, simply had a right to occupy and cultivate a certain plot of land, subject to payment of land revenue. But he could not transfer this right, least of all to an outsider, unless the whole body of peasants in the village agreed to it. Moreover, land was in most parts of the country more plentiful than cultivators, so the right of occupation was no use save to a person able to till the land himself. It was no use therefore to the moneylender. Consequently, he sought payment out of the crop and had no ambition to lay hands on the land. With the advent of British rule this was all changed. Owing to the establishment of peace, the development of communications, and the growth of population, land became more valuable and more sought after. At the same time legislative enactment or the silent operation of English ideas and the English legal system converted a mere right of occupation into a transferable proprietary right. The peasant now had a valuable security to offer. This should have led to a great reduction in the rate of interest charged on loans; but, owing to the peasant's ignorance, it did not in fact do so. The moneylender, on the other hand, now had a strong inducement to possess himself of this valuable security, and facilities for so doing quite unknown before. In Mogul times the moneylender depended in the last resort for recovery of his debts on the local executive officer; and he, if he could be induced to attend to the matter at all, generally allowed the recovery of only such an amount as he considered reasonable and compatible with agricultural efficiency. As collector of the revenue, he did not want to see the peasant over-exploited by the moneylender, for if the peasant became discouraged, land would go out of cultivation and the revenue fall. But the mighty fabric of English law soon put an end to these rough-and-ready, easy-going methods. The moneylender, when in trouble, now applied to a civil judge, who, unlike the revenue-collecting executive officer, had no interest in the peasant's well-being and in any case was left with no discretion. Hedged in by elaborate rules of evidence and procedure, dominated by the theory that a written contract is sacred and must be observed down to the last letter—even when one of the parties is illiterate—the civil judge became a mere automaton for registering the moneylender's decrees and setting in motion a well-regulated machinery for the seizure of the debtor's person and property. So under the aegis of British justice the moneylender thrived while the cultivator starved—a direct though quite unintended result of our rule.

THE PEASANT AND POVERTY

'I regard this triumph of a parasitic class as one of the major defects of the 1860–1900 period. We fostered parasites; and, what is worse, we ourselves at the same time began to become parasitic. Do you remember a few months back Sir Dinga Ram saying in a public speech that the English favoured the bania because they were themselves banias? There was a considerable outcry at an Indian Minister saying anything so dreadful. Yet there was an unpleasant element of truth in his remark. Of course there was no conscious causal connection between England's becoming India's creditor and English rule in India favouring the creditor class. Yet there is a certain parallelism between England's relationship to India and the literate moneylender's relationship to the illiterate debtor. In both cases the debtor is relatively helpless—the peasant because he is ignorant and improvident; India because she is not a free country. In both cases the creditor stands on the letter of the contract regardless of the poverty of the debtor. The full pound of flesh is exacted. In both cases the creditor gets something for doing very little.'

'But surely,' Greenlane interrupted, 'whereas the peasant borrows foolishly and throws the money down the drain on litigation and marriage ceremonies, the borrowing which our Government out here has done on India's behalf has on the whole been wise and for sound productive purposes. Indeed, our whole financial management has been so skilful that India's credit stands very high and she has been able to borrow very cheaply.'

'True in the main, quite true. But the criticism which I mentioned earlier of the way in which the railways were constructed shows that there may be two opinions whether borrowing has been wise or unwise. After all, a debtor can hardly feel that his interests are entirely safe when exclusively in his creditor's hands. Yet this is India's position so long as her financial and exchange policy is in English hands. What we do may always be in India's best interests, but it is bound to be suspect. And as for those investors who put up money for railway construction on the strength of a Government guarantee of 5 per cent, an unfriendly observer might, I think, regard them as parasitic.'

'Yes, I suppose he might.'

THE PEASANT AND POVERTY

'This, then, was the relationship between England and India which came into existence in the 1860–1900 period. There were, of course, solid achievements to our credit; we had rendered India real service; England was not just a functionless creditor. The peace which we established and kept, the railways and canals which we built, greatly increased the wealth of the country. But they were not enough; and unfortunately our general attitude of complacency—already illustrated by our failure to save the peasant from the moneylender—made us too ready to believe that they were enough. We were too prone to draw our dividends and rest on our oars; and we could not afford to rest on our oars; for every year a steadily increasing population was pressing more and more heavily on the land. The cultivated area had been increased by our efforts, but the population was growing almost *pari passu*. There had been a considerable addition to the total wealth of the country, but not much, if any, to the wealth per head.'

'Well, you can't blame us for that,' said Greenlane. 'We could hardly have been expected to introduce universal birth control in India fifty to sixty years ago.'

'I agree. But though we could not check the growth of population, we might have attempted to increase more rapidly the production of wealth. As I shall explain in a minute, we did in fact, about 1900, bestir ourselves; but for the last twenty to thirty years of the nineteenth century, we were distinctly sluggish. You may be under the impression that we were helpless as the growth of population in India was something quite abnormal and peculiar to this country. But this is incorrect. Down to 1921 the rate of increase here was less than that of any country in Europe and much less than that of England and Wales. But in England during the nineteenth century, though the population increased very fast, the wealth of the country increased still faster. Consequently the bulk of the population was raised well above the level of bare subsistence and the concept of a standard of living to be maintained became widely diffused, and began to operate as a novel check on further increase. In India on the other hand, wealth and population both increased at a moderate and about equal rate, with the result that the major portion of the population remained, where it began, at the bare subsistence level; while we looked on with infinite complacency and admired the blessings of British rule.

'Then, just at the end of the century, Lord Curzon arrived on the scene as Viceroy. He really did try to get things moving. He gave a fresh impetus to railway construction and irrigation works; he reorganized the agricultural department and laid the foundations of organised agricultural research; and he had the sense to see that the salvation of the peasant might lie in Co-operation and passed the Co-operative Credit Act of 1904. These were well-conceived constructive measures and, in this Province, at any rate, we are still reaping their fruit.'

'We certainly are,' said Greenlane. 'A year in the canal colonies teaches you that. It is amazing what acres and acres of desert have been brought under cultivation and what magnificent crops are grown. And then the Agricultural Department with their improved varieties of cotton and wheat have put lakhs and lakhs of rupees into the cultivator's pocket.'

'Yes, and I think there can be little doubt that, as a result of these efforts, there has been in this Province, and possibly in India as a whole, a real rise in the standard of living in the last thirty years. In this Province figures prove it. The cultivated area has increased more rapidly than population and we know that most of the new cultivated area is good canal-irrigated land, bearing excellent crops. We also know that compared with thirty years ago a larger proportion of the population now eat wheat instead of inferior grains, that there is a greater consumption of meat, and that fruit and vegetables are beginning to find their way into the diet of the common people. But Curzon's viceroyalty marked the last attempt at constructive leadership in the economic field. Since then we have followed faithfully enough the lines already laid down, but we have made little attempt to explore new paths. We have ceased to lead, although the task of increasing the country's productive capacity remains as urgent as ever. You can see yourself how urgent the problem is. Look at all those hundreds of people who gathered to see us this morning at Gandiwind. Of course they had notice of our coming and made a point of being present. But it is the same wherever you go. Heralded or unheralded, within a few minutes of your reaching a village a crowd collects; the reason being, of course, that except at

37

harvest time the male population has quite insufficient to do. Every village is full of idlers. We are simply witnessing a visible symptom of mass rural under-employment. While this persists, the general economic level is bound to remain low.'

'But why do you say that in this matter we have ceased to lead? What could we be expected to do about it?'

'My dear Greenlane, in the last twenty years instead of leaders we've become obstructionists, obstinately resisting new ideas and damning those who spread them as Congress-walas, Communists, anti-English and seditious. Obviously the situation calls for a pretty radical revision of our whole rural economy. On the one hand we require to draw off from the land the large surplus population, and this can only be done by a great speed-up of industrialization. Experience has already shown that private enterprise will not achieve this. The old policy of *laisser-faire* won't do. Yet any suggestion that Government should take a hand is met with a "non possumus". In India we can't make this, and we can't make that. Why not? Oh, we haven't the necessary skilled labour. Well, why not train it? It would be too expensive and really quite impossible. Indians are congenitally incapable of attaining the high standard of accuracy necessary in so much of modern industry. You know the attitude—making difficulties instead of trying to overcome them.

'On the other hand we require to devise a new, more productive system of agriculture to replace the present peasant system with each family cultivating a tiny holding of often hopelessly fragmented land. Some form of large-scale co-operative farming, perhaps on a village basis, is what we seem to want. This would have to be preceded by a veritable seisach-theia—a huge writing down or writing off of agricultural debt; and, in those parts of the country where landlordism exists, a considerable revision of landlords' rights.

'Changes of this sort are no doubt rather revolutionary— perhaps beyond the capacity of an alien government. If so, this is all the more reason for hastening the day of Indian independence. A hundred years ago we set out to abolish widow-burning and infanticide—a fairly drastic interference with social custom; we had then more courage and self-confidence than we have to-day. We felt ourselves to be leaders and as

38

such we were admired by Indians. The best of them wanted to imitate us—to understand our ideas, to adopt our methods, to partake of our culture. It was the reactionary elements that opposed us—the decaying remnants of the broken Mogul power. To-day exactly the opposite holds good. Princes and landlords support us, but all the youth of India, all the progressive ardent elements in the country, find no inspiration in England. They look for light to Russia. And we, with obstinate folly, try to prevent them. It is really rather extraordinary. To-day,[1] in Russia, an experiment is being conducted which is patently of the highest relevance to India. They are attempting there simultaneously a rapid industrialization of the country and a new form of co-operative farming. God knows whether they will fail or succeed. But what they are doing has an obvious bearing on our Indian problems and ought to be of the greatest interest to us. Yet we take no notice of this grand experiment except to proclaim it a disaster while it is still in progress. Russia is the root of all evil; and therefore Russia must, so far as possible, not be mentioned. Russia must not be studied. Russia must not be visited. And anyone coming from Russia must be put in gaol. Do you know that you can't even get your passport endorsed for Russia in this country? I intend when I next go on leave to travel through Russia and try to see something of it for myself; but what do you think I've had to do? Last year when at home I had to slink up surreptitiously to the Passport Office in London and get my passport endorsed for Russia there. It would be useless to try here.

'Now, as I've already said, it may be that foreigners like ourselves cannot carry through the drastic, far-reaching policy which seems to be called for. But there is much that we might do by way of preparation for it. For instance, we could study the Russian technique of economic planning, instead of saying that a planned economy is impossible. We might even try to get out a five-years' programme of industrial planning for the whole of India. Then again our continually growing canal colonies afford a splendid opportunity for small-scale experiment. Instead of just reproducing everywhere in these new areas the old type of peasant community—each man cultivating his own small diminishing plot with primitive home-made

[1] The reader is reminded that this conversation took place in 1934.

39

implements—we could try the experiment of large-scale State farming or of co-operative farming or, if you like, of large-scale capitalist farming. Or we might try giving peasant grants on the condition that the rule of primogeniture would hold, so that the land would not be subdivided in a couple of generations among a host of sons and grandsons. Yet we do none of these things ourselves and discourage those who would like to do them. No wonder the socialist wing of Congress, which, I believe, sincerely desires to help the Indian masses, regards us as the greatest obstacle. During the last twenty years probably the best work done for the rural masses has been due simply to the initiative and enthusiasm of individual officers, acting more or less on their own, often in the face of official discouragement.'

'You're thinking of Brayne[1] and his Rural Reconstruction.'

'Yes of him amongst others. I also have in mind those officers who have devoted themselves with real enthusiasm and faith to the co-operative movement, and endeavoured through co-operation not merely to rescue the cultivator from the money-lender and provide him with cheap credit, but to develop in him a community spirit, enabling a whole village to embark on joint enterprises; for instance, the consolidation of holdings, the purchase of agricultural implements, the sale of produce. Brayne and these other officers realized that the regeneration of village life must come largely through the villager himself. Though the practical results of their efforts may now seem transient and negligible, some day we may reap an unexpected harvest. Moral and material progress are closely allied. These officers have attempted to provide the moral basis; but the material basis is lacking. That could only be provided by action on a scale beyond the scope of individual officers. Don't however, despise their efforts. They are a small item on the credit side in a rather lamentable twenty years.'

'Well,' said Greenlane, 'your rapid review seems to have

[1] F. L. Brayne, C.S.I., C.I.E. As district-office Gurgaon, just after the last war, he attempted to reform village life by a combination of better farming, e.g. use of improved seed and cattle and more scientific collection of manure, and better living, e.g. greater cleanliness, less litigation, more enlightenment in the home through education of women.

40

taken us from the seventeenth century down to the present day; but you have not yet answered the question which I suggested at Gandiwind this morning—whether we have impoverished the Indian masses.'

'I'm sorry for being so tedious; but I thought we'd better remind ourselves of some of the main Congress criticisms. I think, however, I can now give some sort of answer to your question. The people of Gandiwind, so far from being impoverished, have been somewhat enriched as a result of our rule. This is mainly due to the very rapid extension of irrigation in this Province. Irrigation has outstripped procreation. Though the people of Gandiwind have not gained directly—I don't think anyone from that village has obtained land in the canal colonies—indirectly they have gained through the general relief of the pressure on the soil throughout the Province.

'As regards the Indian masses in general, I feel less confident. I should say that as a result of British rule they are not worse off than they were and probably a bit better. Since 1900 at any rate, industrial and agricultural production have increased slightly faster than population. But they are still miserably poor. They began at a low level and they still remain at a low level. That is about all one can say.'

'And Congress say that we are responsible.'

'Well, they are inclined to throw a good deal of the blame on us. I have tried to indicate some of our mistakes and short-comings, and also some of the unfortunate, though often not consciously intended, consequences of our association with India. But the truth is that English rule and England's whole relationship with India during the last 150 years are only factors in a huge complex of conditions determining the present level of existence of the Indian masses. Their poverty is largely due to factors beyond our control, and even beyond our ken. We cannot control climate, rainfall and the distribution of natural resources. We can only mitigate their deficiencies, generally at much expense. Social customs and institutions we can only slowly modify—and then sometimes through ignorance in the wrong way. As for the movements of population and all the unintended social consequences of the cumulative action of individuals, motivated by their own individual purposes—we have hardly begun to know the first thing about them.

41

THE PEASANT AND POVERTY

'Much modern Congress criticism of English action or inaction assumes that our grandfathers possessed the same knowledge and social purposes as we do to-day. To that extent it is invalid. The idea that society by taking thought can raise its standard of living is comparatively novel. Our fathers and grandfathers cannot justly be blamed for failing to make the sort of plans which we to-day are just beginning to see are possible. A great deal of what the English have consciously undertaken and accomplished has been for India's benefit. Peace and order, political unity, railways and canals—these are foundations of prosperity and were consciously laid by us. But impressed by these achievements we have been too ready to shut our eyes to some of the less deliberately intended results of our dealings with India. The Indian sees that England has grown rich while his own country has remained poor, and draws an easy inference. We English, conscious of the rectitude of our declared intentions, overlook the cumulative effect of numberless individual Englishmen seeking to make money out of India. It is the old story of God and Mammon. That curious but unsuccessful Governor-General, Lord Ellenborough, saw it all quite clearly. Let me quote from a letter which he wrote to Queen Victoria.'

Mr. Lightfoot reached for a book and read:

'Lord Ellenborough can see no limit to the future prosperity of India if it be governed with due respect for the feelings and even the prejudices, and with a careful regard for the interests, of the people, with the resolution to make *their* well-being the chief object of the Government, and not the pecuniary advantages of the nation of strangers to which Providence has committed the rule of this distant Empire.'

'Rather good, isn't it?'

'Yes,' said Greenlane, 'but you can't expect that degree of idealism in practice.'

'True, but without it you can't expect the generous thanks of a grateful India. You can only expect what we're getting. And we might, I think, have approached a bit nearer it. After all, tearing aside the considerable pecuniary advantages which we have reaped at India's expense, we have not in our behaviour towards Indians exactly had regard for their feelings. For years we treated them with scorn, excluded them from our

42

clubs, heaped upon them social insults and regarded them as unfit for any post of honour and responsibility. All this might have been avoided.'

'But surely we may claim the merit of never having said, "Evil be thou my good". However much we may have exploited India in practice, exploitation has never since the eighteenth century been our deliberate policy.'

'That may be. One may hope that other nations will give us credit for it. But you mustn't be surprised if Indians sometimes fail to appreciate the point. Personally, in viewing the relationship of England to India, I like to think of her, in Marx's phrase, as just "the unconscious tool of history." I am proud that our country should have been chosen by fate, nature, God or whatever you like to call it, to clear up the debris of the Mogul empire and to unlock for India the treasures of Western thought. I think on the whole we were worthy of it. But I must get on and do my files, and I expect you've some judgments to write.'

'Yes, I've one or two to do before to-morrow.'

'Mind you convict.'

'I'll try to.'

'Good.'

III

THE PEASANT AND THE LAW

'Your Honour must know', says this judicious person, 'that the great evil is that men swear falsely in this Country. No judge knows what to believe. Surely if Your Honour can make men to swear truly, Your Honour's fame will be great and the Company will flourish. Let Your Honour cut off the great toe of the right foot of every man who swears falsely, whereby Your Honour's fame will be extended.'—MACAULAY.

On the outskirts of a remote village in Northern India Greenlane, with a retinue of clerks, servants and orderlies, is encamped. The scene is not an attractive one. The village, a collection of 500 or 600 mud huts, rising somewhat above the level of the surrounding dun-coloured plain, looks as though it were built on the accumulated manure of past generations. Its sandy lanes are littered with more recent refuse, and every vacant site is occupied by sprawling heaps of filth and rubbish. Seedy fowls and emaciated curs scratch and rummage in the garbage; naked, blear-eyed children scrabble fitfully in the dust; and hard by a solitary, sore-backed donkey stands mournfully—a picture of somnolent and dejected resignation.

A large number of the inhabitants have gathered round Greenlane's tent, obviously expectant. His visit to the village, though of no special significance, is in itself something of an event, and it has by chance coincided with a happening of much interest to all the villagers; for only yesterday morning one of their number, a young man of twenty-two named Karam, was murdered in broad daylight as he was driving his cattle from the village pond. His corpse has already been despatched on a charpoy[1] to the nearest town, twenty miles away, for a post-mortem examination. Its return is expected in a few hours. Meanwhile the police have been busy investigating and have arrested

[1] See note on p. 25.

44

two men named Raja and Jahana. The case seems clear enough. The deceased was attacked from behind by the two arrested persons, who mercilessly battered his head to pieces with heavy, iron-shod clubs. There was no attempt at concealment. They set upon him boldly in full view of the village, and having accomplished their purpose walked off unhurriedly to their houses. This is the story the police have elicited from three alleged eye-witnesses, one of them the white-bearded grandfather of the deceased. The motive for the murder is also plain. The dead man had been making love to Jahana's wife, who was also Raja's sister. Husband and brother had taken revenge.

Greenlane being the magistrate of this area, the case is to be put into his Court for committal to the Court of Sessions. It is so simple and straightforward that the police expect to be able to bring most of the witnesses before him while he is still encamped at the village, and thus save trouble and expense. Meanwhile the villagers have gathered round Greenlane's tent, hoping that he will presently emerge and question them about the murder or ask them to show him the spot where it occurred, thus affording them (so they imagine) an opportunity of influencing his mind one way or the other. Relatives both of the murdered man and of the two arrested persons are present in force; for each side is afraid lest in its absence the other will impress him too keenly with the justice of its cause.

But they are to be disappointed. Greenlane has no intention of exposing himself to the noisy importunities of the rival factions. He sticks firmly to his tent, and presently his Reader comes out and tell the assembled villagers to go home, 'No, the Sahib is busy with office work and will *not* be going to see the scene of the crime. It is no use hanging about round his tent.' But the villagers are disinclined to move. Each faction fears that the other will somehow contrive to get the ear of the Sahib alone. Each, therefore, will stay as long as the other does. The Reader's admonitions make no impression, until he is joined by Greenlane's servants and orderlies, who in more peremptory and offensive language bid them be off. Then at last, slowly and with evident reluctance, they scatter to their houses.

But at about nine p.m. a vague clamour arises. Lights and torches are to be seen approaching the western side of the village, and presently mingled with the fierce discordant shouts of men the regular rhythmical wailing of women can be heard. Gradually the noise increases and becomes a loud confused uproar as the lights reach the edge of the village. It is the return of the corpse, and friends and relatives have gone forth to meet it.

Suddenly above the babel of sounds and voices a shout is heard, 'The Sahib has come, the Sahib has come.' The moving multitude stands transfixed, the hubbub ceases and amid profound silence Greenlane steps quickly out of the darkness into the circle of the torches' light. The bearers of the charpoy, on which the corpse is laid, set it on the ground; he goes up to it, glances for a moment at the dead man's face, which shows no traces of violence, stoops down, removes the turban and examines closely the crown and back of the head. Then without a word he rises and turns to go; but, as he does so, the silence is broken, as suddenly as it fell, by a fierce and deafening outcry. As though moved by some invisible signal the crowd of friends and mourners burst forth in unison, 'Justice, justice! Cruel wrong has been done. Justice! You are our ruler. Justice!' But Greenlane makes no response. Still without a word and apparently unmoved by their cries he vanishes into the darkness in the direction of his tent. The tumult quickly subsides and the crowd moves off in procession to the burial ground on the far side of the village.

Greenlane was not really unmoved, but he knew what value to place on these cries for justice. Although during the whole afternoon he had never stepped outside his tent, inside it he had received a number of visitors; and from some of these— notably the local zaildar,[1] an excellent young man of his own age who belonged to this very village—he had learnt a good deal about the murder. The relatives of the dead Karam called for justice; but it was not what Greenlane understood by justice. In the name of justice they were demanding the death of an innocent man, and Greenlane knew that they had so planned and plotted, so tutored and taught the witnesses that, so far as the law and legal evidence was concerned, they had every chance of obtaining it.

[1] The leading man of a 'zail' or group of villages. He receives a small emolument in return for services rendered to Government officials and enjoys considerable local prestige.

The facts, as elicited by Greenlane from his visitors and confirmed by subsequent inquiries, were as follows: The murder was the work of one man, not two. Raja, the brother, was responsible; Jahana, the husband, had no hand in it. It had been witnessed by none of the alleged eye-witnesses; it had been witnessed in fact by no one save a single timorous shopkeeper, who had not the courage to give evidence or to make a statement to the police.

Raja had been moved to commit the murder by anger at Karam's attentions to his sister which aggravated a long-standing dispute about Karam's cattle trespassing in his fields. Jahana, who was innocent and who had disbelieved the stories of his wife's infidelity, had been falsely implicated by Karam's relatives, partly because they thought he might have been privy to the murder, but mainly because they could not procure satisfactory evidence against Raja without roping him in as well. Karam's white-bearded grandfather was ready to give any evidence that might be required of him. But a solitary eye-witness, and he a near relative of the deceased, clearly would not satisfy the Courts. More eye-witnesses, unconnected by blood or marriage with Karam's family, were essential. Two men were available, who were willing to pose as eye-witnesses; but they demanded a price—Jahana's blood. One of them simply bore Jahana a grudge; he thought that Jahana's influence had prevented his son's betrothal to Jahana's niece. The other hoped that some land belonging to a distant relative would eventually come to him, if Jahana was out of the way. Both felt that this convenient opportunity of removing Jahana was too good to be missed; and the relatives of Karam, provided they got Raja, were quite willing to have Jahana thrown in as well.

All, therefore, was arranged accordingly, and the three eye-witnesses carefully instructed in their parts before anyone was sent off to the police station to call in the police.

Greenlane was by now only too familiar with this type of case. Since leaving Mr. Lightfoot in the autumn of 1934, he had been posted as Sub-Divisional Magistrate to an outlying part of the Derajat district, and for many months had daily been hearing criminal cases. But though familiar with every refinement of falsehood, he still constantly found himself baffled and quite uncertain what to do. Justice was so passionately demanded, but seemed so rarely obtained, so hard to give and so little deserved. Yet justice was one of the very things that the English were supposed to have given India. Only a few years back, Sir Samuel Hoare, as Secretary of State, had said, 'You have given India justice such as the East has never known before. You have laid deep the foundations of justice in great legal codes.' And Greenlane at that time had believed him and taken comfort at his words. Whatever unfriendly critics might say about exploitation and the tribute which openly or disguisedly England had drawn from India, at least she had established the reign of law and sent out generations of upright officers to judge the people righteously. The open plunder of the nabobs, the honourable but solid pensions of officials, the more glittering fortunes of cotton merchants—all the diverse streams of wealth that had flowed from India to England, to England's great advantage, found, so it seemed, in this a partial justification, that English rule had ensured justice, rescued the dumb millions from oppression and arbitrary caprice, and given them the protection of a beneficent system of English law.

Greenlane had believed this. He now knew from bitter experience that the truth was otherwise. The ignorant peasant had not been protected by English law; he had perverted it and been perverted by it. As for the great legal codes, they and the whole legal system of which they were part defeated the best efforts of an honest man to do justice. And there seemed now no remedy.

The next day at noon, sitting out in the open air, Greenlane duly took up the murder case against Raja and Jahana. All the principal witnesses were present except the doctor; and his evidence would be practically formal. His written report showed that the whole of the back and top of the deceased's skull had been smashed to pieces. There could be no doubt of the intention to kill Karam. The evidence of the eye-witnesses was just as Greenlane had expected. All three told exactly the same story; all three were unshaken in cross-examination; indeed cross-examination was necessarily ineffective; the story they told was so brief and so simple. They had seen Karam driving his cattle from the pond. As he passed by a big tree where the lane was narrow, Raja and Jahana had jumped up from behind a low wall, attacked him in the back and hit him on the head with heavy clubs. At the second blow he fell down on his face. They hit him several times more on the head as he lay on the ground, and then walked off in the direction of their houses. The witnesses had been unable to intervene. Two of them were infirm old men. The third was unarmed and did not dare to approach alone the two murderers with their heavy iron-shod clubs. All that the witnesses could do was to raise an alarm and look to the dead man.

Greenlane finished the evidence soon after four p.m. Witnesses, lawyers, police, Court officials and idle spectators dispersed, and he retired to his tent to have tea. About half an hour later his orderly, Saddique, came in and said:

'Sir, the faqir[1] has come to salaam you.'

'Bother the faqir. I don't want to see him.'

'Sir, it is the faqir who owned the dogs and arranged the dog-fight, which you saw on the way here yesterday morning, and so much enjoyed. He is a very good faqir.'

'Well, what does he want? I suppose he has come for an inam.[2] I will give him his inam, if that is what he wants.'

'Oh no, Cherisher of the poor. He does not want any inam. He is a very good faqir. He does not trouble anybody or beg for money. You need not give him an inam.'

'How does he live then if he doesn't beg?'

'Sir, he is a very wonderful kind of faqir. He begs money from no one, but every morning at ten o'clock he produces a ten-rupee note from his armpit.'

'Produces a ten-rupee note from his armpit! Who told you this, Saddique?'

'Sir, the people say so. God knows whether it is true or false. People speak both falsehood and truth. I myself have not seen this thing with my own eyes. Why should I deceive you and say that I have? I am just telling you what people say. But this I know, he is a very good faqir. May I tell him that your Honour will see him?'

'But if he doesn't want an inam, what has he come for? What is it he *does* want, Saddique?'

'Cherisher of the poor, he doesn't want anything. He only wants to salaam your Honour. Nothing more. Sir, his heart

[1] A mendicant devotee.　　　　[2] A reward.

will be broken, if you do not see him. It will only take one minute. May I bring him in?'

'All right. Let him come in.'

The faqir entered Greenlane's tent wearing nothing but a loincloth and with a staff in his hand. He was a youngish man of medium height with a small, round, closely cropped head. He had large eyes, but his face bore no particular expression. He stood silently before Greenlane as though waiting for him to speak.

'Well, faqir sahib,' said Greenlane after a few moments. 'I hope you are quite all right. It is nice of you to come and see me.' The faqir remained silent and did not move. 'I am very pleased to see you again,' Greenlane went on after a pause, not quite knowing what to say. 'Is there anything you want?'

The faqir still remained silent.

'Oh, I see you've no special request. You've just come for salaam. Very good. Well, I hope all will go well with you, faqir sahib, and that your dogs will win many fights.'

The faqir murmured as though trying to speak, but uttered no articulate words. Greenlane waited for some seconds and then said, 'Is there nothing then you want?'

The faqir at this point found his voice and said suddenly in a ringing tone, 'Release Jahana.'

Greenlane was taken aback. 'But I'm afraid I can't do that,' he said, 'I don't know what the final result of the case will be, but it is not possible for me to release Jahana. The evidence against him is so strong that he will have to be committed to Sessions. I am sorry, faqir sahib, but I can't release him.'

The faqir screwed up his mouth and remained silent. His large eyes filled with tears which trickled slowly right down his cheeks. Then he turned and went out of the tent. Greenlane never saw him again.

A week later Greenlane had taken the doctor's evidence and committed Raja and Jahana to the Court of Sessions on a charge of murder. He could do nothing else. Yet he was certain that Raja alone had murdered Karam and that Jahana was innocent. But how could he prove it, and who would believe him? His own knowledge of the real facts was based on hearsay —on the reports of reliable men of the locality. They in turn had got the true story from the timorous shopkeeper, who was the solitary real witness of the occurrence. But this shopkeeper, a mild Hindu, unconnected in any way with the factions and enmities of the turbulent Muslim peasants, was never going to embroil himself with them by giving evidence in a case of this nature. And without his evidence the real facts could not be brought before the Court. Greenlane might himself represent the matter privately to the Sessions Judge or even to higher authority. He had tried this once in a previous case, and been severely snubbed. A very senior officer had told him that he shouldn't listen to gossip outside Court and quoted Gibbon at him to the effect that an indiscreet and intemperate zeal for justice is the last temptation of virtuous minds. He didn't feel inclined to try it again. In any case how could he convince the Sessions Judge? He himself could arrive at the truth, because he was in constant touch with the people of the countryside and knew which of them were good men and true whom he could trust to tell him honestly all the relevant facts, concealing nothing, and adding nothing. But the Sessions Judge, sitting seventy-five miles away in Derajat, knew none of these people; and why should he believe the hearsay report of Greenlane, a quite junior officer whom he had only met once? Why indeed should he listen to him at all?

So Greenlane did nothing; and Jahana was hanged along with Raja.

Greenlane was still young enough to feel intensely the wrong of innocent men being sent to gaol or to the gallows. He was appalled at Jahana's execution. Yet he knew that it was only a particularly glaring instance of what in a lesser degree was happening continually. In Indian conditions the whole elaborate machinery of English law, which Englishmen tended to think so perfect, simply didn't work and had been completely perverted. Greenlane and myriads of Indian magistrates daily spent hours in their Courts solemnly recording word for word the evidence of illiterate peasants, knowing full well that 90 per cent of it was false. Even if the events described had actually occurred, the alleged eye-witnesses had not seen them. Even if the accused were guilty, it was perjury which proved their guilt. False evidence was always in demand, as much to prove what was true as to establish what was false. Against innocent and guilty alike it was equally necessary.

51

THE PEASANT AND THE LAW

It was amazing to Greenlane that anything so unsuited to a simple people as the English system of law should ever have been foisted upon India; and all the more amazing when he discovered that the early English administrators had again and again inveighed against it. Warren Hastings thought it a monstrous injustice that Indians should be subjected to laws designed for quite different social conditions. Macaulay wrote, 'All the injustice of former oppressors, Asiatic and European, appeared as a blessing when compared with the justice of the Supreme Court.' Metcalfe[1] had complete contempt for our Courts 'which are meant to perform so much good' and knew that the people dreaded them and at the same time were debauched by them. He left a description of them which; Greenlane felt, was still, 100 years after, absolutely applicable to his own Court. 'Our Courts are scenes of great corruption. . . . (The Judge) sits on a bench in the midst of a general conspiracy. . . . Everyone is labouring to deceive him and to thwart his desire for justice. The pleaders have no regard for truth.'

Thus at quite an early stage the unsuitability of the English legal system and formal English Courts had been recognized. What was really needed had also been fully understood and frequently stated. Again and again Governors, Councils and Boards of Administration had framed most promising policies and passed most admirable resolutions. 'Our object,' wrote some of these wise men, 'is that substantial justice should be plainly dealt out to a simple people, unused to the intricacies of legal proceedings. We should avoid all technicality, circumlocution, and obscurity, and aim at simplifying and abridging every rule, procedure, and process. Our endeavour must be to form tribunals which shall not be hedged in with forms unintelligible to the vulgar, and only to be interpreted by professional lawyers, but which shall be open and accessible courts of justice where every man may plead his own cause, be confronted face to face with his opponents, may prosecute his own complaint, or conduct his own defence.'

In Greenlane's own Province these intentions were for just a few years after annexation partially fulfilled. Unhampered by the maxims of lawyers or established legal principles magi-

[1] Charles (afterwards Lord) Metcalfe, served in India from 1801–1838, and acted as Governor-General 1835-36.

strates freely admitted 'hearsay' as evidence and punished offenders, not on the legally proper but fictitious evidence of alleged eye-witnesses, but on the common report of the countryside. Only too soon however, the temptation to advance asserted itself, and in less than twenty-five years the Province was equipped with codes of law, rules of evidence, a Chief Court, a corrupt Bar and all the legal apparatus which had already worked such havoc elsewhere.

What was the result? Greenlane was the unhappy witness of it. A simple people had become habituated to systematized perjury, had been corrupted by unscrupulous lawyers, had been taught to flock to the law courts, and to revel in the tainted atmosphere of bribery and chicanery that surrounds them. Litigation had become a national pastime and the criminal law a recognized and well-tried means of harassing, imprisoning and even hanging one's enemies.

Greenlane was quite unable to understand why we should have introduced a legal system which was in every particular precisely the reverse of that which had been seen to be required. A layman, still more an illiterate peasant, who endeavoured to 'prosecute his own complaint or conduct his own defence' in one of our Indian Courts had not the remotest chance of success. The procedure and rules of evidence were so elaborate that even educated persons did not understand them; and the proceedings were conducted in a language unintelligible to the majority of the litigants. The Courts were a sham and a mockery in which police, witnesses, lawyers and judges all played their part in producing or using evidence which they knew to be quite false.

Everyone who had anything to do with the criminal administration was aware of this and deplored it. But as the system was now well established and supported by the vested interests of the lawyer class, no one showed the slightest inclination to alter it. Most English officers simply washed their hands of the whole matter. Having worked as ordinary magistrates for a short while during their early years of service, and having decided that hearing criminal cases was a futile waste of time, they put all this behind them at the earliest opportunity. Some became revenue experts; some found their way into the Secretariat; even those who remained ordinary district officers usually, in their capacity as District Magistrates, confined themselves to a routine supervision of the work of subordinate Indian magistrates. The challenging problems of criminal administration they just avoided. Greenlane could get nothing out of them.

Even Lightfoot was not very helpful. He was, of course, fully alive to the problems, and always gave personal attention to criminal work which he regarded as the foundation of good administration. Unlike most district officers, he regularly heard criminal cases himself and took considerable pains both to encourage and to control the police; for in his view the police were what the people most feared and yet most needed. Greenlane, from conversation with Lightfoot at Sawanpur, knew well that he abominated the existing criminal system. He was always talking about its evils and how it had corrupted the people instead of being the means of creating a sound public opinion. Yet as regards remedies he was defeatist.

'My dear Greenlane,' he used to say, 'it is no use just tinkering with the law, omitting a section here and changing a word there. The whole criminal administration requires to be scrapped and built up afresh. But do you imagine that Governors and other elderly gentlemen, who have for thirty years been content to watch this system grinding out its injustices and demoralizing the people, are at their age going to try to replace it? It will go on for another thirty years without any cataclysm, so why bother? If attention is drawn to unpleasant facts, for instance, that innocent men are often imprisoned and sometimes hanged, and that respectable, honest men, the natural leaders of the countryside, are continually required by the police to give false evidence—why, you just deny them. It is an easy technique which you'll soon learn—though, I hope, never employ. In any case, it is probably impossible for sophisticated people like ourselves to provide an appropriate criminal system for a peasant society, whose customs and outlook are so entirely different from our own. A primitive people's conceptions of justice and methods of securing it are crude and even brutal. Blood is paid for with gold, and truth elicited with the aid of ordeals and compurgators. These were the methods of our Saxon and Norman forefathers and they are still to-day the methods really natural to much of the rural population of

India. If you can successfully keep cases out of court, you will
often find them settled by compurgation, or by some strange
ordeal. But our Western enlightenment cannot tolerate such
methods. It must have something more up to date, something
which it can show to the word as the rule of law. You will never
therefore get the system changed while we rule this country.
We have not the energy and we have not the imagination.
Attempts at reform will be met with a denial of the facts.'
And Lightfoot proved right.

There came out to the Province from England a new High
Court Judge, a downright vigorous man, with no knowledge
of India, but with every intention of serving her well. He soon
became aware of the features of the criminal administration
which had struck Greenlane with such surprise and horror, and
he began laying about him with considerable energy. He denounced the police for manufacturing false evidence; he denounced the judges and magistrates for believing it; he
denounced the members of the public for giving it He frankly
confessed that in the existing state of affairs he was quite at
a loss what to do when hearing appeals; for he could hardly
ever feel certain that a man had been rightly convicted. The
whole of the evidence against him might be false, as even the
agents of the Crown did not hesitate to utilize false witnesses
and concoct false evidence.

In setting to work to tackle the evils which he so vigorously
denounced, the Judge was handicapped by an unquestioning
belief (the result of his purely English training), in the 'beauties
and benignities' of the English law. Still he did at least have the
honesty to recognize the evils and a very real determination to
combat them. Greenlane, in his lonely subdivision, heard of
his prowess and longed to discuss with him the problems of
which they both seemed so keenly conscious. An opportunity
came. The new Judge in the course of a tour through the
Province decided to pay a visit to the small country town where
Greenlane was stationed. They quickly fell into animated
conversation.

'You know, if people in England became aware of what goes
on in our criminal courts out here,' said the Judge, 'they would
be absolutely shocked. As a matter of fact they simply wouldn't
believe half of what you told them. The corruption and un-

scrupulousness of the police is staggering. I believe there are even some English police officers who always keep handy a supply of human blood so that blood-stained garments can be made available when required.'

'I don't think, sir, you should be too hard on the police,' said Greenlane. 'Often they are not to blame for false evidence and false cases. They simply bring before the Court the story told by the complainant and his witnesses. If it is false, it is not the fault of the police.'

'They oughtn't to prosecute when the story is false.'

'Sometimes they are not quite certain that the story *is* false. Sometimes they are afraid that if they don't prosecute they will get into trouble. Suppose for instance there is a murder, and the story told by the deceased's relatives is all wrong. If the local sub-inspector[1] of police doesn't accept their story and prosecute the alleged murderer, they may complain against him and say he has been bribed. Generally, much the safest course for him is just to pass the baby to the magistrate, and let the magistrate make what he can of the evidence. Of course, I admit that quite often the police themselves manufacture false evidence to strengthen a case; but the temptation to do so is very strong.'

'They ought to resist that temptation,' said the Judge. 'It is not for the police to decide that a man is guilty. That is for you and me. Their business is simply to collect and put before us the available evidence; not to try to fill up what they think to be gaps.'

'I fancy that if you were a police sub-inspector, responsible for peace and order and the control of crime in a rural police station, you would see things in rather a different light. After all the general public consider it the business of the police to catch the criminals. It is not much good the sub-inspector catching them if the magistrate lets them out the next day because of the weakness of the evidence. The public won't think much of him nor will his superior officers. They judge him by results.'

'It is up to him by skilful investigation to get the requisite evidence, not just to take the easy course of concocting it.'

'But our law of evidence and the rulings of various High Courts make his task so impossibly difficult.'

[1] An officer in charge of a police station.

56

THE PEASANT AND THE LAW

'I know that there are a few silly rulings, but I intend to have them revised and corrected. I am fully alive to the difficulties of the police and want to do what I can to help them. But monkeying with the evidence is quite intolerable. It has got to stop.'

'Well, I wonder what you'll think of this which happened in a neighbouring district recently. The police rounded up a whole gang of cattle thieves and recovered from their possession over fifty head of cattle. With great labour they traced out all the various owners from whom the cattle had been stolen, and intended to cite them as witnesses to identify the animals, and say that they were theirs. But the thieves were rich and influential people, and before the case had reached Court the police learnt that they had got at the owners and persuaded them to deny that the cattle belonged to them. The case seemed bound to fail. So the police went out into the highways and hedges and brought in twenty to thirty other persons who were not the owners of the cattle in question, but were prepared to swear that they were. They were duly produced in Court and their evidence was believed. The thieves were convicted and imprisoned; the real owners, who had played false, lost their cattle; and the sham owners and the police sold the cattle and divided the proceeds. That was fair enough, wasn't it?'

'Bah! No civilized government can tolerate such methods.'

'But what if it is dealing with a relatively uncivilized people? Don't you think such methods may then be appropriate? In any case a civilized government, if it introduces formal Courts and formal rules of evidence among a backward people, compels the adoption of such methods. Take another very simple little example. There is a burglary in a village. The thieves make a hole in the mud wall of a peasant's house, and carry off clothes and ornaments. The police get on to the tracks of one of the culprits, who has temporarily hidden his share of the loot under some bushes in a piece of waste land. After some interrogation—to use a polite term—the culprit offers to produce the stolen property. He takes the police to the bit of waste land and the property is duly recovered from under the bushes. But if the police tell this story in Court, the case is bound to fail. It will be held, on the strength of so many High Court rulings, that as the property was recovered from an accessible place,

57

not in the exclusive possession of the accused, he cannot be presumed to be the thief or the receiver of stolen property; he may have just seen someone else put it there. Our formal Courts would have to give him the benefit of the doubt arising out of this remote possibility. So the police will say that they searched the accused's house, and recovered the stolen property from there; and they will produce several respectable persons of the locality to testify that this is what happened. A very ordinary, venial, but necessary bit of falsification. Can you blame the police?'

'I cannot possibly condone such conduct. Don't you see, Greenlane, it strikes at the root of any civilized, scientific system of reaching the truth? If the Crown's own agents are permitted to tamper with the evidence, no Court can find any solid basis for its reasoning.'

'But I am doubtful whether your so-called civilized, scientific system is at all required in a country like this. It seems to me to be out of place. Do you know the story of the Algerian tribesman to whom a French officer was explaining that the Code Napoléon was about to be introduced and all the inestimable benefits that would flow therefrom? The tribesman, after listening to the officer for some time asked one question. "Does it mean that in future witnesses will be required?" "Yes," replied the officer. "In that case," said the tribesman, "I am afraid there will be no justice".'

'That's all very well, Greenlane, but do you imagine that there would be any more justice *without* witnesses? Of course, amid a backward society of illiterate peasants you can't expect to find justice such as one looks for in a highly civilized society like our own. But the same general principles are applicable everywhere. We have evolved in England by a process of trial and error extending over many centuries a body of legal principles and a system of jurisprudence which there is nothing to beat. It is no good your telling me that it won't work in India. We've got to train the people to work it, and you won't do that by gaily allowing the police to manufacture false evidence.'

'Well, sir, you may be right, but I am afraid my experience in this sub-division has made me very sceptical of our system. There may be nothing to beat it in England, but I think almost anything would beat it in India. Consider for a moment one quite minor feature of it which we've not yet mentioned.'

'What is that?'

'I'm thinking of all the enormous amount of petty criminal litigation which it permits and encourages. Such a dreadful waste of time, money, and energy. You know the sort of thing. Two villagers have a slight scuffle and one of them gets a black eye. Immediately he rushes off to Court, perhaps fifteen to thirty miles away, and starts a case. Both sides hire witnesses, engage pleaders, bribe petty officials and incur ruinous expenditure. The case drags on for months and ends probably in an acquittal or in mutual apologies. Could anything be more futile? Yet I believe that in this Province out of a population of about 25 million nearly 300,000 persons are annually brought to trial in respect of these petty, personal quarrels. They ought of course to be dealt with in the villages and never to come before formal Courts at all. But under the existing law you can't prevent it.'

'I quite agree with you about these petty cases. We ought to have more panchayats[1] and leave petty cases to them to settle. I don't deny that some changes and reforms are necessary, and as a matter of fact I am planning to get Government to appoint a committee to go into the whole question of criminal administration and make recommendations. As you seem so interested I'll suggest that you should be put on it.'

'Oh, I am afraid I'm much too junior for that, sir. It would be much better if you would have Mr. Lightfoot put on it. He is a great expert in all these matters.'

'I've heard of Lightfoot, but not yet met him. A gentleman of refreshing candour, I believe. Well, we'll see what can be done. Meanwhile, Greenlane, don't you let the police have it all their own way. I hope we'll have further opportunities of discussing these things.'

Greenlane wrote off in high glee to Lightfoot about the Judge's visit and his proposed committee on criminal administration. He really thought something was going to come of it. But months passed and he heard nothing; till at last one day, during a short holiday in Delhi, he ran into Lightfoot, who asked with a somewhat mischievous smile, 'Well, Greenlane, what happened to the committee on criminal administration?'

[1] Village councils.

'I don't know. I've heard nothing more about it. Were you asked to serve on it?'

'Good Lord, no. When Government want to ignore awkward facts they steer clear of me. And perhaps facts are better ignored when they are unpleasant and nothing can be done about them. But I've had a report about its deliberations. At an early stage in the proceedings a very senior officer, who was acting as chairman, said that in all his experience as a magistrate he had only once known the police to produce false evidence. Anything of that kind was very rare. "Yes, very rare indeed," chimed in two police officers who were present. No one ventured a contrary opinion, and so the discussions soon ended. The committee confined itself, I think, to a recommendation that magistrates should wear black coats in Court.'

'How ridiculous and how intolerable! I can't think how you can take it so lightly.'

'Simply because I knew it was bound to happen. To get rid of the existing system would be an enormous task. No one wants to take it on, and no one knows what to put in its place. Besides, in two to three years we'll be handing over provincial government, and with it criminal administration, to popularly elected Indian ministries. So why not leave it all to them?'

'We might at least before we hand over try to thrash out the whole question honestly and formulate a few proposals. I had been thinking things over during the last few months, and had got one or two ideas which I had hoped, if you were a member of the committee, might have been considered. But it's no use now.'

'You might as well let me know them in any case.'

'I am afraid they are very obvious and I haven't worked them out in detail. I imagine that in big cities our formal Courts would have to continue. What I say therefore doesn't apply to them. But in the rural areas three main changes seem to me to be required. First of all much more discretion must be placed in the hands of judges and magistrates, especially in regard to the admissibility of evidence. The Evidence Act should be scrapped and magistrates allowed to use any evidence which they think has a useful bearing on the case.'

'You would be placing enormous power in the hands of magistrates many of whom, I fear, would be corrupt and

60

oppressive. Still I would be in favour of taking the risk. You must trust people with responsibility if you are ever going to get any improvement. In any case it is easier to change a bad man than a bad system. Probably no part of the country would have to endure very bad magistrates for very long. Neros would be followed by Trajans. What next?'

'The people must be more closely associated with the administration of justice. What seems to me to be required is a rudimentary jury system. Magistrates should be empowered to select assessors from among the leading men of the locality to assist them in the trial of difficult cases. These assessors should be required to give their opinion as to the real facts after taking the most solemn oath *coram populo*. Their opinions would often include much hearsay evidence which the magistrate should be entitled to take into consideration. I am sure that to give our rural notables the honourable position of assessors —which would be a position of real trust, reserved only for those who showed themselves worthy of it—would be better than compelling them to come and give false evidence in Court on behalf of the Crown. Instead of demoralizing the people, we should be laying the foundations of a healthy public opinion.'

'I like the idea. I have not the slightest doubt that we ought to have done this from the beginning. But I'm afraid it may be too late to begin now. The people have become too much habituated to lies and chicanery. Have you any other suggestions?'

'There should be a simplification of procedure, and all the vast number of petty cases which clog the lower Courts should never come to Court at all. They should be heard at or near the spot by panchayats.'

'I am afraid that in most villages you would not be able to establish a panchayat which would command confidence and work harmoniously.'

'But in some villages panchayats work all right. A few of these might be expected to acquire a good reputation, so that people in surrounding villages would gladly apply to them for justice in petty disputes. Moreover the District Magistrate could be given very extensive powers of control which would enable him to remedy any glaring injustice by a stroke of the pen.'

'Once again I would say that your idea should have been acted on from the very start. As a matter of fact Munro and Elphinstone did endeavour to preserve and develop judicial panchayats, but their efforts were not followed up. They will be much more difficult to develop now.'

'But it would be worth trying.'

'It probably would be. But we shan't try it, my dear Greenlane. We've given up trying. We're simply treading water. You'll have to wait for an Indian ministry to try it, and they'll probably spoil it all by political and other corruption.'

'And I shall probably feel too discouraged to wait for an Indian ministry. It all seems so hopeless.'

'You've been too long all alone in a sub-division. Don't take things so tragically. Remember that an Indian villager who is sent innocently to gaol or to the gallows regards it just as one of the chances of this mortal life. One can't expect justice in this world. Remember too that whatever the defects of our system, we have at any rate introduced into India the conception of the rule of Law; and though we may live to see a new crop of tyrants in India and Law replaced by individual caprice, that conception will not die. It is firmly planted in the Indian mind. It will survive tyranny. It will remain as an ideal.'

'In the existing state of society human caprice might well be preferable to the rule of Law. It could hardly be worse.'

'My dear Greenlane, as I said before, you've been too long all alone in a sub-division. You ought to have a move. I hear that Sandikot State have asked for the loan of a revenue officer. Why not try for the job? They want someone with about your service.'

'I daresay a change would be a good thing. I'll think it over.'

IV

THE STATES

'The situation of these feudatory States, checkerboarding all India as they do, are a great safeguard. It is like establishing a vast network of friendly fortresses in debatable territory. It would be difficult for a general rebellion against the British to sweep India because of this network of powerful loyal Native States.'

L. F. RUSHBROOK-WILLIAMS.

'Ugh!' said Mrs. Lingsdon, wife of the Commissioner of Bandelpur, 'I could hardly bring myself to shake hands with him. Nasty, horrid, fat, greasy creature. And we were all kept waiting half an hour while he and the Maharajah of Sidpur had a private talk in another room. Talking sedition, I've no doubt. I was furious. If he wanted to talk sedition with Sidpur, why should he elect to do it when he had asked a lot of other guests to dinner, and keep them all waiting?'

'I don't see why you should assume that the Maharajah of Ramrutta was talking sedition,' said Mr. Lightfoot.

'Oh, yes, I know he was. I could tell by his face when he came out of that room. Such a crafty, wicked face. I had to sit next to him at dinner, and do you know I couldn't help thinking all the time of all his wives. I can't tell you how many wives he has, Mr. Lightfoot.'

'I don't expect he could tell me himself,' said Lightfoot. 'He must have lost count by now.'

'How horrible it is to have to kowtow to such awful rakes! I didn't want to go over to Ramrutta for his beastly dinner party or to have anything at all to do with him, but my husband said I must.'

'Well, I expect he gave you a very good dinner, Mrs. Lingsdon, and that you enjoyed it. Now would *you* like to give me another little drink?'

'Why, of course. I didn't see your glass was empty. Help yourself. And you too, Mr. Greenlane. Let me see, you served recently in a native State? You must tell me all about it.'

63

THE STATES

Lightfoot and Greenlane helped themselves to whisky and soda. They had come into Bandelpur from their respective districts for a conference on crime and had decided to pay an evening call on the Commissioner and his wife. They found the latter alone. Mrs. Lingsdon was a lively attractive lady of thirty-eight who devoted her life to dancing, flirting, bridge and gossip. She was a good bridge player, and Greenlane had played quite a lot with her at one time. With Lightfoot she had really nothing in common, but he liked her vivacity.

'The Maharajah of Ramrutta may have lost count of his wives,' said Greenlane as he resumed his seat, 'but I'm told on good authority that he is very well up about all his children. He gives a tea party for them once a year, and though there are several hundred of them he knows all their names and takes quite a personal interest in them.'

'I'm glad he takes an interest in something besides himself,' said Mrs. Lingsdon. 'He takes precious little interest in his State and his miserable subjects. Last year, when there was a great plague of locusts in this part of the country, he just buzzed off saying, "Let the locusts dance here. We're going to dance in Paris." But tell me, Mr. Greenlane, how did you get on with your Maharajah? You were only there about a year weren't you?'

'They parted by mutual consent and with mutual respect,' interjected Lightfoot. 'You see, Greenlane went off to Sandikot State without taking the precaution of seeing me first. If he had done so, I should have warned him what to expect. As it was, he arrived at Sandikot, in all innocence, expecting to find there the Rule of Law, Habeas Corpus and other such modern inventions and was naturally upset to discover they had never been heard of.'

'You use such a lot of strange Greek and Latin words that I never know what you're talking about, Mr. Lightfoot. Now I would like Mr. Greenlane to explain to me quite simply what happened.'

'There is nothing much to tell, Mrs. Lingsdon. I was lent to the State as a Revenue Officer, but for some unknown reason I found that amongst my other duties I had to pay periodic visits to the gaol. I was provided with some printed instructions for gaol visitors and these stated that among other things

64

visitors should attend to complaints from prisoners that their cases were being delayed in Court. On my second visit I came across two men who said they had been in gaol for over four years, but that the cases against them were still pending. I made some inquiries from the gaol officials but couldn't find any record showing what the charges were against them and in what Courts the cases were pending; so I left a note in the visitor's book suggesting that the matter should be looked into. On my next visit the two men were still there, and it was obvious that no action had been taken on my previous note. So I recorded a further note and also sent copies of both of them to the Chief Minister. To my surprise he was very much annoyed. He sent for me, and said it wasn't my business as a visitor to the gaol to probe into the reasons why prisoners were being detained there, but simply to see that they were being properly treated. I drew his attention to the instructions for visitors to the gaol. It would appear that either he had never seen them or had forgotten all about them. They were obviously just eyewash, meant for the benefit of any stray wanderer from the outside world who might chance to pry into the affairs of Sandikot. I took the line that in the presence of the instructions it was my clear duty to inquire why two men were lingering in gaol for four years without trial. Either the instructions should be amended or my inquiries should be regarded as proper and not objected to. The Chief Minister did not quite know what to make of this and referred the matter to the Maharajah, who solved it very easily by deciding that he wanted a more experienced revenue officer than me. So I returned and was posted to Dandot and Jameson was sent in my place.'

'And the two prisoners remained to complete their fifth year?'

'I suppose so, and their tenth year too, probably. I was rather worked up about it at the time. In my ignorance I hadn't imagined that in any part of the British Empire people could in peace-time be thrown into prison for an indefinite period without charge or trial just as a matter of course. Now I realize that it is normal practice in an Indian State. I daresay most of the victims deserve it.'

'How can you be so heartless?' said Mrs. Lingsdon. 'Probably the only fault of those two poor men you saw was that the Maharajah had seduced their wives or daughters.'

'Mrs. Lingsdon,' said Lightfoot, 'your recent meeting with the Maharajah of Ramrutta has obsessed you with the idea that the interests and vices of all Maharajahs are exclusively sexual. I can assure you that this is not the case. I should say that those two men were either obscure relations of the Maharajah who wanted to poison him, or dangerous political workers who had suggested that he oughtn't to spend so much as 50 per cent of his State's revenue on himself. Such persons must obviously be shut up in gaol, with or without trial— preferably without. In a medieval society you require medieval methods.'

'You're always so annoyingly sarcastic Mr. Lightfoot, that one never knows what you're really driving at. But I'm sure Mr. Greenlane is very lucky to have escaped from Sandikot. It must be awful to live in a place like that, where the wretched people are groaning with poverty while the ruler flaunts his luxury in an enormous palace. Did you find the people very much oppressed, Mr. Greenlane?'

'To tell you the truth, I didn't notice very much difference in their general condition from that of the people of British India. The police and magistrates and other officials are no doubt rather more corrupt than here, but they're also more easygoing and less hampered by rules and regulations.'

'Corruption often goes hand in hand with common sense,' said Lightfoot. 'In native States oppression is mainly the result of human caprice, which is far more tolerable than our unintelligible system of impersonal idiocy, which produces gross injustice by a scrupulous application of law and rules.'

'Be quiet, Mr. Lightfoot. I don't want to hear your unintelligible talk about unintelligible systems. I want to hear more about Sandikot from Mr. Greenlane. Tell me more about it, Mr. Greenlane.'

'There was one feature of Sandikot which was novel to me and very trying to the ordinary villager. Some of the near relatives of the Maharajah kept huge herds of cattle and camels, which roamed at large over the countryside, devouring and trampling upon the crops. No one, of course, dared to drive them away and put them in the pound, and no police officer or other official would do anything about them. I started a regular campaign against these cattle and rounded up a great number

66

of them myself on horseback and put them in the pound, and then made the owners—though they were the Maharajah's uncles or cousins—pay large sums for their release. I don't think my action was appreciated. In fact, I think it was one of the reasons why the Maharajah decided he wanted a more experienced revenue officer.'

'The ravaging of crops by the ruler's cattle or his deer or other game is a regular feature of feudal society.' Lightfoot was clearly irrepressible. 'Even to-day it is still vestigial in England, witness the fox and the red deer. Here, in India, where a medieval feudal society still in part survives, you would expect to find it. You'll remember that when in 1932 the oppressed people of Alwar at last rose in rebellion against their Maharajah, one of their principal grievances was that the State was absolutely overrun with deer, which no one except the Maharajah was allowed to kill or destroy.'

'Oh, wasn't it about Alwar that I heard all those funny stories? I can't tell you how amusing they were.'

'I'm sure you can't Mrs. Lingsdon, for they would be quite unsuitable for you to repeat before a young bachelor like Greenlane. But the whole Alwar episode threw a remarkable light on the working of the Political Department.[1] The Resident who might be expected to know something about the affairs of the State, took occasion in a public speech to praise the Maharajah to the skies. You would have thought he was the most enlightened ruler since Hadrian. Only two to three weeks later this enlightened prince was asking the Government of India for aeroplanes with which to crush his unruly subjects. And shortly afterwards he had to leave his State and hand over its management to a British officer.'

'I don't see what you're getting at,' said Greenlane. 'There is nothing very surprising in an officer of the Political Department proving himself quite ignorant of the affairs of the State in which he is Resident. Their motto is "otium cum dignitate",

---

[1] For the management of relations with States there is a separate Service recruited from officers of the Indian Civil Service and Indian Army. Its members serve as Political Agents or Residents in the States, in which capacity they exercise a general, vague, and variable supervision over their affairs and act as intermediaries between them and the Government of India.

and so long as they're treated with exaggerated respect and given enough tigers and ducks to shoot at, they don't care what happens.'

'You're prejudiced, my dear Greenlane, by your recent experience in Sandikot, and the indifference of the Resident to the untried prisoners, vagrant camels and other enormities you found there. Of course, I admit there is much to be said against the Political Department. Old eighteenth-century corruption dies hard there. They are lax about perquisites, shameless about allowances, and shower upon themselves undeserved honours. They also often appear slack and careless. But this appearance of carelessness really masks considerable cunning. You see, in face of the growing political discontent in India the loyalty of the Princes is an important British asset. We don't want to lose it, and we might lose it if we meddled too much with the internal affairs of their States. Hence, though as Paramount Power we have long recognized our obligation to protect the peoples of the States from gross misgovernment, the Political Department has found it increasingly advisable to regard only actual rebellion as the criterion of gross misgovernment. Until therefore rebellion actually breaks out, you have to pretend that there isn't gross misgovernment. For if you admitted its existence, it would be your duty as Paramount Power to intervene. It follows too that the more plain the signs become of unrest and discontent within a State and the louder the complaints of its people, the more necessary is it to assure the world that the Maharajah is an enlightened philanthropist. In doing so, you run a risk that you may be disproved by events. But the risk is not great. Open rebellion, which cannot be hushed up and concealed, occurs rarely. It has so little chance of success.'

'I hope Mr. Greenlane knows what you're talking about; I'm sure I don't,' said Mrs. Lingsdon. 'But I think it is disgusting the way we have to put up with all these profligate Maharajahs and treat them as though they were almost as important as members of the Royal Family. The very thought of that dreadful Ramrutta, with all his jewels and European women and crafty leering face, gives me the creeps. I hope I never have to sit next to him again.'

'You mustn't complain,' said Lightfoot. 'Ramrutta and his

brother princes are, to use the Congress phrase, bulwarks of British rule. So when you sit next to him again, you must just console yourself with the thought that you're doing your bit to uphold the British Empire. As a matter of fact it could well be argued, Mrs. Lingsdon, that, if it weren't for these bejewelled princes, you wouldn't now be sitting here sipping sherry in this comfortable house as wife of the Commissioner of Bandelpur.'

'Oh, you could argue the hind leg off a donkey. I believe you simply do it to annoy, Mr. Lightfoot.'

'Mrs. Lingsdon, how could you think that? Of course, I don't do it to annoy. I do it in the hope of affording you some enlightenment and entertainment.'

'Well, I'm sure you're a very mischievous man and a very bad companion for Mr. Greenlane. I always think I detect a seditious note in your conversation.'

'Not at all. All you detect is an unfamiliar aspect of the truth. Nothing more. But Greenlane and I must be running back to our respective satrapies.'

'There you go again. Why can't you say "districts" instead of "satrapies"?'

' "Satrapies" sounds grander, Mrs. Lingsdon. Well, good-bye. Thanks very much for the drink.'

'Good-bye. Mind you both come and see me again when you're next in Bandelpur.'

Mrs. Lingsdon's attitude to the Maharajah of Ramrutta was typical of unthinking Anglo-Indian society. Her disgust at the contrast between his ostentatious luxury and the poverty of his subjects was genuine, but quite superficial and not unmixed with a little subconscious jealousy. Like so many English people in India she vaguely felt it was wrong that her countrymen should countenance and support worthless, immoral, unprincipled rulers who cared nothing for their people, but (less vaguely) she felt it still more wrong that she, the wife of the Commissioner of Bandelpur, should have to mingle with them on terms of less than equality and treat them with deference and every outward mark of respect. As for the real place, actual and prospective, of the States and their rulers in the Indian Empire, she understood little and cared less.

THE STATES

Greenlane had been too much upset by recent experiences to take a balanced view of the States and their system of government. He had been only a year in Sandikot, but this was enough to tell him that he never wanted to serve in an Indian State again. He was as yet too young and inexperienced to appreciate fully the merits of medieval methods in a medieval society.

Some of Lightfoot's remarks showed more sympathy and understanding. There were hints of a realization that the States, besides being bulwarks of British rule, enshrine a valuable and truly Indian tradition. But the exciting influence of the attractive Mrs. Lingsdon had made him flippant and sententious. In order to shock her, he deliberately underlined the darker side of the Indian States as reactionary elements sustaining British Imperialism. This, though an aspect of their character, does not exhaust their significance. We must therefore leave the idle chatter of Mrs. Lingsdon and her admirers and consider more fully the past history of the States and their future prospects.

The Indian States are about 560 in number, occupy nearly one half of the total area of India and contain nearly one quarter of its population. They range in size and importance from a great territory like Hyderabad, which is about as large as Italy, and has a population of over 14 million, to petty areas, like the Simla Hill States, of only a few square miles. One hundred and eight of these States, with a combined population of over 60 million, are classed as major states and their rulers are entitled of right to inclusion in the Chamber of Princes. One hundred and twenty-seven more are represented in the Chamber by twelve members elected by themselves. The remainder are States only in name. Their rulers have a very limited jurisdiction and for practical purposes may be regarded as landowners with certain feudal rights.

Some of these States, e.g. the Rajput States of Rajputana are of great antiquity; but most of the better-known ones originated in the eighteenth century during the confusion which followed the break-up of the Mogul empire. Some were founded by Muslim Governors who threw off their allegiance to the Emperor at Delhi and became practically independent. Others, e.g. the Maratha States of Central India, represented the resurgence of Hindu nationalism against Muslim domination. Others were territories forcibly appropriated by military adventurers. But all alike, whether old or new, survive to-day by the grace of the British who either tolerated their existence, preserved them from extinction, or actually created them.

The British policy was the result partly of accident and partly of design. During the struggle for supremacy over the ruins of the Mogul empire, the East India Company, which became involved owing to rivalry with the French, allied itself with some of the native powers, notably Hyderabad and Oudh, and waged war against others, notably Mysore and the Maratha chiefs. By the beginning of the nineteenth century, after the defeat of the Marathas by Lake and Wellesley (the future Duke of Wellington), the Company, though by no means yet master of the whole of India, had emerged as the strongest power and was regarded by many as the proper heir to the Mogul empire. But it could not very well proceed straight away to swallow up its own former allies. Nor did it wish to do so. For it was primarily a commercial concern and the Directors viewed unfavourably expensive commitments which brought in no dividends. They were not eager to take on too much. Hence they readily allowed a number of chiefs, some of them former allies and some of them former enemies, to continue as independent rulers so far as the internal administration of their States was concerned. The Company simply assumed responsibility for their military protection, which meant that they had to admit into their territories and pay for a force commanded by British officers and under British control. The arrangement was convenient to the Company as it was a cheap method of maintaining and developing military power. Gradually other chiefs, who feared destruction at the hands of more powerful neighbours, sought the Company's protection and acknowledged its suzerainty. In this way many of the States of Rajputana and the Sikh States of the Punjab saved themselves from extinction.

As the nineteenth century wore on and British power and self-confidence became stronger, many British officers began to regret that so many States had been left unabsorbed. Assured of the superiority of Western methods and standards, they looked with disfavour on the tangled confusion of feudal States, sprawling over more than half of India and sheltering all the barbarisms which they were endeavouring to suppress elsewhere. These views were fully shared by Dalhousie (Governor-General from 1848–56) who held that 'such rightful opportunities of acquiring territory or revenue as might from time to time present themselves should not be neglected'. Acting on this principle he proceeded to annex a whole string of States (of which Oudh[1] was the most important) on grounds of misgovernment or failure of male heirs. It seemed probable that in no great length of time all the States, except perhaps a few of the largest, would be absorbed into the Company's dominions.

This natural process was abruptly checked by the Mutiny. Even during Dalhousie's regime there had not been wanting voices to protest against his vigorous policy of annexation. Many of the older officers considered that the natives States afforded restless and ambitious Indians a useful field for the exercise of their talents which was denied to them in British India. Some of them also felt that, though the States were usually misgoverned, the people preferred the misrule of their own chiefs to 'our strict and meddling system' with its incomprehensible laws and growing hordes of rapacious petty officials. Moreover, Dalhousie's swift elimination of several substantial States was calculated to have an unsettling effect on the rest. One officer of this school of thought, Sir William Sleeman, warned Dalhousie of the danger in particular of annexing Oudh which, he said, 'would cost the British power more than the value of ten such kingdoms and would inevitably lead to a mutiny of the Sepoys'. The native States, he said, were 'breakwaters, and when they are all swept away we shall be left to the mercy of our native army'.

The swift fulfilment of this prophecy by the Mutiny of 1857 made a profound impression. The policy of annexation was clearly dangerous and was abandoned for ever. 'We shall respect the rights, dignity and honour of the Native Princes as our own,' ran the Queen's proclamation of 1858. The Native States were retained as an essential part and safeguard of Britain's empire in India.

[1] Now part of the United Provinces of Agra and Oudh.

THE STATES

Thus that the Native States still exist to-day is the result of deliberate policy; that they exist in the confused, illogical profusion which makes the map of modern India so bewildering is largely fortuitous. Boundaries have been preserved just as they happened to exist in 1858.

But we must carry the story further. During the half-century which followed the Mutiny, the relationship of the States to the Supreme Government, though remaining somewhat nebulous in theory, came to be defined by custom and usage. On the whole the tendency was for the Crown gradually to assert a rather more definite Paramountcy than had normally been exercised by the Company. The States were saved from elimination, but came under a closer tutelage. In the event of a minority the Government claimed the right to approve and even appoint the Regent; misrule might lead to the deposition of the ruler; and there was a tendency for the 'advice' offered by the Residents[1] to approximate to 'orders'. Readiness to interfere with the internal administration of a State depended, no doubt, to some extent on its size and importance, the past history of its relations with the British and the terms of its treaty with them. But the principle was laid down that 'treaties should be read together', and this naturally encouraged a greater uniformity of practice.

Despite the fact that during this period, owing to the development of communications and commerce, the matters of common interest to the States and the Provinces of British India multiplied greatly, the States were throughout kept very much in the background and remarkably isolated both from British India and from one another. Lord Lytton put forward a proposal in 1877 for the formation of a consultative body of eight Princes to be called 'Counsellors of the Empress', but nothing came of it. Later, Lord Curzon produced a similar scheme for a Council of Princes, alleging that they 'yearned for practical association in the cares and responsibilities as well as in the compliments and trappings of Empire'. But the authorities in England did not respond warmly to the idea of treating the Princes as 'partners and allies in the administration', and his proposals were not approved.

[1] See note on p. 67.

THE STATES

A few years later there was a marked change of attitude. Lord Curzon's immediate successors all took occasion to consult the Princes on important matters of common interest. A Prince was nominated to sit in the Imperial War Cabinet and to take part in the Peace Conference of 1919. In 1920 an advisory body called the Chamber of Princes came into being and the Princes were cordially invited to share in the political development of India.

The cynic will not fail to note that this change of attitude coincided almost exactly with the beginning of large-scale political agitation in British India. It was certainly unfortunate that this moment should have been selected for discovering that the Princes, for whom for fifty years 'compliments and trappings' had been deemed sufficient, were something more than picturesque puppets. Yet, quite apart from selfish imperialist motives, this change of attitude, coming when it did, corresponded with realities. The old order of direct British rule in the Provinces could not change and give place to Indian self-government without profoundly affecting the system of indirect British rule through the Princes which existed in the States. Hence, once the status of a self-governing dominion had become the goal of British India, the Princes were bound to emerge from the background and inquire 'What is to become of us?' Obviously, with the disappearance of British control, the puppet Princes would either have to disappear too, or else become real Princes, standing on their own legs and justifying themselves by their own fitness and ability to rule. In the latter case their rôle in India's future was destined to be greater than in the past.

The British, sensitive to the growing hostility of British India, were not averse to the Princes stepping into the limelight. For the Princes, in face of the rising tide of democratic nationalism, felt themselves more than ever dependent on the British for the maintenance of their autocratic rule, and were therefore for this, if for no other reason, loyal to the British connection. Their loyalty could be usefully exploited for propaganda purposes —the loyalty of men who were the true representatives of Indian India, India's own hereditary Princes, the rulers of vast territories with teeming populations—a not inconsiderable fraction of the whole country. As Lightfoot rightly reminded Mrs. Lingsdon and Greenlane, their loyalty was an important British asset.

But on fundamental issues there was considerable confusion of thought. The Montagu-Chelmsford Reforms (1919) laid the foundations of parliamentary democracy in British India. This then was regarded as the form of government proper for it. But what is sauce for the goose should be sauce for the gander. If democracy was enthusiastically prescribed for half India, why should pure autocracy be preserved in the other half?

Many Englishmen, who looked at India through Western eyes, now began to regret that Dalhousie had not completed his work so that the tide of democracy could sweep the whole of India, unchecked by those tiresome 'breakwaters', the Native States. They hoped, however, that gradually the Princes would themselves take the path of constitutional reform, so that the whole of India would fairly quickly assume the pattern of parliamentary democracy.

Others, more discerning, who knew from experience how strong is the tradition of personal rule in India, propounded the opposite theory, viz. that the Provinces of British India should approximate to the pattern of Native States instead of vice versa. But they were in a minority, and their views were considered interesting and original rather than practical.

The British Government, with lack of logic but characteristic acumen, refused to impale itself on either horn of the dilemma. In the Provinces nascent democratic institutions were cheerfully applauded. In the States it rested 'with the rulers themselves to decide what form of government they should adopt'. The British Government would not obstruct proposals for constitutional advance initiated by the rulers: but 'it had no intention of bringing any form of pressure to bear upon them to initiate constitutional changes'.

Meanwhile, the attitude of the Princes themselves was determined by a natural instinct of self-preservation slightly coloured by national feeling. They were still dependent on the Crown, both immediately for support against political agitation—above all agitation conducted against them from inside British India —and more remotely for their continued independent existence in a self-governing India of the future. The last thing they wanted was to become subordinate in any way to a popularly

75

elected Government of India. They were careful, therefore, to emphasize that they owed allegiance to the Crown and to request that the Paramountcy vested in the Crown should in no circumstances be transferred to an Indian Government.

But though still dependent on the Crown, they were not unaffected by prevalent nationalist sentiments. If British India was beginning to free itself from British control, why should they not do likewise? Why should they not put a check on the Paramount Power's unwelcome meddling with their internal affairs? It was an awareness of their growing inclination to assert themselves that made Mrs. Lingsdon assume, on quite inadequate evidence, that the Maharajah of Ramrutta had been talking sedition.

During the years following the end of the last war the Princes, hoping that what was defined would thereby be limited, attempted to obtain a definition of Paramountcy. In this they were unsuccessful. But they did secure a general relaxation of the Political Department's control: at any rate interference with their internal affairs was undertaken much less readily after Lord Curzon's departure (1905) than it had been during and before his term of office. This was natural enough. The more store the British set by the Princes' loyalty, the more cautious they were of weakening it by unwelcome intervention. Political officers were reminded that 'often not the least valuable part of their work was that which they left undone'. Prudent inactivity became a strong tradition. Hence Greenlane's evident contempt for the Political Department and Lightfoot's sarcastic exaggeration that rebellion was the sole criterion of misgovernment.

The weakness of the British position in regard to the States did not, of course, escape the notice of Indian politicians. The country, which elsewhere professed to be the champion of democratic faith, in India preserved and leaned for support on obsolete autocracies. Yet though the line of attack was obvious, the politicians were comparatively restrained. Many of them, like certain Englishmen, regretted that the States had not been swept away years ago and considered that they should now be brought into line with British India by the gradual introduction of responsible government. But they did not actively agitate to secure this result. 'The Congress', Mr. Gandhi declared at the Round Table Conference (1931), 'has endeavoured to serve the Princes by refraining from any interference in their domestic and internal affairs.' The Princes, whatever their faults, were after all, Indians, and the States had enjoyed and still enjoyed a greater degree of freedom from foreign rule than any other part of India. The reluctance of Indian nationalist leaders to attack them was, on this ground alone, quite intelligible.

This policy of non-intervention has been consistently followed by Congress, save for a brief period during 1938–9. But the reasons for this shortlived departure from their normal policy and subsequent reversion thereto throw an interesting light both on Congress and on the political significance of the States.

The Montagu-Chelmsford reforms of 1919 were experimental, transitional and to be reconsidered after ten years. When the time for this reconsideration arrived, the wiser Princes had begun to realize that they could not hope to survive in splendid isolation from a self-governing India. Their own real interests and the larger interests of India required that they should link up amicably with British India, and it seemed likely that the earlier they made a move in this direction the more favourable the terms which they might hope to obtain. Accordingly, in 1930, at the first Round Table Conference they sprang a surprise by declaring that they were willing to join an Indian Federation. This declaration was greeted with acclamation. It was particularly welcome to the British for reasons set forth with great candour by an ex-Viceroy, Lord Reading.

'If the Princes come into a Federation of All India . . . there will always be a steadying influence. What is it we have most to fear? There are those who agitate for independence for India, for the right to secede from the Empire altogether. I believe myself that it is an insignificant minority . . . but it is an articulate minority and it has behind it the organization of the Congress. It becomes important, therefore, that we should get what steadying influence we can against this view.'

Accordingly the new constitution for India was drawn up on the assumption that there would be an Indian Federation of democratic Provinces and autocratic States; and the assurance of the Princes' 'steadying influence' was rendered doubly sure by giving them greater representation in the two Chambers of the Federal legislature than could be justified on a purely population basis.[1]

It was a strange marriage of dissimilars. For by the new Act of 1935 the Provinces were to be advanced to the status of fully fledged parliamentary democracies with almost complete autonomy in regard to purely provincial affairs. The British Governors were to be metamorphosed into constitutional monarchs and the members of the Indian Civil Service into servants instead of masters. Yet most of the States remained undiluted autocracies, and their representatives in the Federal Legislature were to be nominated by the Princes, not chosen by the people.

The provisions of this Act relating to Provincial autonomy came into force on 1st April 1937. The Federal Sections were to come into force at a later, though, it was hoped, not distant date. The Princes had stipulated that accession to the Federation must depend on the discretion of each individual Prince. Federation could not therefore be inaugurated till a substantial number of them had signified the accession of their States thereto. There was necessarily an interval during which Provincial autonomy was in operation, but Federation still unrealized.[2]

It was at this stage that Congress abandoned their usual moderation towards the States and launched a direct attack upon them. However unwise, this attack was a very natural consequence of the political situation created by the 1935 Act. Though the Act had been variously described by Congress sympathizers (with perhaps pardonable exaggeration) as a 'cup of poison' and a 'charter of slavery', nevertheless Congress contested the elections to the new Provincial Assemblies, and

[1] The population of the States is just under one quarter of that of the whole of India. In the Upper Chamber of the Federal Legislature the Princes were allotted two-fifths of the seats and in the Lower Chamber one-third. It must be remembered that this over-representation of the Princes could be defended on the plea that it was necessary in order to induce them to accede to the Federation.

[2] In point of fact the agreement of the necessary number of Princes had not been obtained before the outbreak of war. so the Federal Part of the Act never came into force and its introduction has been indefinitely postponed.

met with overwhelming success. In six[1] out of eleven Provinces they secured absolute majorities. In two others (Bengal and Assam) they came out as the strongest single party. Only in four Provinces (Bengal, Punjab, Assam, Sind) could a stable government be formed without them. After some hesitation Congress decided not to look a gift horse too closely in the mouth and proceeded to take office and form governments in seven Provinces.

The Provincial elections had clearly shown that Congress was the only well-organized All-India party. The Muslim League had failed miserably at the polls. In the predominantly Muslim Provinces of the Punjab and North-West Frontier it had only secured one seat. Other parties were only Provincial in character and had no All-India basis. Elated by their success and the gratifying position of power which they now enjoyed in seven Provinces, Congress began to wonder whether they might not in due course make a successful bid for the control of the Federal Government also. Of course, according to their official programme, they were pledged to have nothing to do with the Federal Scheme embodied in the Act of 1935; but then they were equally pledged 'not to co-operate with the Act in any way'; and yet here they were running the government in seven Provinces. Clearly there would be no objection to working the Federal part of the Act also, if they could dominate the Federal Legislature. But here the Princes were the stumbling block. Despite all the seats reserved for Muslims, Indian Christians, Europeans and other minorities, Congress might still hope to dominate at the centre were it not for the solid block of seats allotted to Princes' nominees—125 out of 375 in the Lower Chamber. How could this solid block be broken up? It could be broken up if a sufficient number of Princes were frightened or cajoled into introducing responsible parliamentary government and agreeing to their representatives in the Federal Legislature being elected by the people instead of selected by themselves. For those chosen by the people would be Congressmen.

[1] Madras, Bombay, United Provinces, Bihar, Central Provinces, Orissa. Shortly afterwards they also gained a majority in the North-West Frontier Province through the adhesion of eight non-Congress members.

THE STATES

With Congress Governments in power in seven Provinces the moment seemed particularly favourable for bringing pressure to bear on the Princes. The Governments of Native States have their own methods of dealing with their own political agitators, and though these may not always bear inspection they are generally effective. But it is not so easy for them to deal with agitation fomented by outsiders and fed by a continuous influx of 'volunteers' from a neighbouring Province of British India. In such an event they look to the Provincial Government to assist them to suppress the agitation; but when members of Congress constituted the Provincial Government they might look in vain.[1]

In these favourable and tempting circumstances even Gandhi, generally so considerate in his references to the States, began to adopt a minatory attitude. In February 1938, Congress declared, with Gandhi's approval, that it 'stands for the same political, social, and economic freedom in the States as in the rest of India', and, though Congress as an organization could only offer 'moral support and sympathy' to the people of the States in their struggle for freedom, individual Congressmen were free to 'render further assistance in their personal capacities'. In December Gandhi became more outspoken. Total extinction or acceptance of full responsible government were the only alternatives open to the States and he warned the Princes that they had better 'cultivate friendly relations with an organization which bids fair in the future, not very distant, to replace the Paramount Power'.

There ensued a more or less systematic agitation against a number of States in which, in some instances, leading members of the Congress Working Committee took a prominent part. The high lights of this agitation were the murder of a British Political Officer in an Orissa State, a fast by Gandhi in connection with political reform in Rajkot, and a civil disobedience movement in Jaipur.

[1] Under the Act of 1935, the Governors had a special responsibility for safeguarding the rights of the States and Princes and in discharge of this responsibility they could use their special powers even in defiance of their Ministry. But they would be reluctant to do this, and in any case there would certainly be delay and hesitation. Agitation would not be nipped in the bud.

The net result was a small constitutional advance in a number of States. Though the success was not great, Congressmen claimed to be satisfied. But as early as the spring of 1939, Gandhi had decided to abandon the campaign and revert to the old policy of non-intervention. He called off the civil disobedience movement in Jaipur, apologized for his conduct in regard to Rajkot, and advised reformers in the States to hasten slowly towards the final goal. Save in Hyderabad, the agitation now everywhere collapsed and no attempt was made to revive it.

So ended the brief campaign against the States. The political motive for it had been strong. But apart from this political motive many Congressmen, who had been brought up on the textbooks of English Liberalism, were influenced by the sincere belief that the States are 'relics of feudal oppression' which ought to be wiped out on their own account as soon as possible. There were plausible grounds for this opinion. In many States there is still no rule of law, no fixed civil list, and no modern Civil Service. Representative institutions are rudimentary, where they exist at all; incompetence and serious misrule are not uncommon, and in several States the luxury of the ruler is in vivid contrast to the poverty of the people. Moreover, the plan of harnessing together in a single federation these feudal States and the modern provincial democracies seemed illogical and even unworkable. The attack made by Congress on the States may have been unwise, but was not entirely perverse.

When the campaign was abandoned in the spring of 1939, the political motive was growing weak. Federation was by this time fast receding into the distant future, mainly owing to the reluctance of the requisite number of Princes to signify their accession. There was therefore less immediate incentive to press the attack on the States.

But two other considerations may also have prompted Gandhi to discontinue the attack. In the first place he probably realized that, if pushed, it was bound to provoke a communal[1] conflict, and this for a very simple reason. In two of the largest States, Hyderabad and Kashmir, about 80 per cent of the people belong to a different community from the ruler and the ruling class. In Hyderabad Muslims govern Hindus; in Kash-

[1] In an Indian context this term has reference to Hindu-Muslim antagonism.

mir Hindus govern Muslims. In both these States, therefore, any agitation against the ruler is liable to arouse communal passions and hence to produce serious reactions in neighbouring and even distant parts of India. This occurred to a slight extent during the 1938–9 agitation; and only seven years earlier agitation in Kashmir had excited the sympathy and active intervention of Muslims in the adjacent Punjab. The danger of precipitating Hindu-Muslim strife throughout India is a strong deterrent against interference with the larger States.

Secondly, Gandhi may have been influenced by an appreciation of the value to India of the political form and tradition which the States represent. It is difficult for the average Congressman to view the States dispassionately owing to their close association with British interests. But Gandhi was born and bred in a State and comes of a family which for two generations had served Indian rulers. He therefore has more sympathy with the States than Congress politicians who have been brought up in British India on modern Western ideas.

And surely any Indian nationalist, looking simply to the welfare of India as distinct from the possible fortunes of a political party, must ask himself whether the extinction of the States or their rapid transformation into parliamentary democracies is either practicable or really desirable. Several of the States are large and the ruling families well established in the affections of their people. Quite apart from the communal danger, attempts to coerce their rulers (whose rights and dignity Britain is morally bound to uphold) into courses which they dislike and of which they disapprove are liable to produce a convulsion and unlikely to succeed.

Moreover, in a country, most of whose people have hardly emerged from medieval feudalism, it does not appear to be wise to overturn hereditary Princes in favour of exotic Western forms of government. The tradition of personal rule is tremendously strong in India. It persists in spite of changing forms and constitutional facts. In British India the district officer is still a ruler, not a Civil Servant. The people still flock to him with every sort of grievance, public and private, and expect him to remedy them with a stroke of his pen. The new Provincial autonomy worked best in the two Provinces where there was the nearest approach to autocracy. In Madras and the Punjab, owing to the character and prestige of the Premiers[1] parliamentary democracy, despite all outward forms, approximated to the personal rule of one man.

The hereditary instinct is also remarkably strong in India. This was strikingly illustrated on the sudden death of Sir Sikander Hyat-Khan in December 1942. Almost immediately a feeling began to spread that he should be succeeded as Premier of the Punjab by a close relative, a cousin or a brother —although the latter had for years been away from the Province in the service of an Indian State. Before this feeling had gathered its full strength, the Governor had invited one of the existing Muslim ministers 'to form a government'. But the desire to associate with the Government some member of Sir Sikander's family became so vehement that in a few weeks his eldest son, a military officer, who had been serving in the Middle East and had no experience whatever of politics, was hauled out of the army, found a seat in the Assembly and made a Minister.

In dealing with the States, therefore, the path of wisdom may be to avoid drastic remedies, based on modern Western ideas. To absorb them all, great and small, into the rest of India is out of the question. Nor should their assimilation be attempted, until it has become clearer what political form the rest of India, when left to itself, is going to take. A distinction must, however, be drawn between the larger States, which may be regarded as more or less permanent features of the Indian landscape, and the innumerable petty States irrationally dotted about the country. States of a few thousand subjects, composed of fragmented territory and governed by Plantagenet ideas, are an absurd anachronism. They cannot survive.

The larger States will continue to exist. The more backward of them may have to make changes in their administration and constitution; but the large States should not as a whole be coerced into policies which the rulers and their ministers instinctively reject. Among these rulers and ministers is to be found much of India's best political wisdom—the kind of wisdom that India needs and British India has lost.

At present, even in the more progressive States, the stage of political development reached is not much in advance of

[1] Mr. Rajagopalachari and Sir Sikander Hyat-Khan.

Tudor England. Popular Assemblies are still mainly consultative and often contain a large nominated element. But though behind the times, these States are not behind the needs and wishes of the bulk of their subjects. Further advance should be left to the clearly expressed will of the people and the judgment of the rulers. British Indian politicians—and other outsiders—would do well not to seek to anticipate them. Maybe they will soon have no temptation to do so.

Power everywhere corrupts, perhaps nowhere more than in India. In the case of the States the presence of the British prevents the operation of self-acting checks—popular revolt, palace revolution or external aggression. An Indian prince does not have to depend on his own virtue or ability. Even if he is guilty of unspeakable enormities and deposed, his son will reign in his stead. He can injure himself but not his House. In these circumstances the wonder is not that some princes are bad, but that any are good.

Once however British support is withdrawn, the standards of the Princes as a whole are likely to improve. Some may be tyrants; they will meet a tyrant's fate. Some may be weak; their power will pass to others. But many will serve their people well, and a few, like the Tudor monarchs, will know how to divine instinctively the popular temper, bending to it when they ought to bend, resisting it when they ought to resist.

If, then, the major Princes are to survive, upholding the tradition of personal monarchic rule, can it be that after all, instead of the States being assimilated to the Provinces, the Provinces should be assimilated to the States? Where divisions amongst people are as deep as they are in India, there is need of some ultimate arbiter, some repository of justice, and this, in the absence of foreigners, can only be found in a Prince, who looks with equal favour on all his subjects as members of one family. Moreover, when British control is withdrawn, and when in each Province the British Governor makes his last bow, someone will be required to replace him as the ceremonial head of the Government. If the new figurehead were to be invested with some of the powers[1] now enjoyed by a British

[1] For the powers of Provincial Governors under the Government of India Act 1935, see the note on recent constitutional developments on pp. 206–8.

Governor, which practice and usage would contract or (more probably) expand, insensibly Provinces and States would come to assume a more or less uniform character. It may be that some Provinces would welcome such a development as making for political stability.

The States then, may have a greater significance for the future than is generally imagined, and Congressmen, if they are wise, will not again depart from their habitual moderation towards them or look upon them with undiscriminating hostility. Gandhi, at any rate, has a regard for the Princes, and he has given charming and characteristic expression to it: 'I feel and I know that they have the interests of their subjects at heart. There is no difference between them and me, except that we are common people and they are, God has made them, noblemen, princes. I wish them well; I wish them all prosperity.'

May Gandhi's sentiments prevail.

V

A COMMUNAL RIOT

'Parva leves capiunt animos'

In the City of Natlum the great Muslim festival of Moharram[1] is celebrated with a pomp and fervour only equalled
at Lucknow. The festival commemorates the martyrdom of
Ali, son-in-law of the Holy Prophet, and of Ali's two sons,
Hasan and Husain. Ali met his death at the hands of an assassin
and his position as Imam or temporal and spiritual head of the
faithful was usurped by outsiders. His son, Hasan, was
wounded and died. Husain, the other son, invited by secret
emissaries to make a bid for power, left Medina and traversed
the waterless desert of Arabia with a small party of followers.
But his expected adherents in Iraq failed him and he found
himself surrounded outside Karbala by greatly superior forces.
Cut off from food and water, he mounted his horse, and, with
sword in one hand and Koran in the other, made a desperate
bid to break out of the ring. But he and his little band were
driven back; one by one his companions fell, till at last, left
alone with a few women and children of the party, he himself,
the grandson of the prophet, was mercilessly done to death.

The memory of Ali and his sons has been held in special
reverence by the Shia sect of Muslims, who maintain, as against
the Sunnis, that they and their descendants to the ninth generation were the true and rightful Imams. Annually at Moharram
they 'abandon their souls to the religious frenzy of sorrow and
indignation' and parade in procession their 'tazias'—tall,
painted, pagoda-like structures of wood or cardboard representing the mausoleums of the martyrs.

Though the Sunnis are supposed to abhor 'tazias' and to
disapprove of all public exhibitions of grief, in Natlum all
Muslims, Sunnis and Shias alike, join in Moharram celebrations with equal enthusiasm. Every Muslim guild—the painters,

[1] Moharram is the name of the month in which the festival occurs.

86

the masons, the carpenters, the weavers—and many other local Muslim fraternities have their own tazias and their own troupes of actors and mourners and during the ten days of Moharram reproduce various scenes of the brave struggle at Karbala. For the first nine days the celebrations take place in the evening or at night; the tazias are placed on the ground and are not moved at all, or at most only short distances The actors and mourners make only occasional excursions into the city streets, and these performances are interspersed with religious discourses and discussions. But on the last day the tazias in all their painted glory are brought out from their resting places, hoisted on poles on to men's shoulders, and carried in slow, intricate procession through the narrow streets and alleys of the city. Every thirty yards or so the bearers halt and set them on the ground, and the accompanying mourners, bareheaded and half-naked, beat their breasts, lacerate themselves with chains and knives and with a rhythmical thrumming call upon Hasan and Husain. From early morning till early afternoon they parade in this fashion through the streets lamenting. Then as the day draws on they leave the city and bear the tazias away to the burial ground outside, where they are dismantled and the celebrations end.

In Natlum there were nearly forty tazias. Some were huge wooden structures, elaborately carved and gilded all over, which fifteen strong men could hardly carry. Others, no less large, were made of lighter material and brilliantly painted; while others, less than six feet in height, made up for their lack of size by the tastefulness of their decoration. Each had its own wealthy patron, each its adherents among the common people, each its own name and tradition, each its own rivals amongst the others.

The route which each tazia should follow on the final day had long been fixed by custom and was now in British times prescribed by law. The manager of a tazia was required to obtain from the police a licence for his procession, and in the licence were laid down the route to be followed, the places where halts were permitted and the times at which important points were to be reached. Breaches of any of these conditions of the licence could be punished by fine or by immediate forcible dispersal of the crowd forming the tazia procession.

A COMMUNAL RIOT

The last day of the festival in Natlum was always an anxious one for the police. The whole city turned out to see the tazias; sightseers crowded the streets and the roofs of the houses. The mourners, excited by the onlookers and fortified with drugs, worked themselves up to a final pitch of fervour and frenzy, which the most trifling incident might turn to blind fury. It was during the early part of the day, when the tazias were still moving about in the crowded walled city, that the danger was greatest. At some places rival processions had to pass close to one another; the routes of several lay right through the centre of the Hindu quarter of the city. An angry word or a slight mischance might easily precipitate a riot. But by three in the afternoon the police would begin to feel that the worst was over. The tazias would now all debouch by one of the city's seven gates onto the circular road, which runs round the city below the walls. Then, marshalled in regular order, each in its own place, they would pass one after the other along the circular road to the next gate, and thence away from the city to the burial ground.

Though the police were always strongly reinforced from neighbouring districts and troops were kept in readiness, there was a long tale of Moharram riots at Natlum. One year the top of a large tazia struck against a telegraph wire; a small bit was broken off and fell to the ground. In a few minutes a rumour spread through the crowds that a Hindu had thrown a stone at a tazia. Hindus and Muslims fell upon one another; hooligans set fire to buildings, houses were looted, and for several days there was an orgy of bloodshed. On another occasion, just as the tazias were being lined up on the circular road, it was heard that four Muslims had been stabbed by Hindus on the other side of the city. Dropping their tazias on the road, the mourners and bearers rushed back into the city to loot the Hindu shops and murder any Hindu they might meet on the way.

In the early spring of 1938, Greenlane was temporarily sent to Natlum to officiate for a few months as District Magistrate. Moharram began only a week after his arrival. As the last day approached he felt considerable anxiety. He had no experience of handling big crowds; and he had never witnessed a communal riot. He realized that he would have little idea what to

88

do should any mischance occur. The omens were not altogether favourable. During the early days of the festival, the partisans of one of the largest tazias, known as the Master, had fallen foul of the police. The police, thinking that they were bent on mischief, moved the City Magistrate, an experienced old Hindu officer, to demand Rs.500 security from them for keeping the peace. Some of them furnished the required security; but two of them refused to do so and were sent to gaol. All this took place before Greenlane was well aware what was afoot. When he came to know of it, he felt uneasy; but did not like to interfere for fear of seeming to let down the police and the City Magistrate.

Very soon the manager of the Master tazia came with a crowd of his partisans to petition Greenlane. They asked him to release the two men from gaol and to discharge the rest from their security bonds. How could they celebrate Moharram when subjected to such disgrace? How could they mourn the martyrs when two of their own men were in gaol? And how could Greenlane have any doubts about their good behaviour? Had they not always obeyed the directions of the police? Never in any of the disturbances in the past had the followers of the Master tazia caused any trouble. This year too they would be absolutely obedient. They were ready to swear any oath. So why should not Greenlane cancel the orders of the City Magistrate and let them go?

Greenlane would have liked to do so; but the Hindu City Magistrate and the Muslim Inspector of Police both said that they were a pack of rascals and not to be trusted; so they were sent away disappointed and disgruntled.

The final day of Moharram came. Troops in the cantonment stood to within easy call; police and magistrates patrolled the streets; and the tazias started their slow progress through the city. But the Master tazia and its neighbour, the Pupil, a tazia of almost equal size, did not move. They had been brought out and set down on two bastions of the city wall hard by the Kap Gate, through which in the afternoon all the tazias would pass. And there they stopped, in full view of the crowds, towering up above the level of the adjacent roofs, their gilded splendour gleaming in the sunlight. Around them, in sullen groups, sat the mourners and bearers, murmuring of the tyranny of the police and the unkindness of the magistrates; while intermittently from inside the city there floated out the dull rhythmical thudding of beaten breasts and the jingle of chains, as the mourners with the other tazias lashed themselves in frenzy.

Greenlane didn't like the look of things. If two of the biggest tazias refused to move, there might be all sorts of trouble. But the City Inspector made light of it. 'If they won't take their tazias in procession, that is their own funeral,' he said. 'It doesn't matter to us. In fact it will give us some more men. I'll withdraw the constables who were to accompany these two tazias and use them elsewhere. Meanwhile I don't think you need wait about here, sir. The City Magistrate and I will manage everything. You and the Superintendent[1] of Police can go and sit in the police station. We'll ring you up if you're required.'

Obedient to his subordinate, the City Inspector, Greenlane went and sat down in the police station and chatted to the Superintendent of Police. At 3.15 p.m. a telephone message came through. 'The City Inspector says would the District Magistrate and the Superintendent of Police come at once to the Kap Gate. The tazias have halted and won't come out of the city.' With anxiety in their hearts, but with a studied air of leisured nonchalance, Greenlane and the Superintendent of Police made their way along the circular road to the Kap Gate. Women and children, standing on the roofs of houses high up on the walls of the city, gazed down at them as they passed. If all the tazias refused to move, what would the two English officers do? Perhaps something exciting was going to happen.

The narrow streets leading down from the city to the Kap Gate were thronged with people and blocked by the painted tazias. Greenlane could see them rising up one behind another like fairy castles; while in the foreground, on the bastions of the city walls, there still rested the huge golden Master and Pupil tazias—sullen, immobile, and aloof, but majestically imposing. 'It's better than the Lord Mayor's Show,' Greenlane thought to himself, as childish memories flashed across his mind. But he had no time to enjoy the scene. On the road, just outside the Gate, a large crowd had collected. In the middle of

[1] The Superintendent or District Superintendent of Police is the head of the police force in a district. Sometimes an Englishman, sometimes an Indian.

it were the City Magistrate and City Inspector, gesticulating and arguing furiously with a queer, wizened, unshaven little man, clad in the most filthy garments. Greenlane and the Superintendent of Police thrust their way forward through the crowd and inquired from the City Inspector what was the matter. He quickly explained the situation to them. It was the custom for the Master and Pupil tazias to lead the procession through the Kap Gate and along the circular road. But they were on strike. Number three in the order of precedence was known as Lal Khan's tazia. Its manager said that he couldn't move till the Master and Pupil had passed. Number four refused to move before number three and so on right down the line. Thus all the tazias were grounded.

While the City Inspector was still explaining matters, Greenlane out of the corner of his eye caught sight of the manager of the Master tazia standing near him in the crowd. 'Hullo,' he cried good-humouredly, 'why don't you bring out your tazia? All the people are longing to see it move.'

'Most exalted Excellency,' said the Manager coming forward, 'what can I do? The tazia is very heavy and the police have put my two strongest men in gaol. Without them how can I lift such a heavy thing?'

'I could lend you a couple of police constables to help.'

'Your Excellency is very kind. But the constables would not be skilled men. They might let the tazia fall and break it, or they might upset it and kill people in the crowd. How can I risk such a disaster?'

'Get away, you old scoundrel,' shouted the City Inspector, raising his baton, and the Manager of the Master tazia slunk away into the crowd. 'It is no use wasting time with him, sir, and this fellow,' the City Inspector pointed to the unkempt figure with whom he had been arguing, 'is no better. This is Pir Baksh, the manager of the Lal Khan tazia, who says he can't move without the Master and Pupil. There is his tazia just up that side street.'

'Oh, only a little tiddler!' exclaimed Greenlane. 'Fancy the whole show being held up by that!' The Lal Khan tazia was certainly not impressive. A cardboard structure, scarcely six feet high, shabby and somewhat askew, it was quite unworthy of Natlum's fame.

91

A COMMUNAL RIOT

The City Inspector and the City Magistrate were hot, ruffled, and excited. They shouted at Pir Baksh and abused him. They seized him by the scruff of his neck and shook him. And they kept turning to Greenlane and saying, 'We must get these tazias moving, sir. If they remain halted like this with all these crowds about, there'll be a communal riot. Those rascals up there with the Master tazia are bent on mischief.'

Greenlane addressed himself to Pir Baksh. 'Come on, Pir Baksh,' he said. 'What is the trouble? Why are you holding everything up?'

'I am entirely innocent, Your Excellency,' Pir Baksh replied. 'The police are abusing me without reason. My tazia is number three. How then can I go ahead as number one? It would be against custom; it would be against your Excellency's own orders. It is written in my licence that I am number three.'

'Liar,' said the City Inspector, 'there is nothing of the kind in your licence. He is illiterate, sir. Some mischief-monger has told him to say this. In his licence it is simply written that he should pass through this gate at 3.5 p.m. Nothing is said about the other tazias. They are each given their own timings separately so as to bring them through the gate in the right order.'

'Look here, Pir Baksh,' said Greenlane, 'according to your licence your tazia has to be out of the city by 3.5 p.m. You're already twenty minutes late. Now I'll give you just one minute more to get your tazia moving. You needn't worry about what the other tazias are doing. You just attend to your own affairs.'

'I am always ready to obey your Excellency's commands, and since your Excellency orders it, I would willingly take my tazia as number one in the procession, although its place is really number three. But the men who carry the tazia would not agree to it. They would not understand it. When the Lal Khan tazia has always been number three, how could it go as number one?'

'Very well,' said Greenlane, 'if you don't want to move your tazia, don't. You can remain with it here in the street. It doesn't matter to me. You can remain here all night if you like. It will be a breach of the conditions of your licence and will therefore cost you fifty rupees. But that's all. If you think it's worth while, by all means stay where you are.'

Pir Baksh looked a bit puzzled, but said, 'Your Excellency,

92

I am helpless. I cannot move without the Master and Pupil
tazias.'

Greenlane turned away. The City Inspector and City Magistrate were getting more and more agitated. All the tazias,
they said, were refusing to move forward. It was no good just
telling them that they could please themselves and spend the
night in the road. Hindus and Muslims were all jumbled up
together in the crowds and at the slightest provocation would
start fighting. Very likely as a result of this delay wild rumours
were already afloat in other parts of the city.

Just at this moment a sub-inspector of police, followed by five
or six men, came pushing through the crowd and whispered to
Greenlane. 'The Painters and the Carpenters are quite ready to
bring out their two tazias. They're right back there, numbers
eleven and twelve. If you'll just speak a word to the men, they'll
move forward the tazias at once. They say that you know them.'

Greenlane glanced at the men with the sub-inspector and at
once recognized their faces. They had been negotiating with
him for the purchase of two tiny plots of public land in the
city and the bargain was not yet struck. What a Godsend! 'We
want to bring forward our tazias,' they said, 'may we do so?'
They smiled at Greenlane to make sure that he had recognized
them. 'Yes, by all means,' he replied. 'Well done. Come along.'

Back they hustled through the crowd, quite delighted at their
business skill and their good fortune in being able to oblige
Greenlane at such an opportune moment. In a few minutes the
Painters' and Carpenters' tazias were hoisted on to the shoulders
of the bearers and came swaying forward towards the Kap Gate.
The police pushed the other tazias to one side to make way for
them, and there was a general stir. All up the street the grounded
tazias began to be lifted up and moved slowly forward. The tension had relaxed. The trouble was over. The City Inspector and
the City Magistrate were mopping their brows and laughing.
Inwardly Greenlane heaved a sigh of relief. He surveyed the
scene with a smile of pleasure.

Suddenly he became aware of a submissive figure grovelling
at his feet and murmuring, 'Forgive me, forgive me! I forgot
myself. Have mercy!' It was Pir Baksh, manager of the Lal
Khan tazia. He had never expected that the other tazias would
move without him. Now that they were all astir, he and his

93

companions were seized with panic. What if they were now made to wait till last? And what if the police made this an excuse for relegating them permanently to the back and they lost for ever their proud position at number three, immediately behind the two big tazias? The thought of such humiliation and such a break with age-old custom appalled them. So with folded hands and watery eyes Pir Baksh now cringed and grovelled before Greenlane and besought him to let him bring forward the Lal Khan tazia. 'No, let him wait till last,' said the City Inspector. 'He has given us trouble enough. These are only crocodile's tears.'

But Greenlane's heart was melted by Pir Baksh's tears and the look of abject misery on his wizened face. Even if it was all put on, such excellent histrionics deserved a reward. The Painters' and Carpenters' tazias were just approaching the gate. 'Let him wait a minute and follow on immediately behind these,' he ordered. But Pir Baksh was waiting for no one. Leaping in the air with delight, he made a signal to his men; and at once the miserable, measly Lal Khan tazia came hurrying down the slope through the gateway, scattering the crowd helter-skelter, knocking down the City Magistrate who tried to bar the way, barging past the Painters' and Carpenters' tazias, till it had got out into the circular road, clear of everyone, at the head of the whole procession. The crowd applauded, Greenlane laughed, the City Magistrate picked himself up out of the dust, the mourners began beating their breasts. Everyone was happy.

Greenlane walked back to the police station. The women and children looked down at him from the housetops. So he had got the tazias to move after all. They waved and smiled at him as he passed. But amongst the adherents of the Master and Pupil tazias there was resentment. Their Moharram had been spoilt.

A week passed. All seemed quiet. The Superintendent of Police went off on a few days' holiday, and Greenlane, anxious to see something of his new district, decided to go out on tour. He left in the afternoon to motor to Chungawala sixty miles away. On arriving at his destination he was handed a telegram:

'Communal riot in Natlum. Please return at once. City Magistrate.'

Greenlane turned his car round and drove straight back. Visions of a frenzied mob and blazing bazaars rose before his mind. He urged his car forward, but it was old and the road was bad. He couldn't hope to reach Natlum much before nightfall.

The sun was setting as the domes of its shrines and mosques came into view. Was it his imagination or did he see columns of smoke rising above the city? It must be his imagination. Bang! A tyre burst. The car lurched violently to one side of the road and came to a halt. He had been driving too fast.

His servant and orderly began changing the wheel. He himself leaned against the car and looked towards the city. So it wasn't his imagination after all. He could now see quite clearly, beyond any possibility of doubt, three columns of smoke; and, as the light faded, a slight red glow tinged the sky over one corner of the city.

Well, there was nothing for it but to wait patiently while the wheel was changed. If the city was burning, he couldn't help it. But ought he to have foreseen and prevented the outbreak? Lightfoot, he remembered, used to say that any fool could quell a communal riot, but a good officer never let one begin. Ought he to have known that something was brewing? Had he unwittingly made some stupid mistake during his few weeks in Natlum?

At last the wheel was changed and he drove on. On the outskirts of the city there were no signs of life. He hurried to the police station to learn the worst. Eight killed, thirty injured and in hospital, a cinema, four houses and the Congress office burnt to the ground—this seemed to be the extent of the damage. It had all started with the stabbing of a Hindu in a narrow alley near the Kap Gate. A Hindu mob quickly collected, looted some small Muslim sweet shops in the vicinity, marched to the house of a local Muslim leader and began yelling abuse at him and his family. This enraged the Muslims, who in their turn formed a mob and set fire to the headquarters of all Hindu insolence—the Congress office. This was the signal for general hooliganism. Fires started simultaneously in different parts of the city. Gangs of roughs roamed the streets attacking without provocation any member of the opposite community they might see. The police hurried from one point to another, always arriving too late or in insufficient numbers. Towards evening, however, they had managed to clear the streets. The injured had been collected and sent to hospital and arrangements were being made to dispose of the corpses without fuss. 'I don't think we'll have any more serious trouble,' said the City Inspector. 'It has been short and sharp and both sides have had enough of it. The troops have been asked to take up stations in the city at sunrise to-morrow.'

There was no further outbreak, but for several weeks the disturbances continued to reverberate in mutual recriminations, and Greenlane had many anxious arduous days while the city cooled down. He was conscious that his own part in the whole affair had been singularly inglorious and he continued to reproach himself for not having anticipated the trouble and been present in person to deal with it. Lightfoot wrote to him sympathetically. But he felt sure that Lightfoot, if he had been at Natlum, would never have let it happen.

He went over the whole history of events with Lightfoot a few months later. 'The mistake you made, my dear Greenlane, is obvious,' he said. 'But you needn't worry. Government will never spot it or blame you for it. And it was a natural mistake and in a way creditable to you.'

'I wish you would tell me what it was.'

'You should never have upset those people during Moharram by keeping their men in gaol or on security. When you saw they took it so much to heart, it was harsh not to relent; and it was quite unnecessary. If you had released them they would have been so grateful to you that, so far from giving you any trouble during Moharram, they would have done all they could to make things go smoothly. Gratitude is a virtue of unsophisticated people. It is certainly an Indian virtue; indeed, feelings of personal gratitude and loyalty account for much of what we consider their failings and even corruption in public affairs. Those followers of the Master tazia, rascals though they may be, would have shown their gratitude to you all right if you had been a little kind to them.'

'As a matter of fact I wanted to release them.'

'Yes, I have no doubt you did, and it was only loyalty to the police and to the City Magistrate which prevented you. Nevertheless, it was a mistaken loyalty. In this country government

96

officials suffer from wrong notions of prestige. Something which merely offends their *amour propre* they represent as a deadly blow to the whole administration. Perhaps it arises partly from government having been for so long government by a mere handful of foreigners, who, feeling that their position depends largely on bluff, don't dare to cast any doubts on their own infallibility. Anyhow, the results are deplorable. No one is willing to admit a mistake or withdraw from a false step. The whole security of a district, or a Province, or even of the whole of India is represented as being dependent on persistence in some palpable error. The little mistake of your police in Natlum and your loyal support of them is in its small way illustrative of what continually happens in India on a vast continental scale. But I'm straying from the point.'

'You are a bit. What I want to know is what precise connection you see between the behaviour of the Master tazia at Moharram and the riot a week later. There was no visible connection between them.'

'No, but a clear psychological connection. Because their Moharram was spoilt, the followers of the Master tazia felt resentment against authority, and the normal inhibitions deterring them from flouting authority were relaxed. They were in the mood to seize any opportunity of having a smack at the police and the magistracy. For all you know, it was one of them who was responsible for the murder of the Hindu, which started all the trouble. It occurred near the Kap Gate where the followers of the Master tazia reside. Anyhow, they must have formed a considerable fraction of the Muslim mob which set fire to the Congress office. I would say that if a lot of Muslims round Kap Gate had not been in an angry, resentful mood, that mob would never have formed so quickly and started doing mischief. The abusive crowd of Hindus swarming round the Muslim leader's house would have been dispersed by the police and the situation brought under control before the Muslims were ready for concerted action. As it was, a great number of them were just looking for trouble. It only needed an appropriate signal for the whole herd immediately to assemble and start burning Hindu buildings. My instinct tells me, therefore, that it was resentment engendered by the Moharram incidents that was the real cause of the riot a week later. I can't prove it to you. It is just an intuition. I've seen the way things happen in this country.'

'I realize that you're probably right,' said Greenlane. 'How difficult all these things are! With the best intentions in the world one seems to put one's foot in it. I sometimes wonder whether we English don't unconsciously provoke communal strife. There doesn't seem to be much of it in the Native States. Yet we're never free of it in British India. Do you think there is anything in the Congress allegation that we are responsible for it?'

A mischievous gleam came into Lightfoot's eyes. This was an opening he couldn't easily resist. Greenlane smiled. He knew what he had let himself in for. 'All right,' he said, 'go ahead. I'm prepared to listen.'

VI

THE COMMUNAL QUESTION

'The truth plainly is that the existence of these hostile creeds side
by side is one of the strong points in our political position in India.'
                                        SIR JOHN STRACHEY.

'Congress allege that there is no communal problem,'
said Lightfoot. 'Alternatively that if there is one, we
have created it; and in any case that it will disappear
with our departure. As you and I know from our daily experience, the first proposition is ridiculous. There *is* a communal
problem; and it is the only serious obstacle to immediate Indian
independence. For this very reason the Congress try to conjure
it away. If it didn't exist their dreams would at once come true.
So they are strongly tempted to say that it doesn't exist. You
and I know better.

'But, like all district officers, we're apt to get a wrong impression of it. We are always so taken up with disputes about
processions, cow-killing, mosques and music, and so concerned
to settle these without a brawl or an outbreak of hooliganism,
that we easily forget the real character of the communal conflict. These petty squabbles and the disorders to which they
sometimes lead are at most only symptoms; and often they
would most properly be regarded simply as manifestations of an
excitable people's tendency to bicker and fight. As you must
have noticed, in villages communal strife, where it occurs, is
generally nothing more than ordinary village faction. In towns
our so-called communal riots are in one aspect just the brawls
which inevitably arise among an undisciplined city riff-raff. If
the Hindu-Muslim division didn't exist, the city rowdies would
discover or invent some other division. We take too seriously
these ebullitions of the unlettered multitude. They are not
serious in themselves. They are only serious because they are
linked with an unresolved struggle amongst the higher classes
of society. It is this struggle which is important.

'It comes to our notice, of course, as district officers. We see

99

something of it whenever we preside over a scramble for posts in government offices. But because it gives us less trouble than disputes about mosques and processions, we tend to think less of it. It is significant,[1] however, that one of the first acts of the first purely Indian ministry in this Province was to work out formulas so as to ensure that in recruitment to the various government services each community would get its due share down to the last decimal point. The Indian ministers fully understand what it is that has been for so long the root of the trouble. For years the communal conflict has been in essence a struggle between different sections of the middle classes for posts. And this struggle for posts is turning into a struggle for power—a struggle for power between two different sections of the upper and middle classes.

'The basis of the difference is religion. But religion is not the cause of the quarrel. The two communities are not fighting for the supremacy of their own faith. They do not each feel that they are possessed of some important truth or means of salvation which they must force upon the other. There is no particular proselytizing zeal. At most there is a determination to preserve their separate identity. But differences of religion have been accentuated by differences of culture, tradition, and social habits, and by the fact that each community prohibits intermarriage with the other.

'Race does not enter much into the quarrel. Only a comparatively small proportion of the various Muslim invaders of India settled here permanently. The vast majority of the present day Muslims are descended from Hindu converts. In the northwest of India, where Muslim influence was strongest, the Hindu peasantry embraced Islam *en masse*. To this day some of them remember their Hindu ancestry and boast that they are Rajputs. Elsewhere there were extensive conversions among the lower caste Hindus. This is one of the reasons why the Muslims as a whole are comparatively poor and backward. The effects of their lowly origin still persist. They persist and often give an economic colouring to the quarrel. Indeed, economic factors almost everywhere aggravate it.

[1] The reader is reminded that this conversation took place during the summer of 1938. The first Indian provincial Ministries were formed in April 1937.

'But in essence the struggle is one for posts and political power between two communities distinguished by religion and culture.

'So much for the general character of the communal problem. Now let us consider Congress's second proposition—that we are responsible for it. This proposition is not true; but it is not wholly ridiculous. There are elements of truth in it which we ought to recognize. We didn't create the divisions; but our mere presence has helped to keep them alive; and both consciously and unconsciously we have made use of them for our own purposes. Our presence has kept them alive simply because we have been a more or less impartial third party. Left to themselves one or other side would have gone under, or some compromise would have been reached—possibly with the Muslims masters of parts of India and the Hindus masters of the rest. In any event the weaker party, if it did not cease to exist altogether, would have bowed to the inevitable. This was more or less the position in pre-British times. When the Mogul emperors and their Muslim Wazirs were in firm control of the country, the Hindus kept quiet and took what they could get. Similiarly when Muslim rule broke down and Ranjit Singh and his Sikh Sardars made themselves masters of this part of India, the Muslims here kept quiet and took what they could get. But under our rule both parties have been allowed to clamour and found that clamouring paid. The divisions couldn't just be quietly forgotten.

'That we should make use of these divisions for our own purposes was so natural and so inevitable that I see no need to be apologetic about it; and to deny it is absurd. In the early days of our rule we made no bones about it. "Divide et impera" was freely acknowledged as a proper principle for our Government of India. It is only latterly that we have grown more squeamish and driven the principle from the conscious to the subconscious regions of our mind.

'It is interesting to note how in the course of 150 years we have leaned first to one side and then to the other. When we conquered India, it was mainly a Muslim ruling class that we displaced—the Nawabs, Wazirs, and other grandees of the Mogul empire. These were the people who we feared might turn against us, not the mild Hindu; and it was currently assumed that the Muslims were the real instigators of the Mutiny. For many years after the Mutiny we were content to see them steadily lose ground both economically and politically, while the Hindus forged ahead in business and captured all the best places in our new clerical system of administration. But with the growth of the Nationalist movement, which from the start was primarily Hindu, there was a swing over. The Hindu became the irreconcilable foe; the Muslim a friend and loyal to the British connection. And this has been the prevalent view for the last fifty years.

'Probably our most conscious application of the divide and rule principle has been in our management of the army. We have been careful to keep the communities balanced both in the army as a whole and even within the several units. In the political field its most glaring application was dictated more by force of circumstances than by any Machiavellian policy. By conceding in 1909 the Muslim demand for separate electorates, we ensured an accentuation of communal antagonism and division; but it is difficult to see how we could have acted otherwise. The Muslim demand was so strong and so cogent. Still, the effect of our action was to keep the communities apart. And subconsciously we welcomed this effect. It suited us. The estrangement of the two communities we viewed with satisfaction, their rapprochement with disquiet. I well remember during the 1919 disturbances the surprise and alarm caused by the unprecedented fraternization of Hindus and Muslims. It seemed to us a most perturbing symptom. And you yourself must occasionally have heard British officers, perhaps even me, say with mingled relief and amusement, "Now they've begun to fight amongst themselves!" Wearied with direct attacks on Government, that is on ourselves, we welcome a diversion.

'Now this sort of attitude is not confined to the ordinary rank and file of British officials. It is to be found in higher circles also, and influences the conduct of statesmen and Viceroys. I have only twice met a Viceroy, but on each occasion he made the same remark, "I've never known communal feeling worse than it is now. Have you?" This may be just a stock remark which Viceroys make to district officers to keep up their spirits. But its tacit implication is quite clear. If communal feeling is worse than ever, then the barometer is

THE COMMUNAL QUESTION

"Set Fair" for a continuance of British rule—a reflection comforting to the Viceroy if not to the district officer. This attitude of mind affects policy. I don't suggest that it causes us wantonly to aggravate the communal problem, but it does diminish our readiness to perceive or devise ways of solving it. It encourages us to lie back and leave Hindus and Muslims to their sterile negations. That is why I say that subconsciously we make use of their divisions. And I am afraid that we shall go on doing so, until our whole attitude of mind is changed by a realization that Hindu-Muslim agreement is as much now a British interest as their disagreement may have been in the past.'

'What do you mean by that?'

'Simply this, that until there is some sort of Hindu-Muslim agreement, some reasonable prospect of the two communities settling down together in peace and amity, it is difficult for us to shuffle off our responsibilities and leave India. Yet the longer we remain in India, the more likely it is to become a second Ireland. Hence Hindu-Muslim agreement is now a British interest. But to obtain it is becoming increasingly difficult. For, as I have said, the communal struggle is turning into a struggle for power; and such struggles are not easily resolved by agreement.

'The communal struggle is a struggle for power. If we recognize this, we cannot fail to see that, whatever elements of truth there may be in the Congress allegation that we created the communal problem, fundamentally the allegation is false. Our departure from India simply reopens the old eighteenth-century struggle for power which Plassey interrupted and, for the time being, decided. Just consider the matter historically. When the Mogul empire broke down, the Mahrattas in Central India and the Sikhs[1] in the Punjab formed strong Hindu successor States. On the other hand many rich and populous areas were still in the hands of Muslim Wazirs, owing nominal allegiance to a shadowy Emperor. It was therefore an open question whether India would be ruled by Hindus or by Muslims or by both. The actual answer was "by neither". We English stepped in and excluded all the other claimants to power. But we didn't proceed to make the whole of India English and Christian. So, with our departure, the question must necessarily arise once

[1] The Sikhs were in origin a reformist monotheistic sect of Hindus.

103

more, "Is it to be Hindu Raj, Muslim Raj or a combination of the two?"

'If you look at it in this way, you'll have to admit that the communal problem couldn't be avoided. Possibly some far-sighted policy might have prevented it taking shape again as a struggle for power; but the course which, in perfect good faith, we actually adopted was perhaps least likely to prevent this. With some misgiving, but urged on by educated Indians, we introduced into India the English system of representative Government. Now in England we count heads to save the trouble of breaking them. But in India to count heads is the surest way of getting them broken. For by mere counting you simply make a present of political power to the Hindus, who enjoy a permanent majority. The Muslims, who number ninety millions and ruled India before we did, cannot be expected meekly to accept this arithmetical logic and just content themselves with such crumbs of power as a Hindu majority may allow them. In the absence, therefore, of some agreement for sharing power, they must necessarily prefer breaking heads to counting them.'

'But', interrupted Greenlane, 'our system of parliamentary democracy is already functioning all right in the Provinces without leading to any particular breaking of heads. No doubt, during the last twenty to thirty years, since we began introducing elections and other democratic machinery, there has been a considerable increase of communal feeling and communal rioting, but no major communal crisis has been provoked.'

'Yes, but the comparative smoothness with which democratic self-government has been introduced in the Provinces is deceptive. If it can function in the Provinces, you may say, why not at the centre also? But the Provinces are many; the centre is only one. In the Provinces political power is shared. Hindus dominate in some; Muslims in others. Both are therefore more or less satisfied. But how can the centre be shared?

'People in authority, who are now all agog to bring into operation those sections of the 1935 Act which provide for a Federal Government at the centre, imagine that the main difficulty will be to secure the accession of the requisite number of Princes. They have not perceived that the main difficulty will

104

be to obtain the acquiescence of the Muslims. For the Muslims will never accept lying down what they believe to be pure Hindu domination at the centre; and this is what they are coming to think the Federal portions of the 1935 Act involve—permanent Hindu Government by a permanent Hindu majority. Consider what it means to them. One of the main subjects with which a Federal Government would deal is Defence. As you know, the Muslims have long had a privileged position in the army. Proportionate to their population they have a larger share in it than the Hindus. How then can they afford to place their position in the army at the mercy of a Hindu majority? Similarly, how can they allow a Hindu Government at the centre, through the management of currency and tariffs, to exercise a general control over the whole economic life of the country? They know that the Hindus are more experienced in business and finance than they themselves and at present have an advantage over them. They fear that Hindu dominance at the centre will mean their permanent relegation to back seats in the business and industrial world.'

'That's all very well,' said Greenlane, 'but when we were hammering out the new constitution embodied in the 1935 Act, the Muslims accepted its main features. Even Jinnah's chief complaint was not that Muslims were put at the mercy of Hindus, but that in the proposed Federal Government too much power was retained in the hands of the Viceroy and not enough transferred to popularly elected Indian Ministers.'

'Yes, but since then the Muslims have been frightened. They have been frightened by the conduct and apparent policy of Congress.'

'How do you mean?'

'Well, it's like this. The Muslims can't feel happy unless power at the centre is shared. How can this be done? One answer is by always having coalition governments; and there is no doubt that the framers of the new constitution intended that the Federal Government should be a coalition government in which real Muslim representatives, not mere stooges of the Hindus, would be included. In other words, there would not be pure majority rule. This, you will note, is the type of government that already exists in the Punjab. Though the Muslims are in a majority, there is not pure majority rule. The

Government is a coalition government and the Hindus and Sikhs between them have as many members in the Cabinet as the Muslims. Now, if at this moment the Muslims were fully assured that this sort of composite government would be formed at the centre, and that the Muslims in it would be real representatives of the Muslim community and not merely nominees of the Hindus, they would probably be satisfied. But owing to the recent conduct of Congress they feel no such assurance. They believe that Congress's aim is to establish Hindu Raj at the centre. They may be wrong—I think they are —but Congress policy has certainly created this impression. For after their sweeping victories in the provincial elections, Congress proceeded to form pure Congress ministries in every Province in which they had a majority. In none of them would they admit the principle of coalition. They have, no doubt, included Muslims in their ministries, but they are their own men—Congress Muslims—not representatives of the Muslim League or any specifically Muslim party. It is pure Congress Raj and this can be only too easily represented as pure Hindu Raj. Matters are being made worse by the strict control exercised by the Congress "High Command" over the Congress provincial ministries. None of them are independent. They have to take orders from the Congress Working Committee. Gandhi and a small Hindu clique have become All-India dictators, issuing orders to Provincial Governments from the ashram at Wardha. So, at least, they are represented to be by Jinnah and other Muslim politicians. The result is the spread of a general feeling of disquiet among Muslims. This disquiet is strongest in the Muslim-minority Provinces, which have already tasted Congress Governments, and especially in the United Provinces where the Muslim minority includes many Muslims of wealth and standing. But even the Muslims in predominantly Muslim Provinces, who need have no fear of Congress or Hindu Raj in their own Provinces, are beginning to take alarm. If Congress majorities insist on pure majority rule in the Provinces, this is what they will do at the centre also, when a Federal Government is formed. Muslim interests will be entirely at the mercy of Hindus. It will be pure Hindu Raj.

'It is easy to see the mistake Congress are making. Unwittingly it is they who are now creating the communal problem

106

or at any rate making it more dangerously intractable. But the mistake is very natural and intelligible. They are so desperately afraid that we shall exploit communal divisions and thereby delay the attainment of independence that they want to cover them over and make it appear as though they do not exist. This they hope to do by saying that Congress represents everybody and speaks for the whole of India. It certainly does include within itself the most diverse and contradictory elements. Its claim to represent everybody, though not true, except in so far as all Indians want independence, is not without plausibility. And after the recent provincial elections, in which Congress was so strikingly successful, it really did seem that the claim might be made good. The Muslim League, the one party which might rebut the claim, had suffered a heavy defeat. Why not ignore its existence and make a drive to bring all Muslims within the Congress fold? To recognize its existence by gratuitously entering into coalition pacts with it would be for Congress to give their case away. It would be an admission that the League and not Congress really represents the Muslims. This admission once made, we could make differences between Congress and the League a ground for withholding independence indefinitely; and Congress would have no answer. They could no longer challenge the League's claim to speak for the Muslims. So Congress have gone all out for no compromise and no coalition with anybody.

'But this policy of Congress, though intelligible, is simply not going to work. It is provoking a strong reaction amongst Muslims and a resurgence of the League. By ignoring the League Congress have given it a fillip.

"This is one of those occasions when we ought to be alert and constructive, preventing the gap between the communities widening and promoting agreement; but we are inhibited by our subconscious adherence to the divide and rule principle and by our dislike of Congress. We enjoy the spectacle of Congress leaders making fools of themselves and Jinnah pitching into them. We would rather like it to go on. We have no strong desire to rescue them from their mistakes. They have made their bed. Let them lie on it. We overlook the fact that we. by the distrust we have inspired in them, are partly responsible for their mistakes. For if it were not for their fear that we will exploit the communal divisions, they would not be at such pains to pretend they don't exist and thus alarm and enrage the Muslims.

'I am afraid, therefore, that just at the moment when, perceiving the dangers, we ought to be actively mediating between the two communities, clarifying the issues, privately suggesting solutions and possible lines of agreement, and above all encouraging contacts between Hindu and Muslim politicians who have shown themselves to be moderate and practical, we shall remain inert and let things drift, until the whole problem becomes quite intractable.'

'I take it then', said Greenlane, 'that you don't agree with the Congress's third proposition, that with our departure the communal problem would settle itself?'

'My dear Greenlane, I am afraid I had quite forgotten about it. However, now that you have reminded me of it, I had better discuss it. I think the best one can say is that it is by no means so foolish as it seems. For one must admit that if the leaders of the two communities saw that either they had to reach an agreement or to fight, they might be more disposed to reach an agreement. As it is, they can just go on raising their terms against each other and making demands which bear little relation to practical possibilities. They can lightly talk of civil war without really thinking what it would mean to organize and launch it. The presence of a third party certainly encourages intransigeance and irresponsibility. I think we ought to recognize this element of truth in the Congress proposition. But whatever truth the proposition may contain, it is, of course, from a practical point of view quite unhelpful. The suggestion that we should just clear out and everything will settle itself overlooks the fact that we have to hand over the government of the country to someone. We cannot leave it to "the effortless custody of automatism". Moreover, even if it were actually possible for us simply to disappear without making any arrangements for the further conduct of the government, it is quite unreasonable to expect us to do anything so irresponsible. Indians often say that they would prefer chaos to the present slavery. Perhaps they would. But British Government in India, whatever its mistakes or crimes—and we shouldn't disguise them—has for over a century had a strong feeling of responsibility towards its subjects. It cannot therefore abdicate in favour of chance or chaos. It must try to find a more suitable successor. This means that before abdicating it must try to solve the communal problem—by agreement if possible; if not by force.'

'By force? Do you really mean that?'

'Well, if we can't get an agreed solution, our only course will be to impose a solution—to impose, if necessary by force, a solution which we consider just and fair. I can't say what that solution would be. It might involve the partition of India. It might involve considerable regrouping of existing Provinces and States. It might involve the introduction of novel constitutional expedients or even of forms of government of which we do not much approve. But whatever it might be, having decided that it was fair and having made the necessary constitutional arrangements for giving effect to it, we should have to help to power persons who accepted it and support them, if necessary with military forces, through any initial disorders till they appeared reasonably firm in the saddle. Failing agreement, there seems no alternative. We can't ourselves remain here indefinitely. My own belief is that if we showed ourselves determined to enforce some solution which was reasonably fair, the necessary measure of acceptance of that solution would be forthcoming and force would not be required. Let us hope so. Forcible solutions are not often satisfactory.'

'No, indeed. But, Lightfoot, the Muslim objection to "majority" rule at the centre, which I confess I had not fully appreciated, seems pretty insuperable. How do you envisage that we should get over that?'

'I don't really know. But I should say that if the functions of the Federal Government were reduced to the minimum, which would mean, I suppose, Defence and Foreign Affairs, Tariffs and Currency and Communications, and if Muslims were given some definite assurance regarding the sharing of power, their fears would be sufficiently allayed. For instance, instead of just trusting to good sense and tacit convention, one might make statutory provision that the Federal Government should always include a certain number of Muslims possessing the confidence of the Muslim members of the legislature. Or one might give so much weightage to the various minorities in the central legislature that the Hindus would only be able to obtain a majority by combination with one or other of them. Of course agreement is impossible unless leaders on both sides show some moderation and good sense. But we have quite a good basis of moderation and good sense on which to build, if only we will make use of it.'

'I am afraid I see precious little moderation or good sense in Congress or the Muslim League.'

'In these two bodies as such there is little, but in individual members there is much. What about Sikander[1] and Rajagopalachari?[2] Each is a recognized leader in his own community, each is liked by the other community, each has for the other considerable respect, and each is Premier of his Province. Here are two moderate and sensible men who, if encouraged and brought together and shown that in trying to reach an agreement they will have our backing, are quite capable of effecting a compromise. You must remember that the Muslims in the Muslim majority Provinces, though perturbed by Congress tactics, have not yet themselves been affected by them and therefore have no strong emotional urge to go to extremes. They would prefer a settlement to a break or to some drastic and startling remedy. But much is going to depend on us. We have got to be alert and constructive, perceiving the dangers in advance and selecting the right means and the right men to avert them. Above all the right men. You can't hope to be successful if you try to work through noisy and extreme communal leaders. You must make use of moderate men and bring them together in good time so that they can quietly work out a settlement and convince the extremists of its merits, before the latter have committed themselves to wild and impossible demands. But shall we do this? I have no confidence that we shall; in which case the outlook will be black indeed. For as you know, the worse a communal quarrel grows, the more is authority distrusted and blamed by either party. Unless therefore a settlement is reached soon, we shall become increasingly incapable of exercising a useful, mediating influence, and increasingly hated by both Congress and the Muslim League.'

[1] Sir Sikander Hyat-Khan, Premier of the Punjab from 1937 till his death in December 1942.

[2] Congress Premier of Madras from 1937–9.

Lightfoot paused. The lecture was apparently at an end. Greenlane also remained silent for a few moments. Then he said, 'You know, Lightfoot, I find you most depressing. You analyse things so clearly that you show up their hopelessness. In India every turning seems to be a blind alley. You can't get a move on in any direction. And we, who are partly responsible for the mess, simply aren't wanted and in any case aren't contributing anything.'

'You're putting your own gloss on what I said. I never said that the problem was hopeless; and we certainly could contribute much, if we could be more clear and more sincere about our aims. The trouble is that we're in two minds. We've promised India self-government, but we don't really want to relax our hold, and we don't really have much faith in the form of self-government that we are trying to give her. Still this doesn't mean that the communal problem cannot and will not be solved.'

'Well, somehow it doesn't look to me as though we're going to solve it.'

'You're unduly pessimistic. Natlum, a communal riot and the hot weather seem to have got you down. I must admit, however, that I often wish a monstrous crow would come along.'

'What on earth do you mean?'

'Well, wasn't it a monstrous crow that made Tweedledum and Tweedledee forget their quarrel? That's surely what we want out here.'

'Perhaps. But can you produce or invent one?'

'Possibly a war might serve the purpose. I can think of nothing else.'

But the war didn't serve the purpose. The hope that Hindus and Muslims would unite in the defence of India was not realized. Nor was any use made of the possible Sikander-Rajagopalachari bridge; and by the end of 1942 Sir Sikander was dead and Mr. Rajagopalachari had gone into the political wilderness. It was therefore Mr. Lightfoot's fears rather than his hopes which came true. The gulf between Hindus and Muslims steadily widened, till the Muslim League put forward a demand for the partition of India, the Hindus passionately resisted it as 'vivisection', while the contribution made by Congress was to go to gaol.

The Muslim League's demand for partition has now become the main issue between the two communities; so, though Mr. Lightfoot's discussion of the communal problem was sound so far as it went, it requires to be supplemented. Partition, say the spokesmen of the League, is the only way of saving the Muslims from Hindu domination. It is the only way, therefore, of ending the quarrel between the two communities. Since 1940, it has been the League's official policy.

But partition involves dividing India not merely into two, but into at least three. For Muslims are in a majority in both the north-west and the north-east of India, and the League demands that both these areas should be constituted into separate, independent, sovereign States, connected with Hindu India (Hindustan) only, if at all, by treaty. The north-west area or Pakistan[1] would be a federation of the Punjab, Sind, the North-West Frontier Province and Baluchistan. The north-east area would comprise Assam and most of Bengal.

This proposed solution of the communal problem may at first sight appear attractive. But it is beset with difficulties both territorial and economic. The League, perhaps wisely, has been reticent about details. The boundaries of the proposed Muslim States have not been defined. Their economic prospects have not been examined. Their relations with each other have not been explained. The practicability of the whole scheme has been assumed but not demonstrated.

As regards Pakistan or the north-west Muslim area, the presence in the central Punjab of the vigorous Sikh[2] community is a serious complication. The Sikhs cannot forget their past history. Beginning as a mere reformist sect of Hindus, they were turned into a distinct, self-conscious, militant community by the persecuting zeal of Aurangzeb. After long years of resistance to Muslim oppression and of guerrilla warfare against Muslim Governors, they ultimately emerged under Ranjit

---

[1] The name is derived from the first letters of the units which might comprise it, viz. Punjab, Afghanistan (i.e. North-West Frontier Province) Kashmir.

[2] There are rather more than five million Sikhs in the Punjab, including 1·4 million in the Punjab States.

Singh as masters of the Punjab; and they were its rulers immediately before British annexation. This being their past history, Muslim domination is as repugnant to them as Hindu domination is to the Muslims. Their reaction to a Pakistan run by Muslims is the exact counterpart of the Muslim reaction to a United India run by Hindus. It is by no means certain that any concessions would reconcile them to becoming a minority in an independent Muslim Pakistan; and as they are a compact, well-organized, vigorous community, any attempt to incorporate them in a Muslim State against their will would be forcibly resisted. Yet to exclude them from Pakistan and include them in Hindustan means finding a frontier somewhere in the middle of the Punjab; and this seems impossible. Geographically, economically, racially, and linguistically the central Punjab is one. There is no natural dividing line. Any boundary bisecting it in the middle would be wholly artificial. It might conceivably serve as a mere administrative boundary between two units of a single federation, but not as the frontier between two independent National States.

Muslim League spokesmen argue that the small Sikh community would be better off in Pakistan, where they could expect to have considerable weight and influence, than in a United India where their voice would not be heard. This argument is not without force and it is possible that, if certain special concessions were granted to them, the Sikhs might be persuaded that a more glorious future awaited them as members of a Pakistan 'supported by the combined might of Muslims and Sikhs' than as an insignificant fraction of a United India or a Hindu Hindustan. The concessions which they might require would be (a) the grant of rights and privileges out of proportion to their numbers in the management of the affairs of Pakistan; (b) the creation of a separate, mainly non-Muslim Province of eastern Punjab which they could hope to dominate,

But at present there is no indication that the Sikhs are tempted by or have even envisaged the prospect of inclusion in Pakistan on such terms. And until the Sikhs have agreed to inclusion, the practicability of the whole scheme must be regarded as doubtful.

There are also economic objections to Pakistan. Three of the units to be included in it, viz. the North-West Frontier Province, Sind and Baluchistan are deficit areas and receive financial assistance from the Central Government. In other words they obtain support from the whole of the rest of India. But in the event of partition the burden of supporting them would fall on Pakistan alone. The immediate effect, therefore, of creating this separate National State in north-west India would be to make all its inhabitants worse off than they are at present.

There is also another way in which they would suffer. At present a considerable number of the inhabitants of the Punjab and North-West Frontier Province make their living by military service. The rest of India pays these martial people to defend its frontiers. But if India were partitioned, Hindustan would wish to have a Hindu army of its own, and would no longer employ Punjabis and Pathans as its soldiers. The martial classes of Pakistan would have to be supported by Pakistan's own unaided resources.

The obvious economic disadvantages of Pakistan are one reason why Muslim politicians from the Pakistan area have so far shown little enthusiasm for the scheme. The demand for it has arisen from Muslims in the Muslim-minority Provinces (i.e. Provinces which would form part of Hindustan) and not from the inhabitants of Pakistan itself. Sir Sikander Hyat-Khan, the foremost Muslim leader of North-West India, was definitely opposed to it and, though as a member of the Muslim League he subscribed to the official Pakistan policy, he was always anxious to make out that the real meaning of the League's Pakistan resolutions was different from the plain meaning which the words apparently conveyed.

The other proposed Muslim National State in north-east India is open to objections hardly less formidable. Its natural capital would be Calcutta. But Calcutta is a predominantly Hindu city and to have a Hindu city as the capital of a Muslim National State is not likely to lead to harmony. On the other hand if it were excluded, the north-east Muslim State would be economically so weak that it might cease to have any attraction for the Muslims.

It is contemplated that western Bengal, which is predominantly Hindu, should be excluded from the north-east Muslim area. But western Bengal is intimately bound up both culturally and economically with the rest of Bengal and with Calcutta.

An attempt to partition the Province at the beginning of this century provoked such a violent Hindu agitation that it had to be abandoned. It cannot be assumed that the inhabitants of western Bengal would now meekly accept either severance from the rest of the Province on the one hand or inclusion in a Muslim National State on the other.

These difficulties are alone sufficient to show that partition creates as many problems as it solves. Indeed, it leaves the minority question unsolved. Even after partition there would still be a large Muslim minority in Hindu India and large Hindu minorities in the two Muslim States. Muslim advocates of partition welcome these minorities as 'hostages'. Others may regard them as a potential source of friction between Hindu and Muslim India, leading inevitably to war. A number of Hindus believe that war is deliberately intended and affect to see beneath the proposal for two Muslim States a sinister plan for the revival of the Mogul empire. They point out that the nature of the relations between the two proposed Muslim States has been left unspecified. Their nearest boundaries will be almost 1,000 miles apart. They will be separated by the whole length of the United Provinces and Bihar. Are they then to be entirely independent sovereign States? Or are they expected somehow to coalesce? Hindus suggest that the latter is intended and that this is to be achieved by the absorption of the intervening and predominantly Hindu areas of the United Provinces and Bihar. The fact that the keenest enthusiasm for partition is to be found amongst the Muslim minorities of these two Provinces seems to them to confirm their suspicions. For these minorities would not gain from the partition scheme except perhaps indirectly on the 'hostage' principle. Their real hope must therefore be that the creation of Muslim States in the north-west and north-east of India will quickly lead to Muslim rule over the whole of India's northern plains from the borders of Afghanistan to the frontiers of Burma. Such, at any rate, are the fears of some Hindus.

On altogether more general grounds partition is to be deprecated. Geographically India is a unity; and, though seldom united politically, political unity was for centuries a vague ideal, supported by a sense of underlying cultural and spiritual unity. That ideal has been realized; its realization has been the out-

115

THE COMMUNAL QUESTION

standing achievement of British rule. To throw over that achievement now by a deliberate act of partition would be a lamentable retrogression wholly at variance with the real needs of the modern world and fraught with grave dangers. For to partition India may well be the prelude to breaking India in pieces. In a country so full of divisions and diversities loss of political unity may swiftly lead to hopeless fragmentation.

Partition has to-day become a live issue. Yet five years ago it was not taken seriously, and even to-day, though it is the official policy of the Muslim League, there is no general acceptance of it amongst educated Muslims of the Muslim-majority Provinces. As for the Muslim masses, who till their fields or quarrel about tazias, they still know nothing about it. And some people believe that even the League only puts forward the demand for partition as a bargaining counter.

The ultimate fate of the proposal depends largely on the attitude of Muslims in Bengal and the Punjab. Without the support of these Muslim-majority Provinces, partition is out of the question. Sir Sikander Hyat-Khan, the first Premier of the Punjab, was firmly opposed to it. Mr. Fazl Haq, the first Premier of Bengal, was not committed to it. But Sir Sikander is dead and Mr. Fazl Haq has been displaced. Their successors may not have the courage to resist League extremists and to work for the acceptance of something less than partition.

The best hope of avoiding it would seem to lie in concentrating attention less on the forms of a possible Federal Government of India and more on the problems with which that Government would have to deal. Its two main concerns would be defence and economic policy, and these are the very matters in regard to which Muslims fear Hindu domination. But India's defence and her economic development are not merely Indian questions. They are world questions and have to be viewed in their proper international setting. India alone cannot provide for her own defence. This must necessarily form part of a larger scheme for the defence of the Bay of Bengal, Burma and Malay on the one hand and the Indian Ocean and Persian Gulf on the other. Similarly, a five- or ten-year plan for the industrial and agricultural development of India ought to dovetail with the plans of other countries with which India has important economic relations. This means that the general

116

lines of policy to be followed in regard to both defence and economic development would have to be determined in agreement with other countries. It is possible that, in the attempt to reach some such general agreement with other countries, the supposed disagreements of Muslims and Hindus and their mutual suspicions and fears would be seen to be more imaginary than real; for in these matters the real clash of interests is not so much between Hindus and Muslims as between different Provinces or regions of India. Regional conflicts of interest arouse less passion and are therefore more capable of reconciliation than pure Hindu-Muslim conflicts; and if general agreement were in fact reached on broad plans and policies for the defence and economic development of India, suitable constitutional machinery could certainly be devised to enable Hindus and Muslims to unite in carrying them out.

Thus the task of reconstructing peace might furnish just that diversion from the communal quarrel which Mr. Lightfoot vainly hoped would be provided by war.

But these are only speculations. In any case, it is unlikely that the last has yet been heard of partition. Some say that partition is impossible. Others that it is inevitable. But it is neither. It is only undesirable. And though undesirable, it may prove the least undesirable of the alternatives found to be practicable.

VII

THE PEASANT AND DEMOCRACY

'Englishmen are as great fanatics in politics as Muslims in religion.'—SIR THOMAS MUNRO.

'Come and have a drink, Allah Dad,' said Greenlane dismounting from his horse. 'I suppose you're a good Muslim and so it's no good offering you beer; but we ought to celebrate our success somehow. Besides you must be thirsty after sweating about all the morning like this.'

'Though I am a Muslim, sir, I am not so strict in all these matters. I should be very glad to have a glass of beer.'

'Come on, then. We'll sit down outside my tent. I can't say how grateful I am to you for the help you've given me. I could never have settled this wretched boundary dispute without you. It was something of a triumph to have shown those State officials that they were in the wrong and got them to admit it. Your knowledge of measurement work is amazing. You had them beaten all the time.'

Allah Dad smirked and followed Greenlane towards his tent. He was a neatly-built young Muslim officer of medium height, his figure set off by the elegant cut of his breeches and riding coat. On his head, at a slightly jaunty angle, he wore a dark red fez, and he carried in his hand a smart cane. His face was round and full; his expression lively, intelligent and, despite a hint of cunning, attractive. He had an air of subdued self-confidence and respectful, though quite definite, independence.

Greenlane liked him not only for his own qualities but because he was a protégé of Mr. Lightfoot. He had received no University education and had started his official career in the lowly rank of naib-tahsildar.[1] But Mr. Lightfoot had detected his abilities and had steadily pushed him, so that in a few years, in defiance of all rules of promotion, he had risen to be a magistrate of the highest grade. He was now serving under

[1] The lowest grade of revenue officer.

Greenlane in the small district of Dandot, and in view of his special knowledge of measurement work, acquired when he was a naib-tahsildar, Greenlane had called upon him to assist him in the settlement of a boundary dispute with the Native State of Khasrapur. They had spent three days encamped at a village near the river which divided British territory from the State territory. Disputes had arisen about the exact boundary owing to this river changing its course; and, though the area involved was only about fifty acres of inferior grazing land, there had been several sanguinary clashes between villagers from the British-Indian side of the border and villagers from the State. Each party tried to assert their right to the disputed area by grazing their cattle on it; and each, when they found an opportunity, forcibly rounded up and drove to the pound the cattle belonging to the others. The latest episode had involved the death of one of the villagers from the State. He was said to have been killed while trying to protect his cattle, and several men from the village where Greenlane was encamped had been arrested for his murder. According to their version of the affair he had accidentally been drowned when fording the river.

In order to allay this quarrel Greenlane and Allah Dad had spent hours with State officials taking measurements from fixed points on either side of the river; and at last, thanks to Allah Dad's efficiency and his ability to confute all objections, the State officials had been compelled to admit that they had no claim to the disputed area, and that the correct boundary line was exactly where the British-Indian villagers and officials had always said it was.

Greenlane was quite childishly delighted with the outcome of his labours. 'Those patwaris[1] of yours did magnificently,' he said to Allah Dad as they sipped their beer. 'That last fixed point from which they took measurements must have been at least four miles away over some pretty rough country, and yet they managed to bring a line from it dead straight right to the river. The State officials, by demanding yesterday a check from such a distant point, thought they had foxed us and we should have to give up, leaving the whole matter undecided to form the subject of dispute and correspondence for another twenty-five

[1] Patwari = village accountant, in charge of the land records and revenue records.

119

years. But when this morning they saw us solemnly begin measurements from that distant point, they were so astonished that they just crumpled up and threw in their hand.'

'They were wonderstruck to see it, sir. As we started, I could catch them murmuring to each other that they were beaten. That old Muslim officer of theirs with dyed beard, who was so obstinate on previous days, was frankly saying that their tricks had failed. But I had collected some very good patwaris for this work. I didn't just rely on the local ones.'

'You've managed the whole thing splendidly, Allah Dad. I'm most grateful to you. And I'm very pleased with the patwaris. I think we ought to give them some reward for their good work.'

'I was just wondering whether I might suggest this. I would request you, sir, to grant them all certificates.'

"I will certainly do so; but I think they ought to have cash rewards as well.'

'They are poor men, sir. It will be a kind of encouragement to them if you will sanction this. I wanted to propose it, but didn't know how you would like the idea. I've only told them that I would try to get certificates for them. They were more than satisfied with this. If I now tell them that you are considering cash rewards, they will be too much pleased.'

'You mean to say "very much pleased". Well, you just put up proposals Allah Dad. I'll find the money somehow.'

'I am glad, sir, that you appreciate the work of these low-paid officials.'

'I always think patwaris are marvellous people. With little education and pay of only Rs.25[1] a month, often, as it seems to me, half-blind and with one foot in the grave, they contrive to maintain the whole of our vast system of land records and agricultural statistics. Fancy twice a year, at each harvest, in the space of four or five weeks having to write up all the relevant entries—owners, tenants, subtenants, mortgagees, rent payable, class of land and crops grown—for some 5,000 fields of all shapes and sizes and with no proper boundaries; and then having to work out the total area under each crop; and sometimes too, where the land revenue is fluctuating, the amount of land revenue which each man has to pay. Whenever

[1] About £2.

120

THE PEASANT AND DEMOCRACY

I see an old, bespectacled patwari, grasping in one arm an enormous bundle of records, pulling a pen from his turban, a pencil from behind his ear, a bottle of ink from his pocket and a map of the village from somewhere inside his shirt, I am amazed to think what an immense amount we get out of this queer unkempt figure and for how little.'

'Some of the patwaris are very clever men, sir, and they are a very ancient institution. You can trace them, so I have read, far back beyond Mogul times to the days of the ancient Hindu kings. People often abuse them because they are corrupt. It is also alleged that they stir up mischief by making wrong entries in the records and so causing the zemindars useless litigation. I would not deny that there are bad patwaris who do such things. But I do not agree with those who sweepingly condemn the patwaris. No doubt nearly all of them take tips from the villagers. But as the villagers are illiterate, the patwari is useful to them in many ways. They could not get on without him, so they do not grudge these tips, which are also sanctioned by immemorial custom. For long before the patwari was paid by Government he was the servant of the village. And you must have noticed, sir, that generally the people like their patwari. He is part and parcel of their village. They do not want to get rid of him and have another man. If he makes some petty exactions, they don't mind.'

'The patwari is part of a really remarkable organization. I've heard people say that our system of land revenue and land records is the greatest achievement of the English in India.'

'It is a great achievement, but, if you will pardon me, sir, I would say that it is only partly yours. That is why it has been so successful. You have taken over and developed what existed before—a system native to the country and therefore understood by the people. Of course, without the peace which you established this system could not have been so much perfected as it is. Most people nowadays consider peace just an ordinary thing, and do not feel grateful for it. But I have read something of the old times and have come to understand the blessings of peace. I can truthfully say that I appreciate them. But I am puzzled to know why you English, having given us peace, felt such keen interest in forcing on us your own notions of government and law. It strikes me that you must have despised us

Indians too much, and so could never admit that there might be any merit in our ideas and ways of doing things. It must therefore just have been our good fortune that in England you had no regular land revenue and so in this matter were content to make the best of what you found already existing. The result, I would say, is that of all the branches of the administration the assessment and collection of land revenue and the maintenance by the patwaris of the land records works the most smoothly and produces least evils.'

'It works well enough now. But our early assessments were much too heavy. They nearly all broke down as the people couldn't bear them.'

'That is true, sir. The people sometimes ran away and abandoned their land when they heard the English were coming. In this district, in village Bhagtanwala, the people so much dreaded heavy assessments that when the English officers came they all fled away, except one clever fellow who remained behind and claimed the whole village as his own. And it has continued in the sole ownership of his family to this day. No doubt, sir, your early assessments were far too heavy. Having heard that the Moguls used to take one third of the gross produce of the land, you thought you could do likewise. You did not understand how much corruption greased the wheels of the Mogul machinery, and that what was one third in theory might be more like one fifth in practice. But those early errors were corrected.'

'I certainly think, Allah Dad, that in this part of the country our land revenue system has been pretty good; but we made a hopeless muddle of things in Bengal and some other parts of India which we first occupied.'

'I dare say, sir, that was mainly due to your belief in your own ideas and unwillingness to understand the real nature of what existed here. You had in England a landlord system which you thought very good. So you considered it ought to exist in India too. In Bengal you found a class of tax-farmers, survivals of the decaying Mogul empire. Though they were not really landlords at all, but simply collectors of the government land revenue, you decided to make them landlords, ignoring the rights of the actual cultivators of the soil and not bothering to consider whether these landlords of yours could be really useful to the persons whom you made their tenants. I might say that this is one reason why Bengal has always been giving so much trouble. But by the grace of God you did not push these ideas everywhere.'

'I would awfully like to hear you develop this theme, Allah Dad, but I see the thanedar hanging about as though he had some business with me. I had better call him up and see what he wants.'

The local sub-inspector of police had for some minutes been hovering around some little distance from Greenlane's tent. Greenlane now beckoned to him to come up. He advanced and saluted. 'I have here, sir, an accused person who is confessing,' he said. 'I thought that as you were encamped only three miles from the police station, you would be wiliing to dispose of the case on the spot at once. It will only be necessary to examine one witness and to record the accused's plea of guilty.'

'All right, sub-inspector, I'll take it up at once. What is it? Cattle theft?'

'No, sir. It is a case of arson. The accused is a woman.'

'A woman? That sounds a bit odd. Well bring her along.'

In a few minutes the accused, a stumpy, dark-coloured woman of about twenty-five, with a fat, pock-marked face and no obvious physical charms, was brought before Greenlane in the custody of two police constables. A number of villagers, led by the lumbadar, also approached the tent and squatted down on the ground not far off to listen to the proceedings. The principal witness appeared to be just a small bundle of skin and bones, enveloped in an enormous, ill-fitting old great-coat. He turned out, however, to be the woman's husband—a Hindu shopkeeper of well over sixty. As soon as he came before Greenlane he bobbed down in low obeisance. Then, removing a filthy bedraggled turban that he was wearing, he pointed to his head, turning it round so that Greenlane could see it from every angle, touching it gingerly with his fingers, grunting feebly and pretending to cry.

'What on earth's the matter with the fellow?' inquired Greenlane.

'There is nothing much wrong with him,' the sub-inspector replied. 'His hair and moustache got a bit singed in the fire, but he is not badly burnt. He's just making a fuss for nothing.

123

Now then, Mangtu,' he continued, addressing the old Hindu, 'stop all this blubbering and tell your story.'

The old man pulled himself together, and Greenlane had soon recorded his evidence and also taken the statement of his wife, who, after pouring forth a torrent of obscene abuse against her husband, confessed her guilt and asked for mercy.

The case was really one of attempted murder. The old man's first wife had died without leaving him any children, and he had therefore purchased as a second wife for Rs.250 the woman who was now accused. She had been brought for sale from down-country and nothing was known of her origin. But she proved a slut and didn't keep the house clean; nor did she show any signs of bearing children. The old man was always nagging at her and saying she was not worth the money he had paid for her. At last she could bear it no longer. In the middle of one night, as he slept in the courtyard of his house, she quietly tied him down to the bed with cords. Then she sprinkled a little kerosene oil over the sheet which covered him and set light to it. But before it was well ablaze he woke up; and though he couldn't extricate himself from the bed, he made such a hullaballoo that the neighbours came rushing in and rescued him before the flames had done much more than singe his hair and burn up the sheet.

'Well, she's confessed her guilt; but what punishment are we to give her?' asked Greenlane, leaning back in his chair and addressing the world in general.

Allah Dad glanced at him with a leer, but ventured no opinion. The sub-inspector, however, jumped up with a bustle and bluster and said, 'She's been guilty of a most daring crime. I would request you, sir, to inflict a heavy penalty. At least one year's rigorous imprisonment is called for.'

'Why not find out what the lumbadar thinks?' suggested Allah Dad. 'I believe the accused and her husband belong to this very village.'

'A good idea,' said Greenlane. 'Lumbadar, you know all about this case. What punishment do you think the woman deserves?'

The lumbadar rose with dignity and came forward in front of Greenlane. 'Most exalted Excellency,' he said, 'when you, a giver of justice, are present, your humble servant can have no opinion. All the same, I must say this, that the woman ought to be adequately punished. Though this old man may have been a bit harsh towards her, she should have been obedient and given him no occasion to find fault. She has burnt his hair and moustaches in a most merciless manner, and he, poor fellow, has wasted his Rs.250 to no purpose. If your Honour thinks proper, she should certainly go to gaol.'

"All right, lumbadar, she shall go to gaol. But the question is for how long? What do you think, Allah Dad?'

Allah Dad, who had been smiling to himself, now looked solemn and said, 'Sir, you must be feeling for this poor woman. She must have been enticed up here on the pretext that a good husband would be found for her; but instead of this she was just sold away to this foolish old Hindu shopkeeper. I daresay he must have abused her and beaten her till she could no longer tolerate it. To my way of thinking she really deserves mercy. But the people do not have so much sympathy for women. They expect them to be obedient in all things and to bear abuses. We must have some regard for their views. So I would say you should send her to gaol for six months, though this will perhaps be not one tenth of what her husband is expecting you to give her.'

'Very well then,' said Greenlane. 'Let it be six months. That seems to me quite suitable. Six months' simple imprisonment.'

On hearing the sentence the husband immediately began to whimper and whine, and, removing his turban, repeated his previous pantomime, even pulling out from his head a few half-singed hairs and cringingly holding them in his hand for Greenlane to see. But the sub-inspector jumped up and hustled him away; and the two constables marched off the convicted woman. She had throughout taken no interest in the proceedings and appeared quite indifferent to her sentence.

The group of villagers squatting not far off now rose and, headed by the lumbadar, came up to Greenlane and salaamed. The lumbadar at once began a panegyric on Greenlane and Allah Dad for having got the better of the State officials over the boundary dispute. 'We were utterly ruined,' he concluded, with some exaggeration, 'but your Honour has saved us. If you will kindly permit, we would like to show our pleasure by letting off some crackers. If only your Excellency was stopping another night we would have arranged some fireworks; the people are disappointed that you cannot stay. But we hope that you will permit us to let off the crackers.'

'All right,' said Greenlane. 'I hope the State officials won't hear. They might be rather annoyed.'

The lumbadar waved his arm and gave a vague shout. There was a hissing sound some fifty yards off followed by a loud bang. Then another, and another, and another. The horses tethered near Greenlane's tent plunged and whinnied. The syces[1] ran up to hold them; a patwari's pony broke loose and galloped off. There were cries of 'Enough, enough' and a general commotion. At last the explosions ceased. The lumbadar, evidently pleased with his little display, turned to Greenlane and salaamed, 'It is all your Honour's kindness,' he said.

Greenlane felt that something was called for from his side. He pulled Rs.10 out of his pocket and said, 'Lumbadar, I am very glad it has all ended so happily and successfully; and to celebrate the occasion here is Rs.10 to buy sweets for the schoolchildren. I am sorry I have not been able actually to visit the school. The boundary dispute has taken all my time.'

'It is most kind of your Honour to think of the children. They will be very pleased. Indeed, the whole village is pleased at your having come here. You are most just and also most merciful. What mercy you have just now shown to that woman, although she had committed a heinous offence! And we, your humble subjects, also ask for justice and mercy. We have only one request to make. We hope you will grant it. Kindly write to the State authorities to release our men who have been arrested and charged with murder. They are absolutely innocent. The man was drowned while crossing the river. Those people from the State, out of enmity, because we had put their cattle in the pound, have entangled our men in a false case. I take an oath that they are quite innocent. Your Honour can make inquiries. I swear that I am speaking the truth. Your Honour can inquire from the thanedar.'

'I'm afraid it is very difficult for me to do anything about a case pending in a Court in the State.'

'Your Excellency, you can do everything. Your pen is very

[1] Grooms.

126

powerful. You only have to write a letter to the officers of the State and they will immediately release our men. We beg you just to write to them.'

'Do you think they are innocent, thanedar?' Greenlane inquired.

'They are undoubtedly innocent, sir. I have made full inquiries. The sub-inspector from the State was also quite convinced that they are innocent, but he did not have the courage to say so to his superior officer, as all the people in the State are keen to trouble our zemindars because of the boundary dispute.'

'Well, lumbadar, I'll see what can be done, but I'm not very hopeful. And now, Allah Dad, if we're going to catch that train back to Dandot we had better be moving.'

The lumbadar quickly interposed. 'Your Excellency, before you leave, there are two men who want to petition you about their own troubles.' He pulled forward from the cluster of villagers a tall man of about forty. 'This man has suffered very much. I would request you to help him. As you know, sir, we all live in harmony among ourselves in this village, and, in obedience to your orders, we all unanimously agreed to consolidate our holdings, which had become very much scattered. Your officers kindly worked out all the necessary exchanges and after many months each of us received his due share of land in one, two or at most three plots. But it was so fated that this poor fellow lost all his land, and he and his wife and small children are now in a pitiable condition.'

'I don't understand,' said Greenlane. 'How could he have lost his land as a result of consolidation? Each man gets as much land as he owned before. At most there may be a difference of a few square yards.'

The tall man broke in with a torrent of words. 'Sir, I am ruined. My wife and tiny children are starving. I have had to sell all my bullocks and my wife's ornaments. There is now nothing left. My land has all disappeared. It is not a question of a few square yards. I had six acres and now I have none. I and my family are dying.'

'But how can your land have just disappeared? I can't understand it.'

'Sir, it was by magic.'

THE PEASANT AND DEMOCRACY

'By magic? What *do* you mean?'

'Sir, it must have been by magic. I had six acres of land and it has all gone. Not one inch is left. I can only say it is magic.'

Greenlane was quite mystified, but the lumbadar intervened, and said, 'Sir, he is an illiterate man. No doubt it seemed to him like magic. But I will explain the matter to you. Formerly he had ten or twelve small pieces of land scattered in different places all over the village. As a result of consolidation, instead of these scattered fragments he was given a single plot on the south side of the village towards the river. But it so happened that last year there was a heavy flood and the river shifted its course towards our village and made a channel where it had never been before. Several of us suffered some small losses, but he, poor fellow, lost everything. The whole of his land is now part of the riverbed; whereas if there had been no consolidation he would have only lost two small pieces—about one acre in all. It was God's will that it should happen so. But it was a great calamity for him. The whole village feels sorry for him and would like to help him. Most of us are willing to surrender some small portion of our own land, so that he might get two to three acres on which to support himself and his family. But we cannot agree among ourselves about it, nor can we work out how the redistribution of the fields is to be arranged. We would request you therefore kindly to help. If you will just order the tahsildar or an officer of the Co-operative Department to come here, he will certainly be able to make us agree among ourselves so that some remedy is found for this man's miserable plight.'

'That's easy,' said Greenlane. 'I'll send an officer as soon as possible and tell him to see that something is arranged.'

'You have saved me,' cried the tall man. 'I shall never forget your justice. You are very kind and have sympathy with us poor people in our misfortunes. I shall be ever praying for you. My children also will pray for you.'

'Well, so much for one petitioner. Where is the other and what does he want?' Greenlane inquired.

Another villager, a man of about sixty, stepped forward and said, 'Kindly order the thanedar to catch the man who cheated me. I have seen him sitting at the shop of the soda-water seller, quite close to the police station. I have seen him there for the

128

past two weeks. The police can easily arrest him and give me redress.'

'Do you know anything about it, thanedar?' asked Greenlane.

'No, sir, I've never seen this man before. He has made no report at the police station. I don't know what he is talking about. But we'll soon find out. Tell me, old man, who is it that cheated you?'

'I don't know his name, but I can recognize him. He cheated me in a very cunning manner and put me to a loss of over Rs.200. He came to the village one day and told me that he knew some magic whereby he could turn many things into gold. He asked me to put a small lump of silver in a wooden box and give it to him. I did so, and he took it and buried it in the ground close by the graveyard. Then he uttered some strange words, and told me to wait three days and then to dig up the box and look inside. After three days I went and dug it up and found inside a lump of gold not much smaller than the lump of silver. A few days later that man came to the village again. I told him that the magic had worked and I showed him the lump of gold. He said that if I would give him a hundred rupees he would turn them into gold also. I had fifty rupees in my house and I borrowed another fifty. As instructed by him I put them all in a wooden casket and handed it over to him. He promised to bring it back the next day. He came the next day in the evening with the casket. I could see some smoke coming out from beneath the lid. I opened the casket and looked inside. The hundred rupees were still there, but there was no gold. A great deal of smoke was coming out of the casket, yet it wasn't burnt at all. I was very much disappointed and asked that man why there was no gold and what was the meaning of all the smoke. He said that the smoke was part of the magic, but that he had made a little mistake and so the rupees had not yet turned into gold. He assured me, however, that it would be quite all right and that he would just do the magic again. He also said that if I hadn't any more rupees, I should put some silver ornaments in the casket, along with the hundred rupees already there, so that there might be more gold and he could also take a little share of it. So I put some silver ornaments in the casket worth about one hundred and twenty rupees. He then took the casket away and told me that at sunrise on the

129

fourth day I would find it with gold inside it under a certain tree near the graveyard. I went on the fourth day to the grave-yard as he had directed me. I felt a little anxious lest the casket might not be there. But I became very happy when I spied it quite all right under the tree. I ran forward, eager to get the gold. The casket had been sealed up and it took me a little time to open it. But when I had managed to lift up the lid, I found inside no gold at all, but only a few ashes.'

Allah Dad and the sub-inspector laughed, 'Why didn't you make a report at the police station?' they inquired.

'I searched about for that man for many days in the neigh-bouring villages, but I could find no trace of him nor could anyone tell me his name. So I said to myself, "What is the good of going to the police?" But now I have seen him at the soda-water seller's shop and so the police can easily arrest him and get him to give back my rupees and ornaments.'

'I don't expect you'll find he's got them now,' said Greenlane. 'How many weeks is it since this all occurred?'

'Sir, I cannot say how many weeks it is, but it must be about twenty years.'

'Twenty years!'

'It may be a little more or a little less. But it must be about twenty years.'

'Good Lord, how on earth do you expect to get your money and ornaments back now?'

'Sir, it all rests with you. You have been sent to rule over us. You can do everything. You've only got to give the necessary orders to the thanedar.'

'I'm afraid even the thanedar won't be able to recover the things for you now.'

'That cheat is sure to give me some compensation if the thanedar catches hold of him. And if he doesn't, your Honour can send him to gaol. He should certainly be punished for cheating a poor illiterate man like me.'

The lumbadar backed him up.

'It will be very kind of you, your Excellency, if you will do something for this man. That scoundrel who cheated him should certainly be punished. If you will send him to gaol, it will be a lesson to all, and this man, even if he doesn't get back his money, will feel some satisfaction.'

'Very well, lumbadar. We'll see what we can do, but I'm afraid it will be a pretty hopeless case after twenty years. Thanedar, you had better arrest the man and make inquiries. You can put the case into my Court and I'll see what I can make of it.'

'Your Excellency is very kind,' said the petitioner. 'Your justice is renowned. I know that you will give me redress and send that cheat to gaol. I am ever obedient to your Excellency.'

Greenlane rose. 'Come on, Allah Dad,' he said, 'we must get along. Call up the horses.'

They set off together towards the station and for some way rode in silence. At last Greenlane said, 'I was sorry for that woman I sent to gaol. These wretched creatures are treated just like cattle. At best they are the meanest drudges. Even amongst the educated classes women are treated pretty queerly. I often find it odd, when I dine with some educated Muslim, to think that stowed away somewhere in the house, he has a wife and possibly even two or three of them.'

'It may seem strange to you, sir, and I myself am not so much in favour of the pardah system. Nevertheless, when I see the loose morals of European women in this country, I cannot feel certain that pardah system may not be best for people in India. I might agree to some relaxations, but I am totally opposed to women, and especially young women, mixing freely in society. I would request you, sir, not to consider that our ways and customs, though they may seem backward as compared with yours, should be altogether despised; for, to my way of thinking, they are often adapted to our peculiar conditions and the stage of development we have reached.'

'You're back on your old theme, Allah Dad, that we've been too keen on our own ideas, which we believed to be so very much superior. You would say that we've not had sufficient imagination to understand Indian ways of thought.'

'Sir, from what I have read I have come to know that when you first were conquering India, many of you Englishmen had real sympathy with our beliefs and habits. I may cite Warren Hastings, who so much resisted attempts to impose laws and institutions borrowed from England. You may know that he took keen interest in our philosophies and was appreciating them. He was not very contemptuous even of the Hindu religion. I remember to have read that he wrote about their super-

131

stitious ways that the "Being who has so long endured them will in his own time reform them". But later, because it was seen that Hindus worshipped idols and did so many foolish things and were still carrying on barbarous practices such as widow-burning and infanticide, English officers came to think that we were utterly depraved and there could be nothing good in us. No doubt the mass of the people were backward and through various causes our society had become much corrupted. Yet there were a few wise and learned men among us, through whose help, if you had been more sympathetic towards their views, you might have accomplished more solid good for the people. Perhaps too I might make so bold to say that even infanticide, though Englishmen might be shocked to find it, had much use in checking the population, and it might have been better to tolerate it till some other check had been found.'

'I believe it is still not absolutely suppressed. But you may be right that we ought to have winked at it more. After all, the ancient Greeks, who in many ways were pretty civilized, prac-tised it. By the way, that's a good remark you quoted of Warren Hastings.'

'Yes, sir. I think he might have understood that superstitions must prevail for a long time among the common people; for the real Hindu philosophy is far above their comprehension. Though I myself cannot claim to have made a deep study of it, yet it seems to me to be very noble. You must be knowing the famous saying from the Gita, "In works be thine office; in their fruits let it never be." Perhaps that is the fittest maxim for any one in this country, for if he was expecting to see much of fruits he would quickly despair.'

'My God he would!'

'But he would not if he had managed to guide himself by the Hindu philosophy. The danger, however, is that by not caring for fruits he would too easily accept everything, good or bad, without any sort of struggle. And you must be noticing that this is too much the habit of the people of this country, especially, I would say, of the Hindus. We Muslims sometimes look down on them for this. And so do you English. But I believe most English officers do not think much even of our Muslim religion, what to say of Hinduism. Yet, having con-sidered the matter a good deal, I would say that our religion has this one great advantage over others, that its essential dogma is so simple and straightforward that even a highly educated man need have no difficulty in accepting it.'

'I am afraid I don't even know its essential dogma; which perhaps confirms your point that we don't take enough trouble to understand your ways of thought.'

'You must have often heard it, sir, but perhaps were not knowing that it comprised our essential belief. It is simply, "There is one God and Muhammad is his Prophet." We do not much seek to define God's nature; but most men would agree in thinking that in some sense there is God and that He is One. And Muhammad was clearly a Prophet, if we consider a Prophet to be a high personality who proclaims a great spiritual truth. So, in spite of so many advances of knowledge, I do not feel the necessity of giving up the essential dogma of my religion. But from what I have read, I find that educated Christians are nowadays puzzled to know how to reconcile their so much complicated doctrines with other things which we have come to understand. I also notice that these doctrines, when taught to illiterate people of this country, become no more than superstitions. I must, however, say this, that, though English officers may not have taken much trouble to appreciate our religious beliefs, yet in this matter they have not been so much bent to force their own beliefs on us. In fact, English officers have often discouraged the Christian missionaries and in early days would not even allow them in the country. I could wish that they had followed a similar policy in other matters also.'

'Well, I would certainly agree with you so far as English Law is concerned. I cannot get over the absurdity of our applying to this country our legal system.'

'And what about your political system? I sometimes think that you Englishmen must have gone mad to introduce into India, as it is to-day, so-called democratic government. I am simply wonderstruck to see in the papers how big men from England, like Lord Lothian,[1] come out to India and urge us with so much keenness to pay attention to elections and voting for Assemblies and awakening the masses to political issues. Are these people quite ignorant of the ordinary zemindar to

[1] Lord Lothian toured India as Chairman of the Franchise Committee.

whom they have now given a vote? I wonder what they may imagine illiterate villagers can at all understand of voting, what to say of political questions. You, sir, have now got some experience of the people of this country. You and other English officers must be knowing fully well that it is totally ridiculous, I might say mad, to expect these people to understand such things. What, for instance, may one think of those three men that came before you to-day? That old Hindu shopkeeper, and those two petitioners, who, though quite illiterate, were zemindars, must all have been voters at the last elections for the Provincial Assembly. You must have been noticing that they were quite simple. And they belong to a village that is better than most. For at any rate those villagers had shown that to some extent they could manage their own affairs and understand their real good; otherwise they could not have consolidated their holdings. Yet I dare to say that they could never have come to agree to it by themselves and without so much help and persuasions from the Government officers. And how can such illiterate, simple people ever learn to understand political matters by listening to speeches of so-called politicians, who speak so many white lies just to pleease them? Truthfully speaking, sir, these meetings and speeches and votings at elections are just a "tamasha" for the zemindars. They are a mere show. You must be knowing what went on at the 1937 elections. I was on duty at one of the polling stations and it was crystal clear to me that most of the zemindars were thinking it was just a "mela".[1] Many of them did not know at all for whom they were expected to vote, but they came along because other people were going; they felt it was a kind of an outing for them. They were very glad to have a free ride in a lorry and a free meal which the candidates provided. I saw several of them who, when they came into the booth to have their ballot paper marked for them, had forgotten the name of the candidate for whom they had been told to vote and had to be reminded. I remember there to have been one zemindar who was utterly bewildered when it was inquired from him for whom he was voting. He could not be made to understand what was expected of him. At length he was sent out again from

[1] A gathering of people for a fair or for rustic sports, usually associated with some festival or shrine.

134

the booth, and immediately he got outside the agents of the two candidates both seized upon him together and each was loudly shouting into his ear the name of their candidate. That old man was quite bemused, and felt no desire to enter the booth again, but only to get away from those two men who were pestering him. At last they gave it up and left him. But later one of the two, who was perhaps more clever, managed to catch hold of him again when he was alone, and without much trouble was able to persuade him to finish the matter by voting for his candidate. There was another zemindar too who simply did not know what for he was made to go into the booth. Instead of coming up to the table, where the officer was sitting to mark his ballot paper, he just salaamed the officer and went out of the other door.'

'Yes, I know all these absurdities. I was also on duty at the elections and had similar experiences.'

'We may also consider the matter, sir, from the point of view of the candidates. I made some inquiries and found that in the district where I was then stationed, which was not so rich, the candidates had to spend from their own pockets not less than 30,000 rupees. And in the colony districts, where the people are better off, and in some other places where the contest was too keen, they had to spend very much more. Now, having spent so much money and perhaps incurred some debts, how can they be expected to attend to their proper duties and be content to call themselves M.L.A.?[1] Must they not necessarily be hankering after jobs for their relations or posts for themselves, and interfering with judicial cases and executive matters so that they may have prestige among the people and taste the sweetness of some power?

'To satisfy these wants of theirs you must have noticed that Government are creating so many new posts and departments and keeping the appointments to these in their own hands. This is nothing short of a calamity for the people, who are already harassed by too many petty officials—sanitary inspectors, vaccinators, agricultural assistants and such like—swarming into their villages like locusts, eating up the zemindars and writing so many fictitious reports, without being able to do any solid work. I was told the other day that Government wanted

[1] Member of the Legislative Assembly.

to invent some new post of "Uplift Worker" and that district officers had been asked to advise to which tahsil in their district one of these workers should be posted. Sir, if I may make a suggestion, I would say you should tell Government that he must be posted to Kandwal tabsil, because the people there are the most mischievous and therefore most deserve this misfortune.'

'Not a bad idea. I quite agree that the multiplication of these petty officials is appalling and with this new form of democratic government we're going to have a spate of them. But I think perhaps it must be much the same in all countries.'

'It may be so, sir, but it must be worse in this country, as petty officials are in the habit of battening on the people who are much too poor to bear it. Moreover, in this country, we are in any case too much prone to hanker after jobs for all sorts of relations. No doubt there is something bad in us which makes us do it; but, of course, from olden times our family ties have been much stronger than amongst you, and we feel a sort of obligation to help even distant relatives when they press us. We cannot easily refuse them. We are perhaps, therefore, not so much to be blamed; though I would admit it is bad. But why should you tempt us, or rather compel us, to give way to our tendency by always introducing more and more elections, which because they put the candidates to so much trouble and expense make them all the more clamorous for some substantial reward?'

'Well, we embarked on this policy a good many years ago and don't feel we can go back on it.'

'Sir, whatever may have been your reasons, I must honestly say that what you have done makes me think that you must believe in magic, and are really not much different from that simple fellow who thought that by uttering a few charms silver might be turned into gold. How except by some magic could you expect that the people of this country in their present condition could within less than a lifetime so much change as to be able to understand and make to work your democratic institutions? Not only are the mass of the people quite illiterate, but from time immemorial they have considered that the officers of Government, the "Hakiman",[1] are quite distinct

[1] Rulers, lit: the givers of orders (Hukm).

from themselves, belong to quite a separate class and, I might almost say, are an altogether different type of being. They cannot possibly imagine that suddenly they have themselves become the rulers and that all the high officers of Government have in some sense come to depend on them. Yet this is what the Ministers are telling them. They go about making speeches to the ordinary zemindars, saying that *they* are now the masters and the Government officers only their servants; though in fact this is all nonsense. Sir, I can confidently predict that just as that poor fellow, believing in magic, got for his silver, instead of gold, only ashes, so too if we persist with these democratic charms of elections and votings we will only get an utter deterioration of the administration, mere ruins, I would call it, of what exists to-day.'

'I'm afraid you're only too likely to be right.'

'I need hardly say, sir, that the mistake arises from ever supposing that just by introducing here some new political forms you can in a twinkling of an eye change the whole character of the people. You seem to have fallen into our great Indian failing of preferring mere outward show to anything really substantial. If I understand at all rightly the true secret of your democracy, it is not elections, votings, and assemblies, but that you people have come to form some habits of tolerance, so that by discussing things together freely, without too much suspicion of each other, you can arrive at some sound compromise. But you, sir, know only too well what trouble we have to bring people here to a compromise. The mass of the people are so ignorant, and all of them, whether literate or illiterate, so full of divisions and party factions and so suspicious of each other, always attributing corrupt and selfish motives, that they cannot for one instant tolerate each other's opinions, but rather are p-one to run after the most mischievous persons who are quite extreme and violent in their views. We may, I think, best change the people and develop among them the habit of compromising things by making them attend to their own quite petty affairs in their villages and qasbas,[1] as we are doing already to a certain extent. But this must of necessity take much time. We are only just beginning to see the people in some places pulling on together harmoni-

[1] Small towns.

137

ously; and this is generally effected by the help and persuasions of Government officers or by some religious leader who has a genuine feeling for the good of the people and does not have to run after them for votes and such like things. But we cannot hope to make any progress if we are impatient and rush madly along our present course. We will only more corrupt the people by feeding them with lies and increasing their natural enmities and appealing only to selfish motives. And I fear that the Government officers will also be much corrupted so that they will not be able so usefully to guide the people. They will always be looking to the Ministers for good stations and fat posts and jobs for their relations, and trying to please them by flattering them with outward show and at their request doing wrong things and injustices and managing for them all sorts of petty shararats,[1] so that they will quite lose the confidence of the mass of the people and perhaps themselves care not at all for their good. The administration will of course immensely deteriorate, as it is already doing, and become like, or rather far worse than it is in the Native States. I can clearly see that all this so-called democracy, because it is quite unsuited to the people in their present condition, instead of giving freedom or any other good thing to them will be perverted into the worst tyranny of the worst men. You will please excuse me sir, if I have spoken my mind too freely in this matter, but I must feel deeply when I see such calamities coming upon my country.'

'There is no need to apologize, Allah Dad. I entirely agree with what you say. I am astonished at our having introduced all this democratic machinery, and I sometimes feel profoundly depressed at the whole business. But I think you should remember that it was not just the English who foisted all this upon India. Many Englishmen saw that it was all wrong; but they had to give way to the insistent demand for self-government made by Indian politicians.'

'Sir, self-government does not necessarily mean democratic government. In the States we can say that there is to a great extent self-government, considering that the work is all done by Indians; yet there is not democratic government. I do not know whether you English deliberately misunderstand what we really want, when we ask for self-government, or whether you

[1] Mischief(s).

138

are just misled by your enthusiasm for your own institutions and too eager to give them to us also, believing that they will be for our good. It is no doubt very kind of you to have such good intentions for us. We really must appreciate it. Perhaps no people but the English would have such noble ideas. But of course what we really want is simply to be free from your control. There may be some of us who feel so keenly the blessings of democracy that they want to have them at once. But most of us, and I am one of them, do not sincerely believe in these blessings; rather we think them a curse. I must frankly say that really we are aspiring to those posts of influence and power which you English have been for so long enjoying; and at the same time we would like to feel that we are not subject to any foreign domination. You will readily agree, sir, that these desires of ours are quite different from any desire for democracy.'

'Yes, but there has all along been a doubt whether there would be enough Indians fit to hold higher posts.'

'English people talk many foolish things about this matter, thereby showing their ignorance. I fully admit that we could not have been expected at once to come up to your standards; but why should you have for so long presumed that we were incapable of improvement? When you first came here, could you not find even one or two Indians who might be worthy of some high post? For instance, I know from what I have heard that my grandfather was a very honest and upright man, much respected by all the people. He had a mind as a young man to enter Government service; but when he considered that he could never hope to become even a Deputy Commissioner, he preferred to remain looking after his lands; for he had some feeling of what was proper for him, considering his position among the people. There must have been some more like him. Surely if you had attracted them to Government service by the hope of rising to some high posts, and if you had been kind enough to let them mix more freely with you and to work with you on terms of equality, they must have become cured of many of the defects you found in them. We may have been very bad, but why should you have imagined that we were one and all incurable? Most Englishmen, who were managing things in Bengal and in Madras when those territories were first conquered, were also very bad, and so corrupt and greedy for

139

money that you must hardly like to read about it. But later, by selecting your officers much more carefully and by giving them a sound education and paying them good salaries, in quite a short space of time you brought about such a wonderful improvement as hardly would have been believed possible. I think the same must have been found with us, though perhaps to a lesser extent. But you for so many years would obstinately persist in keeping us out of all good posts and honourable employment, as though you quite despised us and almost had a zid[1] against us. Only recently you have started taking us freely into the I.C.S. and other Services, and this just when you have begun totally to undermine those Services by your eagerness to give us democratic government. Without any previous experience of responsible posts and without much of traditions of holding power, these Indian officers, in addition to ordinary temptations, are exposed to all those so many pressures which can only be expected when they are subordinate to ministers who are always looking for popular votes. Whereas if you had been kind enough to take us into the highest services many years ago, it is just possible that no need would have been felt for democratic institutions so soon, before the people are ready for them. In any case, if they could by no means be avoided, I dare to say that they would not have caused such a rapid deterioration of the Services as we must now expect.'

'I don't quite know what to say, Allah Dad. I'm afraid you're right in thinking that we made a tremendous mistake in excluding Indians from the highest posts in Government service for so long. I've never been able to understand why on earth we did it; for, so far as I remember, nearly all the most famous Englishmen, who worked in India over a century ago, warned us against it. Somehow or other we disregarded their advice; and now we're in a fine mess. I find the prospects most dispiriting. But look here, if we're going to catch that train, we'll have to bustle up. Let's make these horses get on a bit. I'll race you to the canal over there. Come on.'

Greenlane was quite right in his recollection. Elphinstone, Munro, Metcalfe, and many other of the ablest Englishmen who served in India at the beginning of the nineteenth century,

---

[1] A feeling of obstinate dislike.

repeatedly urged that Indians should be admitted to the higher posts in Government service. But their advice went unheeded. There was, of course, from the outset a laudable and not merely a selfish reason for the policy of exclusion. The corruption of the Company's servants in India in the eighteenth century had been shocking; and one of the contributory causes was thought to be the ease with which they could employ native subordinates to make illegal exactions on their behalf. It seemed therefore desirable to keep them in separate cadres of their own quite clear of contamination by native colleagues and subordinates.

Forty years later, by the time of the Mutiny, the ineradicable corruption of the oriental and the immeasurable moral superiority of the Englishman had come to appear as unalterable facts of nature; and by this time they were bound up with strong vested interests. India had become the paradise of the English middle classes, where they could ape the manners and taste the pleasures of the aristocracy. Despite therefore many excellent professions of policy, all plans for admitting Indians to positions of trust and authority were opposed in principle and thwarted in practice by the men on the spot. Theoretically, of course, the competitive examination, whereby, since the middle of the nineteenth century, the Indian Civil Service was recruited, was open to Indians. But as the examination was held in England, in English, and in English subjects, and as the maximum age was only twenty-one and later nineteen, few Indians could hope to compete successfully. Those few who managed to pass in, appeared in their extreme rarity to be almost like freaks of nature; and, by the very strangeness of their position, freaks of nature they often did in fact become.

The fruits of this obstinate policy of exclusion are being gathered by the present generation. But earlier generations did well out of it. The solid rewards of service in India throughout the nineteenth century are not always fully appreciated. There was nothing, of course, to compare with the stupendous fortunes of the eighteenth-century nabobs. But Metcalfe during thirty-seven years' service (1801–38) accumulated nearly £100,000; and in a still more modest age young William Hunter, who went out to India in the Civil Service in 1862, was shortly afterwards writing to his fiancée: 'If God gives us health and long life together we shall be rich, very rich, before we are

141

fifty. I mean three or four thousand a year from our savings and my pension. Let us be thankful to heaven for its mercies.'

There were therefore sound material as well as plausible moral reasons for keeping the best posts in English hands. And temporarily India also did well out of it. The administration was maintained at a level that would otherwise have been impossible. Yet it was a colossal blunder—probably the prime cause of the distresses of the last thirty years. And because of the far-reaching consequences of the error, it is worth quoting the most famous and the most eloquent of the warnings uttered against it.

'Foreign Conquerors', wrote Thomas Munro to the Governor-General in 1817 'have treated the natives with violence, and often with great cruelty, but none has treated them with so much scorn as we; none have stigmatized the whole people as unworthy of trust, as incapable of honesty and as fit to be employed only where we cannot do without them. It seems to be not only ungenerous, but impolitic, to debase the character of a people fallen under our dominion. . . . The strength of the British Government enables it to put down every rebellion, to repel every foreign invasion, and to give to its subjects a degree of protection which those of no Native power enjoy. Its laws and institutions also afford them a security from domestic oppression, unknown in those states; but these advantages are dearly bought. They are purchased by the sacrifice of independence, of national character, and of whatever renders a people respectable. The Natives of the British provinces may, without fear, pursue their different occupations . . . and enjoy the fruits of their labours in tranquillity; but none of them can aspire to anything beyond this mere animal state of thriving in peace . . . none of them can look forward to any share in the legislation or civil or military government of their country. . . . The effect of this state of things is observable in all the British provinces, whose inhabitants are certainly the most abject race in India. . . . The consequence, therefore, of the conquest of India by the British arms, would be, in place of raising, to debase the whole people.'

The prophecy contained in the last words has a poignant ring, and finds an echo in the speeches and writings of Indian nationalists to-day.

VIII

MERCENARIES OR MISSIONARIES

Throughout the winter of 1938–9 Greenlane struggled on at Dandot, feeling more and more depressed. Now that Provincial Autonomy had been introduced, district life was becoming quite intolerable with politicians continually butting in and working little ramps. Reports reaching him from friends in other Provinces suggested that conditions were no better there and perhaps even worse. A young English police officer with two or three years' service, who was posted for a few months at Dandot, was always saying to him, 'What's the good of our being here? We can't do anything now, and we're not wanted. They would much prefer to have their own officers. So why remain?' Greenlane found himself unable to give any satisfactory reply. The truth was that he too was asking himself the same questions. The administration was getting shadier and shadier, and English officers could not prevent it. What useful purpose then did they serve? They might occasionally smooth over a local communal squabble, but they couldn't settle the general communal question. Nor could they contribute much to the large-scale social and economic reform, which was so badly needed. That now must necessarily depend on Indians themselves, and in any case it was beyond the capacity of foreign bureaucrats. The outlook was certainly gloomy; and over all there hung the shadow of impending war.

In the spring of 1939 an incident occurred which for Greenlane brought matters to a head. There lived in a village in the Dandot district a man named Manak. He was only semi-literate, but he owned considerable land and was notorious as a receiver of stolen property and a 'rassagir'.[1] He had under his control all the bad characters of the neighbourhood; he was in fact a rural gangster. As such he commanded a good deal of influence and even respect among the illiterate peasantry, and

[1] One who receives and passes on stolen cattle.

143

at the elections for the Assembly he had used this influence with great effect on behalf of certain candidates both in Dandot and in an adjoining district. The police had long known all about his criminal activities and for years had tried unsuccessfully to run him in. At last, in January 1939, they managed to arrest him in connection with a daring robbery. The evidence against him appeared to be overwhelming. But, owing to the part he had played in the elections, there were powerful persons supporting him. Greenlane realized that a strong magistrate would be required to deal with the case and therefore entrusted it to Allah Dad. During the course of the trial a large number of people approached Allah Dad with the request that he would acquit Manak or at least only fine him. But Allah Dad took no notice of them and in due course convicted Manak and sentenced him to three years' imprisonment.

The case went on appeal to the Sessions Judge. Allah Dad, who had many private sources of information of his own, warned Greenlane that the Sessions Judge had been successfully approached by Manak's partisans. He had been promised by an influential politician, so the rumour went, that if he would accept Manak's appeal and acquit him, his son, a quite worthless young man, would be given a government post. The rumour, like most ugly rumours of this kind in India, was soon confirmed by events. Manak was first released on bail by the Sessions Judge, and later acquitted. Rockets were let off as he returned in triumph to his village.

Greenlane was furious. He discussed the matter with Allah Dad, vainly toying with the idea that the Session Judges' order of acquittal might be set aside. But Allah Dad was quite defeatist.

'We can do nothing, sir,' he said. 'Manak has got the better of us. Only the High Court can interfere with the Session Judges' order and we can only approach them to do so through Government. We cannot expect Government to take up the matter, when Manak gave their supporters so much help at the last elections. I wish I could feel that we had heard the end of this affair, but I am afraid that Manak's friends, having got him acquitted, will certainly go on to take revenge on me for having put them to so much trouble by convicting him in the first instance.'

'Good God, Allah Dad, they surely won't go as far as that! In any case, what can they do?'

'Sir, you must be knowing that in this country people will do all sorts of things simply out of enmity. I myself have had a bad experience. You may have heard that some years ago, at the beginning of my service, I was nearly imprisoned in a totally false case.'

'I've vaguely heard something about it, but I don't know the facts. I once received an anonymous petition against you in which it was stated *inter alia* that in Sawanpur district you had been caught "enjoying with the chaukidar's[1] wife". Perhaps that's the incident to which you refer.'

'Sir, a totally false charge of rape was brought against me. I had not so much as even seen the woman. It was all a cooked-up case. I was only a naib-tahsildar at the time and was posted at Nawah. Sometimes, when I had been away and came back by train, I used to take a short cut from the station to my house past the quarters of the chaukidar of the post office. One night, as I was passing that way, two men suddenly sprang upon me out of the darkness and pinned me to the ground. At the same time a woman inside the chaukidar's quarters began uttering loud shrieks. I struggled to get away, but several other people, hearing the noise, came to the spot, and they all dragged me away to the police station. I had to spend the whole night in the lock-up; for those two men reported that, on hearing the cries of the chaukidar's wife, they had rushed into the quarters and found me trying to rape her. The next day, with great difficulty, I managed to get myself released on bail, and went to Sawanpur to see the Deputy Commissioner. But he was a Hindu and for certain reasons was not pleased with me. On receiving telegrams that I had been caught raping the woman, he at once, without making any inquiries, suspended me and would not even see me when I went to him. Sir, this false case was made against me simply out of enmity. It so happened that the postmaster at Nawah, who was a Hindu, had an unmarried daughter living with him. I had previously come to know this girl at a mixed club in Karachi, where I used to go with my father. When I was posted to Nawah as naib-tahsildar, that unmarried girl, remembering me from Karachi, wrote and

[1] Chaukidar = watchman.

145

suggested that we might meet again. We exchanged several notes and letters and she also came to my place once or twice. But her father didn't like my intimacy with her, and became much annoyed. He suspected that I had some bad intentions towards her, which was by no means the case. Just because of this grudge he, with the help of his chaukidar, and the local sub-inspector of police, who was also a Hindu, cooked up that false case against me. I was quite at a loss what to do, finding all these people against me and the Hindu Deputy Commissioner also not at all inclined towards me. But as good luck would have it, while the case was still pending, the Deputy Commissioner was transferred and Mr. Lightfoot came to Sawanpur in his place. I had heard from many sources that Mr. Lightfoot was a good officer of independent views who would always hear people and try to do solid justice. So I went and saw him, and told him all about the case against me, and also showed him some of the letters which that unmarried girl had sent me. He was impressed with what I said, especially when he saw the letters. He at once, that very day, sent for the file of the case and also called up the sub-inspector, who had investigated it, and questioned him on several points. He became convinced that the case was false and that I was quite innocent. The next day he sent for the postmaster to come before him, and in my presence threatened him very much and also confronted him with the letters which his daughter had sent me. When he saw those letters, that Hindu postmaster became quite confused. He began to tremble and with folded hands begged Mr. Lightfoot for mercy. Mr. Lightfoot was kind enough to forgive him. He withdrew the case against me and reinstated me as naib-tahsildar, but he took no further action. The postmaster felt thankful to Mr. Lightfoot for not punishing him, and I for my part was amazed to see an officer doing justice so promptly and thus relieving me of my anxieties. I have ever since been grateful to Mr. Lightfoot as, but for him, I must surely have been ruined.'

'Oh, that's the true story of you and the chaukidar's wife, is it? Well, you certainly had a pretty nasty experience. It was lucky for you that Mr. Lightfoot came to Sawanpur just at that time. But really, Allah Dad, I don't see why you should be afraid that something of the same kind will happen again. You

146

surely don't imagine that one of these politicians is going to get a false case started against you simply because you convicted Manak?'

'Sir, they will certainly put me to some trouble, even if no false case is started against me. Either they will get some bad entry made in my character roll that I am corrupt, so that later I may lose promotion, or they will get me transferred to some far-away station where there will be no means of educating my children and I shall have to incur huge expense.'

'Oh, I don't really think anything like that will happen. You are taking an unnecessarily gloomy view.'

'You will kindly pardon me, sir, if I say that I know these people better than you do. I can confidently predict that I will be put to trouble. But I shall not so much feel it. Previously I had a keen desire to be in Government service, as I thought I might be able to do the people some good. But now I have found that there are so many obstacles in the way that it is rather difficult to achieve anything. I am not therefore so much wedded now to Government service, and if I find that I am being put to too much trouble I shall just leave it. I have some land in Bikanir State, which my father left me, and, though I should not be so well off, I should be able to pull on.'

'Well, Allah Dad, I still think you're too pessimistic. I really can't believe that Manak's political friends will get anything done to you.'

But Allah Dad proved right and Greenlane wrong. For a few weeks later Allah Dad was transferred to a remote place in the far corner of the Province.

Greenlane was disgusted. Alone in Dandot and miserable, he confided his thoughts to Mr. Lightfoot.

'I am afraid', he wrote to him, 'I am not likely to remain in India much longer. What goes on disgusts me. And in any case we're not wanted. We are becoming, I feel, in our spiritual isolation more and more like those heroes of the golden age of British rule in India—the Metcalfes, Malcolms and Elphinstones. Just as the British elements were then few, scattered, critical of themselves and of British methods, uncertain masters of their situation, still doubtful whether British ideals and institutions would or ought to prevail in India, so are we to-day—a dwindling band and therefore condemned more and more to loneliness, sceptical of the value of our own liberalism when applied to India, inclined to ridicule even our own integrity, and keenly conscious of the pervasive potency of oriental custom and standards. We, as the rearguard, are in much the same position as they were as the vanguard. The brief days when everything British was best, when Englishmen in India were plentiful in numbers, strong in confidence, proud of their honesty and high principles, which they fondly imagined Indians admired too—those brief days, say seventy-five years in all, are over. They ended finally on the 1st April 1937.'[1]

Lightfoot's reply was to send him a wire, asking him to come and stay with him for the week-end. Greenlane gladly accepted the invitation, and went off on two days' leave to Nanaksar, where Lightfoot was now posted.

They settled down to talk. Lightfoot was at heart very much distressed at the thought of Greenlane leaving India. For Greenlane was his only 'chela',[2] the only young officer who had ever been entrusted to him for training; and he had taken an immense amount of trouble not only to instruct him in all branches of district work, but also to impart to him his own understanding of the people. And now, it seemed, all had been wasted. His own clear-eyed, detached, unemotional outlook, when transferred to Greenlane, had meant only disillusionment, pessimism and a feeling of frustration. He was leaving, and Lightfoot could not help feeling that in some way the fault lay with him. Nevertheless, he approached the matter with an air of careless omniscience.

'My dear Greenlane,' he said, 'the position is surely quite obvious. We English officers out here have now a choice between being missionaries or mercenaries. If we can't adjust ourselves to either of these rôles, we've got to go.'

'I'm afraid I don't quite understand.'

'Well, if we elect to be mercenaries, we have to pocket our pride and our honour along with our pay. Under this new system of government many things have to be done or connived at which are obviously wrong. Officers who are mere mercenaries just shrug their shoulders and say nothing. Theirs not to reason why. It's almost inevitable that this should be

[1] The date on which Provincial Autonomy came into operation.
[2] Disciple.

the attitude of senior officers, with only a few years to run.'

'Oh, I know, Lightfoot, only too well that some senior officers just tend to take the line of least resistance. The morale of the Services is being undermined. What else can you expect when in a country like this you introduce democracy without having trained a governing class? But it makes everything pretty disgusting and intolerable.'

'I share your feelings of disgust but I think we must try to see things in their proper perspective. You remember the old saying that the way to get on in the I.C.S. is either to make yourself useful to other men's wives or to have a wife who is useful to other men. In so far as there is some truth in that cynical observation, we are to-day merely witnessing one form of favouritism and corruption being replaced by another. We must also, I think, consider the matter from an altogether wider standpoint. We English officers in the Indian Services come out to India straight from the Universities and Public Schools with little or no knowledge of the real world. We bring with us our public-school ideals and public-school standards; and we find, of course, when we get here that they are peculiar to ourselves. We are not surprised at this. We think it is just because we are in India. We have always heard that Indians are all more or less dishonest, untrustworthy, and venal. Hence all the dirty ramps and crookery which we come across, from the meanest town committee to the highest department of Government, we attribute to the inherent depravity of the oriental. We imagine that in England, Europe and America everybody follows our public-school standards; that there is in all branches of administration the sort of integrity that you find amongst the British members of the Indian services. But nothing could be further from the truth. Public-school standards exist only in the Public Schools. They don't exist in the real world of practical affairs in England, Europe or America any more than they do in India. In fact less so. For English public servants in India, reacting against oriental corruption, have preserved a sort of virginal purity, which, though perhaps priggish, is probably unique. Our standards of industry and integrity, in the widest sense, are not, I believe, to be found in the Civil Services of England or of any other country. Ask anybody who has experience of both. The evidence on point is overwhelming.'

'Well, what do you conclude from all this? Do you imply that we should just accept a lowering of standards, swim with the tide and do as you say the world does?'

'No. I merely conclude that we should view the inevitable lowering of standards with more tolerance and understanding. We shall then be less likely to underrate Indians and overrate ourselves. But I don't for a moment want English officers to give up their standards and become mere mercenaries, interested solely in their pay and promotion. It is because I foresee that this is almost bound to happen that I have for some time been urging that we should cease altogether to recruit Englishmen to the Indian Services. If by continuing European recruitment at a fairly high level it was going to be possible to maintain the general integrity of the Services, it might be worth incurring considerable political odium to achieve this. But it is not possible to do this and at the same time to have democratic self-government. As you say, English officers are already becoming corrupted, and, unless we're careful, we'll get a reversion to something like eighteenth-century conditions. That will be disastrous. One of the few good things we have given to India is the ideal, and to some extent the example, of an uncorrupt administration. If we now by our conduct show that we have thrown over that ideal, it will be lost to India for generations. For by our defection all India will be completely disillusioned. It is to my mind, therefore, most desirable that Englishmen who remain in India should stick to that ideal.'

'Well, I don't know about sticking to any ideal, but I'm certainly not going to sell my soul to an Indian Ministry. I remember hearing people in England say that British troops could not be used as mercenaries, and that therefore, so long as British troops were required to keep order in India, the British must control the Government. They were most anxious to impress this point on Gandhi. But if British troops cannot be mercenaries, shouldn't the same hold good of British Civil Servants? They don't seem to have thought of that.'

'No, they probably didn't. You see, they probably forgot that we aren't Civil Servants in the usually accepted sense of that term. It might be a rather different matter if we were. Supposing we just had to spend our time writing minutes and drafting letters, as Civil Servants do at home or even out here in the secretariat, remaining quite unknown to the general public, obscure and silent cogs in a great machine. It might then be possible to become mere mercenaries without any serious harm—though I may remark, parenthetically, we should cease to have any *raison d'être*, as plenty of Indians can do that sort of job as well if not better than we. But, of course, as district officers, we are much more than Civil Servants. We are in a real sense rulers and are regarded as such by the people. We are not unknown, obscure, impersonal figures, but live, public personalities whose habits and actions are closely scrutinized and widely discussed. Thousands of people in our districts know our names and our faces. Hundreds come every week to pay us homage and submit petitions. There is scarcely a function of a modern government which we do not, directly or indirectly, influence or control. We are not, and we cannot be, mere self-effacing robots. The concentration of powers in our hands, and the tradition of personal rule in India makes that impossible. We cannot therefore just shuffle off our responsibilities and pretend that in all we do, whether just or unjust, honourable or dishonourable, we are merely the obedient tools of an Indian Ministry. The people expect us to oppose whatever is unjust, foolish, corrupt or wrong. We may or may not be successful, but if we don't make the effort we are held to be accessories. We cannot therefore be mere mercenaries without seeming to be indifferent to the very ideals which we have stood for in this country.'

'Then in your view we haven't really the choice of being mercenaries or missionaries. We either ought to be what you call missionaries or to go.'

'In your case it comes to that. For you couldn't adjust yourself to the rôle of a mere mercenary. You would find it too contemptible.'

'Well, I'm afraid I'd find it too hard to be a missionary. I came out to India with two aims—rather naïve perhaps, but they seemed to me reasonable—to help the wretched peasant and to facilitate the transition to Indian self-government. I find that both of these aims are unrealizable. We can't do anything to relieve the poverty of the masses. That depends now on some large-scale policy which only Indians could carry out. And facilitating the transition to self-government seems to mean conniving at things which you know to be wrong.'

'I think true missionaries don't much bother whether their aims are realized or not. They probably accept the teaching of the Gita. "Be not moved by the fruits of works; but let not attachment to worklessness dwell in thee." '

'It is curious your quoting that. Allah Dad used to be always quoting some such passage.'

'I've several times discussed these matters with Allah Dad. He's a very intelligent and thoughtful man. I think that for people working in India the doctrine of the Gita is the true philosophy. And it is rather interesting to note that Stoicism, the philosophy of the proconsuls of the Roman Empire, with whom we sometimes like to feel a sort of kinship, has very close affinities with the teaching of the Gita.'

'I'm afraid that's all rather beyond me! What I feel is that we English can't really do any more good out here, and that young officers like myself had much better clear out and prepare ourselves for this war which is obviously coming. I remember India Office officials before I came out telling me that our real object in remaining in India was to safeguard British capital. I think they must have been right. If it wasn't so, if we really in our heart of hearts wished to help India to govern herself, why are we always so hostile to Indian Nationalists, whose object is just the same? Well, I'm afraid that just preserving British capital is not an object which appeals to me. And if self-government means democratic government, I think that for this country it is all wrong, and will inevitably lead to the worst form of tyranny and corruption.'

'Well, you may be right. But surely you must have noticed that these new Indian Ministries, with all their faults, have already begun doing some of the very things that ought to be done and that we bureaucrats hadn't the boldness to do. Look at all the debt legislation they've pushed through in this and in other Provinces. Within two years of assuming office they have reversed one of our capital errors, and, for the time being at any rate, rescued the peasant from the clutches of the money-lender. No longer can the moneylender just go to a Civil Court and recover a partially bogus debt plus enormously inflated compound interest by distraining on the peasant's goods and cattle, his land and its produce. Nearly all the peasant's property is now protected by law from attachment and sale. Then again there are the Debt Conciliation Boards which they've set up for the settlement of disputes between creditor and debtor. These non-official Boards, which have no strict rules of procedure or evidence, but carry on more or less as the spirit moves them, are far more suited to the people than our formal Civil Courts. Their methods may seem to us a bit crude —so far as I can make out they just browbeat the parties or harass them with repeated adjournments till out of sheer weariness they agree to what the Board considers a fair settlement—but they work well enough.'

'I don't know about that. In Dandot the appointments to the Board were purely political and two of the members are corrupt scoundrels.'

'Political considerations may mar the Boards to some extent; but they're sound in principle—much sounder than our Civil Courts and boasted rule of Law. In this district I've got such a charming and admirable man as chairman of the Board—an old soldier. Then consider all that is being done by the new Ministries in some of the other Provinces in the way of tenancy legislation. Reforms which were long overdue are now being put through. The new Ministries have also given much attention to another line of development which ought to appeal to you. I seem to remember that you at one time were very keen on encouraging panchayats. Well, that is exactly what the new Ministries are everywhere doing. They're trying to revive the old village council of elders as a real organ of self-government. However disappointing the results may be, can you really doubt that this is a move in the right direction?'

'So far as I can see, the Ministries are interested in panchayats from purely selfish political motives. They hope that every village panchayat will simply become a useful unit in their political organization; and they see a chance of finding jobs for their hangers-on as inspectors of panchayats, deputy inspectors, assistant inspectors and all the rest of it. The whole thing's a sham. It's not sincere; it's not genuine.'

'No doubt politics have a corrupting influence on all that they do. And insincerity is one of the principal faults of Indian character. They have a positive passion for eyewash. That is

153

why they are always talking about "solid justice" and "solid good"; for in this country these two commodities have such a high scarcity value. But when all this is said, you must admit that the new Ministries have been working on sound lines and they have accomplished more in two years than we would do in ten.'

'There may be something in what you say, but as everything is spoiled by dishonesty and political racketeering, which we are powerless to check, I don't see that we can any longer be of any useful assistance. You've admitted as much yourself. You said we oughtn't to be mercenaries and tamely accept all the crookery that goes on.'

'Yes, but you mustn't be so intolerant of crookery. Honest government was probably only an eccentricity of Victorian England, and, like most things Victorian, perhaps not so honest and admirable as it seemed. Apart from this, you've left out my alternative of being a missionary.'

'Well, I don't quite know what you mean by government servants being missionaries. I'm sure I couldn't be one.'

'The character of the mercenary is clear. He's interested in his pay, promotion, and pension. In order to get these he'll do what he's told. On the other hand the missionary civilian remains obstinately the champion, maybe the unsuccessful champion, of certain standards and values, irrespective of personal loss or gain and—here's the real point—irrespective of the success or failure of his efforts. He goes on resisting corruption and injustice, even though his resistance is ineffective and seemingly futile.'

'I'm afraid Lightfoot, I couldn't do that. One must have some results.'

'I'm not sure about that. You know, there are Indian officers who get on without them. Not many, but still a few. You look incredulous. But India is a land of saints as well as of sinners. I know several Indian officers who stick to certain standards even though this seems to produce no results. Allah Dad is perhaps one of them. Any English officer who supports them is probably doing some good. In fact I think this is about the only way Englishmen can now contribute to India—unless they happen to be doctors, engineers or technicians of some kind.'

'I often wish I was a doctor. One could then at any rate feel

154

that one was achieving something. I sometimes think that the missionaries, despite all their follies and narrowness of outlook, have, as doctors and teachers, really done more for India than all the rest of us put together.'

'There's something in what you say. As a matter of fact the best Englishman I've known in India was a doctor; but not a missionary. Curiously enough he was in Government service.'

'I know who you mean. Doctor Toogood, who was Civil Surgeon at Sawanpur.'

'That's right. A single-minded man, and delightfully human and humorous, and a good doctor. I remember our local journalist writing a description of him which, though it amused us at the time, was really very apt. It was just after the Quetta earthquake, and Toogood used to go down to the station to meet the trains of stupefied and often badly battered survivors and see if he could do anything for them. Our local Indian journalist described him as "moving about on the platform like an angel of mercy, begging, nay imploring the Quetta sufferers to let him have the privilege of curing them". In its quaint way that exactly described him. As a matter of fact on that occasion he never got the privilege for which he was begging. The refugees, however knocked about, preferred to go to their homes rather than to a Government hospital. For two days he met the trains to no purpose. At last, on the third day, he got hold of one man with several broken bones who was persuaded to come to hospital. Toogood saw him off from the station on a stretcher in charge of his relatives, and himself in high glee went ahead in his car to be ready at the hospital to receive him. But he never arrived. He was lost en route. His relatives, once Toogood was out of the way, just diverted him from the hospital to his home, to Toogood's chagrin but intense amusement.'

'How typical!'

'Yes. But of course it was just because Toogood really *did* consider it a privilege to cure these poor people that they liked him so. The dumb, driven masses of India, who feel so much and can say so little, were amazed to come into a Government hospital and find a doctor like Toogood speaking kindly to them and making them feel as though he was taking as much trouble for them as he would for a Maharajah. They were quite unaccustomed to treatment of this kind from an officer of his rank. When I used to see him at Sawanpur going round his wards, calm, patient, serious, yet extraordinarily kind, and the faces of the people lighting up as he approached them, I sometimes used to think that perhaps, just because of him, the English were justified in being in India.'

'A grand man! I liked him enormously. Yet officially his merits were quite unrecognized. Government took no particular notice of him, except towards the end of his service to do him down! Again, how typical! But, Lightfoot, we're not doctors, we can't confer any positive benefit on the people. It seems to me that we really are superfluous.'

'You can't mend people's broken bones; but you can in a small way remedy their petty grievances, save them from baseless fears, and lighten their sorrows by convincing them that they are incurable. I think you said that one of your aims had been to help the underdog. Well, don't you think you can do it in some degree as a district officer, just in the course of your normal duties?'

'Oh, I know, Lightfoot, you spend hours every day listening to every sort of petitioner, wasting your time and ruining your health to no purpose. I tried that at Dandot, but found it hopeless. You can hardly ever do anything for them. Most of them want you to give them some land or to recover their runaway wife or something equally impossible. You merely encourage false hopes by listening to them.'

'I'm not sure about that. You may, by listening to them, effectively discourage false hopes; for you may be able to convince them that what they want can't be had or isn't worth having—both are true of a runaway wife—and so induce them to cease fretting and to think about something else. In any case they probably get some consolation just from being heard.'

'I think that's doubtful, and anyhow the game's not worth the candle. Out of all the petitioners you see, for how many can you do any tangible good?'

'Well, I suppose I see about twenty-five a day, and perhaps could say that I positively benefit about three or four a week.'

'It's an absurd result for all the labour and trouble you're put to.'

'It does seem rather small. But I come back again to my old

156

point; you mustn't look for results. They may come or they may not. But they must be a matter of indifference to you.'

'Well, as I've already said, I can't go as far as that, and if that's what you mean by being a missionary, I'm afraid I can't manage it. So, as you've agreed that we shouldn't be mercenaries, the only course left for me is to clear out. And that's what I'm going to do.'

'I'm sorry for that, but I can't blame you.'

'And what about you, Lightfoot? You know you're a bit of a humbug, pretending that you're going to remain on here as what you call a missionary. I can't exactly see you in that rôle, you old cynic.'

Lightfoot's eyes sparkled with mischievous humour. 'My dear fellow,' he said, 'unlike you I haven't got to make any choice. I've been too long in this country and have become too tangled up in it ever to think of leaving. I've said all this about mercenaries and missionaries simply for your benefit. I'm sorry that it has only confirmed you in your resolution.'

So Greenlane left India and was lost in the shadows of war.

IX

POLITICS AND THE WAR

The war came. On the day after its declaration Lightfoot, as he went about his duties at Nanaksar, was conscious that everybody—the clerks in his office, the lawyers, the litigants, the people in the streets—were watching him with more than usual intentness, trying to divine the thoughts and feelings of the solitary Englishman in their midst. He, for his part, was equally anxious to ascertain Indian reactions to the war. In the last war, as a young officer fresh to India, he had got the impression that, despite all the outward expressions of loyalty, there was very little real appreciation, even among educated Indians, of the issues at stake. The war hadn't meant much to them. But India had prospered during the last war. Large fortunes had been made by the trading classes, and the peasants had seen the prices of their produce double and treble. The casualties suffered had been exceedingly small and had affected only a minute fraction of the population. Most of India had memories of war which were by no means unhappy.

These memories coloured the attitude towards the new war. Lightfoot soon realized that nearly all classes secretly welcomed it and foresaw prosperity in booming industry and rising prices. The peasants sometimes naïvely expressed their satisfaction at the prospect. Wheat had touched Rs.10 per maund in 1918. It might do so again. The cunning city merchants said nothing; but they laid in stocks.

The educated classes, so it seemed to Lightfoot, had a greater interest in the war and a much fuller understanding of its significance than in 1914. The general standard of knowledge was higher than it had been twenty-five years earlier. Moreover the events of the past few years had left no doubt as to the character of the Nazi régime. Most Indians had decided that it was something which they disliked, and they were encouraged in this dislike by prominent national leaders. Whatever, therefore, might be their feelings towards the

158

British, they almost all hoped that in the long run Germany would be defeated. But many of them also hoped that the run would be really long and that in the course of it British pride would be humbled by misfortune and defeat. They listened, therefore, with a sort of malicious glee to the German wireless heaping insults on the British and telling of British reverses. They wished that before victory was won Britain should take heavy punishment. Their wishes were destined to be fulfilled.

On the whole then the war was greeted with enthusiasm. Good business, full employment, high prices, defeats for the British, and ultimate victory had, between them, an appeal for most classes of the population. Nor were all influenced by purely ignoble motives. A large number of Indians shared the sentiments expressed in the Central Assembly on 4th September by the Law Member, Sir Muhammad Zafarullah Khan. 'I am certain', he said, 'that every one of us here truly realizes the gravity of the crisis and is determined to do his duty to King and Country.' There were many striking demonstrations of loyalty; many generous offers of help. The Princes assured the Viceroy of their full co-operation. The Premiers of Bengal and the Punjab called upon the people of their Provinces to give ungrudging support to the Allied cause. Even Congress leaders openly admitted that their sympathies were with England and France. Lightfoot, like other district officers, was overwhelmed with letters from persons offering their services or their money. Many of these meant nothing, except that the writers wanted jobs. Many of them were genuine.

No advantage was taken of the first flush of enthusiasm. In India, as perhaps in England, those in authority seemed to think that war against the strongest military power in the world could be waged without actually fighting. There was no immediate attempt to mobilize the forces of India. In the great recruiting areas the villagers were astonished and dismayed to find that recruits were not wanted. The more educated classes wondered why a War Loan was not raised while people, under the influence of their first generous impulse, were willing to lend. Business men and industrialists asked themselves why persons possessed of technical skill were not being registered for war employment, and why arrangements were not being made to train others.

But the policy of those in authority was 'Wait and See'. In war one must not anticipate events. In the making of military preparations it is a mistake to look ahead. You might spend too much. So throughout the winter of the 'phoney' war, there was stagnation in India, while enthusiasm evaporated and Indians asked whether England really meant to fight.

Meanwhile the political situation deteriorated. The Congress leaders, despite their avowed sympathy with the Allied cause, objected to the Viceroy's proclamation of war and promulgation of war ordinances without India's consent. Though they declared that they did not want to take advantage of Britain's difficulties and were not out to bargain, it soon appeared that they would not give any support unconditionally. 'India cannot associate herself with a war said to be for democratic freedom when that very freedom is denied to her.' So ran the Working Committee's resolution of 15th September. They invited the British Government to state their war aims, and they put two specific questions: (1) 'Do [Britain's war aims] include the elimination of imperialism and the treatment of India as a free nation whose policy will be guided in accordance with the wishes of her people?' (2) 'How are such aims to be given effect to in the present?' Presumably if the answers to these questions had been satisfactory, a bargain—in spite of Congress's objections to bargaining—would have been struck.

This was the moment for British statesmen to show imagination. If they had done so, the answers given to the two questions would have been (1) Yes. (2) By a reconstruction of the Viceroy's Executive Council so as to include leaders of the principal political parties. These were in effect the answers given two and a half years later in the draft declaration which Sir Stafford Cripps brought to India in 1942. British apologists say that as the Cripps' offer was rejected by Congress in April 1942, any similar offer would have equally been rejected, if made in the early weeks of the war. But the situation in the autumn of 1939 was very different from what it was in the spring of 1942. Italy and Japan had not yet entered the war. The danger to India seemed remote and hypothetical. The Mediterranean was still open. Hong Kong, Singapore and Rangoon still firmly held. The possibility that the British might be forcibly driven out of India had not even crossed men's minds. In seven Provinces

Congress Ministries were still in office, and for the most part anxious to remain there. Throughout the country there was a strong desire for full support of the Allied cause, of which the Congress High Command were not insensible. The Cripps' offer, if made in 1939, would have seemed to Congress far more attractive and valuable than it did in 1942 when Britain's prospects in the East looked so bleak.

The questions propounded by Congress remained unanswered for just over a month, during which time the Viceroy interviewed over fifty politicians and public men. The purpose of these interviews was not clear. To Congress it gave an opportunity of representing that the Viceroy, by attending to the views of every conceivable minority, was endeavouring to exploit India's divisions. The general impression created was certainly unfortunate. At last, however, on 17th October, the Viceroy made a public statement. Britain's war aims, he said, had not yet been defined in detail, but she sought no material advantage for herself and desired the establishment of real and lasting peace. As for India, the goal of British policy was Dominion Status. (This had frequently been said before.) The stage so far reached in the progress towards that goal was represented by the Act of 1935; but the British Government would be prepared at the end of the war, to consider modifications of the scheme embodied in the Act in the light of Indian opinion. As regards immediate changes, the Viceroy proposed the establishment of a consultative group, representative of all major political parties, as the best way of associating Indian public opinion with the conduct of the war.

This dreary statement—the product of one month's cogitation—was bound to be unacceptable to Congress; and even Indians of moderate views were sadly disappointed. They found nothing whatever inspiring in it. The goal of Dominion Status still remained shrouded in the mists of the future. No time limit for its attainment had been set. And as for the proposed consultative group, nobody could really believe that this was the 'best way' of associating public opinion with the prosecution of the war. Everyone had confidently expected the expansion of the Executive Council so as to include more Indian members.

The Congress Working Committee immediately condemned

161

the statement and ordered the Congress Ministries in the Provinces to tender their resignations. With scarcely concealed reluctance, they obeyed. Non-co-operation, destined to turn to active opposition, had begun.

Meanwhile the Muslim League had also been considering the Viceroy's statement. Unlike Congress, the League, with perhaps commendable honesty, had never concealed its intention of bargaining. Solid Muslim support could be had on two conditions, viz. (i) that pure Congress Raj in the Congress Provinces was ended; (ii) that any further constitutional advance would only be made with the Muslim League's consent and approval. The Viceroy's statement, though it contained a promise that the interests of minorities would be fully considered in the event of any constitutional changes, made no specific mention of the League's conditions. But the Muslim community was already more than half-committed. For the Muslim Premiers of Bengal, the Punjab, and Sind had promised Britain unconditional support in the war and were not likely to go back on that. Mr. Jinnah, therefore, though unwilling to go as far as the three Muslim Premiers (he had been an ardent nationalist in his younger days), deemed it advisable to temporize. The League asked for further discussion and clarification of matters left in doubt.

For several months after October 1939 there was no important development either in the war or in the political situation. In the new year a flicker of hope was raised by a speech made by the Viceroy at Bombay. He announced that Dominion Status was to be attained as soon as possible after the war and that meanwhile his Executive Council would be enlarged. This represented a slight advance, and immediately drew a response from Gandhi who said he liked the speech and hastened to see the Viceroy. The interview was friendly; but nothing came of it. Congress insisted that the people of India alone should shape their own future Constitution through a Constituent Assembly elected on the basis of adult suffrage. The essence of the demand was that Parliament should not dictate India's future; and this was not in itself unreasonable. But the demand could hardly be accepted in the form in which it was put; for to Muslims a Constituent Assembly based on adult suffrage spelt dictation by a Hindu majority. They would not

tolerate Hindu dictation any more than Congress would tolerate the dictation of Parliament—a point which some of the
wiser Congress leaders soon recognized.

So throughout the spring of 1940 the political deadlock
continued and the war effort remained at half-cock.

With the fall of France, India awoke with a shock to the
alarming prospect opening up before her. The war, hitherto so
remote, suddenly appeared real and very near. Some vast, unexpected change in India's fortunes, fraught with unknown
consequences, was felt to be impending. The British Raj, and
with it the habits of a century of peace, seemed about to pass
away. There was an incipient panic—a spate of wild rumours,
withdrawals from banks, hoarding of coin, and a keen demand
for firearms. Crime figures rose steeply. The lawless elements
in the country began to think that their day had come.

With Britain in mortal peril, educated Indians realized in a
flash how much the stability of the British Empire had been
the unconscious assumption of their lives. They knew that all
their hopes for the future were really bound up with Britain's
survival. They had never before contemplated that she would
not survive. But now the odds seemed against her. There was
a curious wave of warmhearted affection and admiration for
her as she stood alone, undaunted by disaster. Many English
officers were touched by the sympathy which Indians, even of
rather extreme views, showed them in those dark days.

Several Congress leaders were carried away by this wave of
emotion. Gandhi paid a tribute to the bravery of the British
people and assured his countrymen that their spirit would not
easily be broken. 'India', he declared, 'does not seek independence out of Britain's ruin.' 'England's difficulty is not
India's opportunity,' echoed Jawaharal Nehru. There were
appeals for calmness and order—and the people of India
responded.

It was perhaps during these weeks that the last real opportunity occurred of resolving the political deadlock. Gandhi,
whatever his sympathy with Britain, was still a pacifist. He was
unwilling that India should defend herself with armed forces
against either external aggression or internal disorder. He
wished Congress to adhere to the creed of non-violence and to
resist the temptation to take office again and lead India in the

prosecution of the war. But most other Congress leaders, including Mr. Rajagopalachari and Jawaharal Nehru, felt that this was hardly the time for pacifism. They, therefore, while leaving Gandhi free to pursue his own ideal in his own way, absolved him from responsibility for the programme and activity of Congress. This meant that if they could reach agreement with Britain over the political issue, they intended to give her not merely non-violent moral support but full material support as well.

The exact terms which Congress now demanded do not appear ever to have been precisely ascertained. 'Full independence for India' was, as usual, one of the demands; but by this was probably intended full independence immediately after the war. The other demand was that a 'provisional National Government should be constituted at the centre such as to command the confidence of all the elected elements in the Central Legislature'. It was not clear what this meant. It might on the one hand have meant a Government wholly responsible to the Legislature. If so, it would have been quite a new departure. Full responsible government had been introduced in the Provinces in 1937, but had never come into operation at the Centre. The Central Government still consisted of the Governor-General and his Executive Council, all of whom were appointed by the Crown and were responsible, not to the Central Legislature, but to the Secretary of State and Parliament. On the other hand it might simply have meant a complete reconstruction of the Executive Council so as to include acknowledged representatives of the principal political parties. Such a Government would have been 'national' in the sense that it was composed of recognized national leaders. Though not responsible to the Legislature, it would have automatically commanded its confidence.

To have introduced responsible government at the Centre would have involved considerable constitutional changes, difficult in any case in time of war, and doubly difficult when Congress and the Muslim League were by no means in agreement as to what those changes should be. Obviously the wisest plan was to retain, so far as possible, the existing constitutional machinery, and hope that recognized national leaders, if they could be induced to co-operate as members of the Executive

Council, would, on the one hand, command in practice the confidence of the Legislature, and, on the other hand, would not fall out with the Governor-General and compel him to use his special powers of overriding his Council.

It is regrettable that the real intentions of Congress at this time were not thoroughly explored. For, now that Gandhi had temporarily stood aside, one of the most influential Congress leaders was Mr. Rajagopalachari. In Madras he had shown himself to be an able and practical man, and it was notorious, both now and later, that he was anxious (for whatever reasons)[1] to come to terms with Britain, patch up an agreement with the moderate elements in the League and form a Congress-League Coalition Government at the Centre for the prosecution of the war. It does not appear ever to have been established that at this stage he would have insisted on nothing less than full responsible government, with all the constitutional changes and communal difficulties which this would involve. Later, no doubt, in 1942 at the time of the Cripps Mission, the Congress showed that they interpreted 'National Government' as nothing less than this. This was in fact one of the main points on which, ostensibly, the Cripps negotiations finally broke down. But it is not safe to argue that their interpretation of it in the summer of 1940 would necessarily have been the same. In 1942 Gandhi, who for reasons of his own was bent on the rejection of the Cripps proposals, was actively influencing Congress policy. In 1940 he had stood aside; in 1940, therefore, Mr. Rajagopalachari had a greater chance of making his views prevail than he had in 1942.

Moreover, Mr. Rajagopalachari was of all the Congress leaders the one most likely to effect a compromise with the Muslims. Moderate Muslim leaders felt that he was a man with whom they could do business; and there were in fact at this very time some *pourparlers* between him and Sir Sikander Hyat-Khan, Premier of the Punjab. The one path which might have led out of the tangle was to promote an agreement between these two men. It is reasonably certain that any proposals which they jointly sponsored could have been safely accepted

[1] e.g. it has been suggested that he felt certain of a British collapse and wanted to ensure that Congress would be well in the saddle before the collapse occurred.

by the British Government. For Sir Sikander was committed to the war heart and soul. He would never have been party to any agreement which might involve Britain being let down and deprived of India's support in the prosecution of the war. But this path was not taken or explored. The *pourparlers*, instead of being helped and encouraged, were actually discouraged. Sir Sikander felt it deeply. From the outbreak of war he had unswervingly supported Britain and done as much as any man to stimulate India's war effort. Yet when it came to high politics, it seemed that his help and advice were not wanted. He instinctively sensed that in the summer of 1940 the last chance of securing Congress support for the war was being let slip.

The British Government, instead of trying to build on the Sikander-Rajagopalachari bridge, came out with the so-called 'August Offer'—a new declaration of British policy. Though not very happily drafted, it did in one respect mark a substantial advance. For it was recognized that the framing of a new constitution was primarily the responsibility of Indians themselves and not of Parliament—a point which Congress had taken at an earlier stage without receiving satisfaction. But the offer was clearly inadequate; it would not appeal even to moderate Congressmen. It contained no reference to the demand for independence, and in this respect alone fell far short of the offer later made in 1942. The principle, 'What you can give, give quickly,' was once more overlooked. Congress rejected the offer—with unnecessary bitterness and scorn. Gandhi regained his ascendancy and once more assumed direction of Congress policy. His lieutenants had been given their chance and had failed. He had told them they would.

Most people now reconciled themselves to the deadlock continuing throughout the war. Of the two big political parties, it seemed a fair presumption that the Muslim League, while withholding co-operation, would refrain from active obstruction. The best hope was that Congress would do the same; and for some time this hope was realized. Gandhi, absorbed by non-violence and pacifism, insisted on asserting the right to preach against participation in the war effort, and in pursuance of this object started a strictly limited, wholly non-violent Civil Disobedience campaign. But it was designed not to embarrass the

British Government, and in fact caused little trouble. Few Congressmen took it seriously and it soon ceased to attract attention. The year 1941 drew towards a close without any significant political development.

Meanwhile the shock caused by the disasters of 1940 began to wear off. Britain had withstood the German onslaught and survived. With Wavell's astonishing victories in Libya the threat to India appeared to recede. The war became once more remote. A number of Indians, who from the outset had shared in the war effort, continued to give all the assistance in their power. A still larger number were determined to lose no chance of making money. Whatever their political views might be, they jostled one another for military contracts. Considerable fortunes were amassed, licitly and illicitly. The war was remote; the war was profitable.

Then suddenly there was a dramatic change. Japan's spectacular victories, her easy conquest of Malay and the Dutch Indies, the temporary collapse of Anglo-American sea power in the waters of South East Asia, brought the war, within the space of a few weeks, to India's threshold. The reaction was similar to what it had been in 1940, but by no means so favourable to Britain. There were calls from many quarters for a united front and resistance to the enemy. But, with an enemy actually at the gate, the will to resist was less strong. In the summer of 1940 India had been impressed by England's courage. In the spring of 1942 she was impressed by her incompetence. The inglorious retreat down the Malay peninsula, the unheroic surrender of Singapore, the hopeless confusion in Burma shattered the reputation which England had gained by her skill and tenacity in the preceding eighteeen months. If Japan should attack India, the English, it was felt, would show the same inefficiency as they had shown in Malay and were showing in Burma. They might talk of defending India, but they would not be able to defend her. It was better therefore to let the invader come and come quietly, than to plunge India into the confusion and miseries of war. Moreover, Japan had no quarrel with India, and would never have menaced her, were it not that she was part of the British Empire and therefore a potential base for Anglo-American military power. Vainly (and mistakenly) English Governors of Provinces dilated on Japanese

atrocities and warned their audiences of the fearful fate await-
ing them if the invader was not repelled. The vast pacific Hindu
population knew better. The atrocities would be reserved for
the British, not for themselves. The Japanese would do no
harm to Indians, if Indians did no harm to them. The difference
in their treatment of British and Indian prisoners captured at
Singapore was no secret. And the Japanese radio was careful
to see that the lesson was learnt.

Gandhi, more than ever confirmed in his pacifism, could
not reconcile himself to India taking part in the war on any
terms. Some of the other Congress leaders had no such scruples.
They were ready for India to fight—at a price. But they differed
as to what that price should be. Jawaharlal Nehru took the
line that she could only co-operate on the basis of immediate
independence. This meant, as Gandhi pointed out, that in
practice Nehru's opposition to India's participation in the war
was almost as strong as his own. Mr. Rajagopalachari, on the
other hand, showed a desire to reach a settlement both with
Britain and with the Muslim League on any terms which would
mean some real transference of responsibility for the defence of
India to Indian hands. He frankly expressed his disagreement
with Gandhi over the war issue and said that this might lead to
'a parting of the ways'. But he and the Congressmen who
thought like him did not receive much support in their courage-
ous independence. For one reason or another, whether anti-
British feeling, fear of the Japanese, pacifism, or loyalty to
Gandhi, Congress as a whole were now definitely opposed to
co-operation.

If the Congress attitude hardened, so did that of the Muslim
League. The proximity of the Japanese evoked a demand, not
for the defence of India, but for its partition. No settlement is
possible, the League declared, on the basis of a Central Government with India as one single unit. The tone of its pronounce-
ments was quite uncompromising.

It was in these unfavourable circumstances that the British
Government made its last and boldest effort to resolve the
deadlock. Sir Stafford Cripps arrived in Delhi in March
1942 with a new Draft Declaration which went much beyond
any previous statement of British policy in regard to India. A
real attempt was at last made to meet the demands both of

Congress and the Muslim League. India was assured that 'immediately on the cessation of hostilities' steps would be taken to set up an elected body (the proposed composition of which was stated) charged with the task of framing a Constitution for a fully self-governing Indian Union. This looked like business. India's independence was no longer relegated to the Greek kalends; the time and manner of achieving it were precisely specified. Moreover, it was to be real independence. For it was made clear that the new Indian Union would be fully entitled, if it so wished, to disown allegiance to the Crown. As for British obligations and interests in India, these were to be settled by a treaty negotiated between the British Government and the Constitution-making body. Congress demands as regards the future could hardly have been more fully met.

Provision was also made for the satisfaction of the Muslim League. Any Provinces which did not wish to accept the new Constitution were to be entitled to remain out of the Indian Union and to frame separate constitutions for themselves, giving them the same full status as the Indian Union. Thus partition was accepted in principle, should the Muslims really desire it.

As regards the immediate present, 'leaders of the principal sections of the Indian people' were invited to participate forthwith in the counsels of the country, of the Commonwealth, and of the United Nations. Clearly the intention was that Indian members of the Executive Council should be nominated not by the Viceroy, but by the various political parties; and that in their share in the common deliberations of the United Nations they should be on an entirely equal footing with the representatives of other countries.

Here at last was real statesmanship; but statesmanship so long postponed that it seemed hardly distinguishable from panic. Such deathbed repentance excited suspicion. Concessions so long refused were now suddenly offered when India's position was desperate. They were not offered freely; they were not (it was unfairly suggested) genuinely meant.

Lightfoot was aware of these doubts and suspicions. The timing of the latest declaration could hardly have been worse. Nevertheless he felt optimistic. There was, he thought, at least a fifty-fifty chance of the mission being a success.

He sought the opinion of a Hindu friend in Nanaksar—a rotund, smiling, astute gentleman, named Gopal Das, who had taken a degree at Oxford and in his younger days had played a prominent part in Congress politics. He dismissed Lightfoot's optimism with a chuckle and a wave of his fat hand.

'Oh no,' he said. 'Oh, dear me, no! Congress will never accept. I know these people; I know them only too well. Whatever you offer them, they'll find some reason for rejecting it. Congress can only agree on a negative. Acceptance would split them. Gandhi will never allow that. He'll preserve Congress unity at all costs. And then, of course, Gandhi is a pacifist. Non-violence is his ruling passion. Don't you remember away back in July 1940, when everyone was in a flap, running about pulling wires and projecting all sorts of political combinations, he wouldn't have anything to do with it? All he was interested in was drafting an appeal to the British to accept the method of non-violence and allow Hitler and Mussolini, as he put it, 'to take possession of your beautiful island, if they wished'. A good idea, don't you think? I'm sure you must have liked it. Well, now, I ask you, how can Congress, with Gandhi at its head, rouse India to resistance, as the phrase goes? How can a party which has for twenty years been preaching non-violence and encouraging anti-British sentiments now join with the British in violent resistance to the Japanese? It's a fantastic notion. They know they can't do it. And, don't you see, the nearer the war approaches, the more pacifist Gandhi becomes, and the more truly he reflects the real instincts of Hindu India? We've for centuries been a conquered people and we don't believe in resistance. We're content to look ahead and bide our time. We know that in the long run non-resistance brings the best results.'

'Yes, Gopal, but not all Hindus are non-resisters, and several important Congress leaders are strongly opposed to Gandhi's pacifism. Rajagopalachari has already made his attitude pretty clear. He would like to accept the Cripps' offer, and Jawaharlal is half-inclined to follow him.'

'When it comes to the point Jawaharlal will follow Gandhi. You know when his father, Moti Lal Nehru, died, his last words of advice to Jawaharlal were that he should obey Gandhi. Since then Jawaharlal has disagreed with Gandhi more than once, but always in the end he has done what he said.'

'It is really rather intolerable that none of these Congress leaders have the guts to break away from Gandhi, even when they think he's wrong.'

'Well, how many English politicians had the guts to break away from Chamberlain when he was trying to appease Hitler? I think you're a bit hard on Nehru and co. Sentiment and personal loyalties mean more to us than to you.'

'You're right there. And the Congress High Command show no mercy to rebels. They're just broken, like Bose. I suppose, Gopal, one oughtn't to condemn them too readily for submitting to Gandhi's dictation.'

'No, especially when his dictation seems good. Though I hold no brief for Gandhi, I should say that, quite apart from his pacifism, he has a strong case for non-co-operating. After all, it isn't exactly a cheerful moment to be invited to share in the government of the country. I should say that if the Japs threw just a little bit of grit into the wheels, the whole machine would stop working. I wouldn't myself like to have to take charge of it just at present.'

'Oh, of course, the administration is rotten. We're all conscious of that. The simplest problem throws the Government of India into confusion. The Japs have only got to land two or three divisions and the whole structure will collapse like a pack of cards. We can only hope that either the Japs won't come or that we'll have enough ships and aeroplanes to break up their armada before it gets here.'

'You may bet the Congress leaders are quite aware of this. Probably some of them think the position even worse than it really is—the wish being father to the thought. Anyhow, the prospect is not very inviting. And what have you got to offer, now that your hold on India is so precarious? Congress leaders have a keen eye for business. It is not very obvious to me what they would gain now by co-operation. They probably figure it out in this way. If England loses, we shall be better off by not having co-operated. If she wins, she'll have to give us independence whether we co-operate now or not.'

'But surely Congress can see the tremendous advantage of getting a National Government functioning while the war is

171

still on. If once they and the League began working together, it is quite likely that the communal problem would solve itself.'

'You're not a business man, Lightfoot. This tremendous advantage which you speak of would at best appear problematic to Congress. They would want something more solid. And at the moment what real advantage is there in any offer which England may make? I'm told that Gandhi is just repeating again and again one sentence, "Why take a seat in a sinking ship?" He goes on saying this. That's all. And it's quite enough. You can take it from me it will be decisive.'

'Yes, I suppose you're right. But I wonder what reason they'll find for not playing. So far as I can see, they've been offered about all they've ever asked for.'

'Oh, you needn't bother about that. They'll find a reason. If need be, they can always ask for something fresh, which they've never mentioned before. Really, Lightfoot, you know, you needn't give any more thought to this Cripps mission. Nothing will come of it. Absolutely nothing. Gandhi will reject the offer because he is a pacifist and because he sees no advantage in it. Others will support him because they are thoroughly anti-British and don't want to co-operate on any terms. The would-be co-operators will find themselves in a hopeless minority.'

'And Jinnah and the League will do exactly what Congress does?'

'Precisely. It'll be just the same old game. Negations all round. I know these people. I've known them for years. Cripps is just wasting his time. Nothing will come of it. Absolutely nothing.' And the fat Hindu relapsed into self-satisfied chuckles.

Lightfoot realized that he was right. Yet, with all his knowledge and astuteness, the fat Hindu was not entirely right. The Cripps mission failed and failed for the reasons he had given. But it had unhappy consequences which neither he nor Lightfoot foresaw.

X

COMMUNISTS AND CONGRESS

August 9th, 1942. A steamy, sultry morning. Lightfoot sat in his office at Nanaksar, dripping with perspiration and listening to petitioners. Soon after 10.0 he rang the bell and ordered his car to take him to the Courts. 'But there's one more man to see you,' said his orderly. 'He's just arrived. He says he has most urgent business with you.'

'I bet it isn't urgent. Who is he?'

'He has given his name as Salig Ram. I don't think he's a good man. He's a political man—a communist.'

'Well, I suppose I had better see him. Show him in.'

Salig Ram was a small, thin rat of a man, with sharp, pointed features, a very sallow complexion, and a crafty expression. But he had an attractive smile which considerably made up for his otherwise unprepossessing appearance. He spoke excellent English, with a slightly American accent.

'Good morning, Salig Ram. Very glad to meet you,' said Lightfoot, lying brazenly. 'I've heard about you. Let's see, you belong to this district, have spent several years in Russia, and came out of gaol a few months back.'

'That's right, sir.'

'Tell me, how did you ever manage to get to Russia?'

'My father was quite an ordinary zemindar, sir, owning only a few acres of land. But one year we had a bumper rice crop and prices were good. My father saved a little money and decided to send me to America, as we had heard that money could be made there and one could also get good education. I spent several years in America and Canada, doing odd jobs and at the same time attending classes. I also did some teaching myself, and altogether saved quite a bit of money. But later I lost most of it, and meanwhile my father died. I had a mind to come home and see to my land. But some Indian friends whom I met in America told me that Russia was a wonderful country and that I should be able to do something useful if I went

173

with them and stayed there for a few years. They themselves had already been in Russia and were returning there again. They said that they could fix me up with a passport and visa. So I agreed, and went to Russia along with them. I spent nearly three years there, studying communist principles and doctrine and, later on, learning about the party organization and methods of forming cells for the propagation of communist views. Then, after the outbreak of war, I was allowed to leave Russia and travel to India overland. But as soon as I got over the border, I was arrested by the British authorities and put in gaol; and I remained there till communist leaders were released some months ago.'

'Very interesting. And what did you think of Russia?'

'They've done wonders there, sir. They've made you people quite out of date; and their leaders are very fine men. We communist workers know that Russia is certain to defeat Nazi Germany.'

'I've long been an admirer of Russia and, so far as I can see, we've got a lot to learn from her in India. But they've achieved what they have at an immense cost in human suffering. Wretched though the Indian peasant may be, I should hesitate to inflict on him, even for the sake of some certain future gain, all that the Russian peasant has been through. What do you think about it?'

'We have to push on with our programme, sir, for that is the only way to free the masses. I find the people are quite ready for it and very enthusiastic.'

'You surprise me. I wonder whether they really understand anything whatever about it. And what *is* your programme? How are you going to improve the lot of the cultivator? Collective farming?'

'Yes, certainly, sir.'

'I'm all in favour of it; but unless you're prepared to use the forcible ruthless methods of the Russians, it's going to take ages to establish collective farming on any considerable scale.'

'The masses are already awakening, sir. It won't take as long as you think.'

'The most ambitious co-operative enterprise that we've yet attempted in the villages is the consolidation of holdings. If you had ever seen the months of patient labour that it takes

174

to get a village to agree to consolidation, I don't think you would be so light-heartedly optimistic about collective farming. You don't seem to realize with what tenacity the peasant clings to the particular little bit of land that he has always cultivated. It might have been a different matter a hundred years ago when there still remained some vestiges of the old village joint community. But for practical purposes that has long been swept away. The peasants are now the most determined individualists. They'll need a lot of persuading to pool their land and cultivate it jointly, which is what collective farming requires. And they certainly won't be persuaded by the speechifying of your young communist students, who stick to the big cities, where there are cinemas, and know nothing of rural life. In his heart of hearts the old, greybearded peasant simply laughs at these chaukras.'[1]

'But I find the people very much like the idea of collective farming and are already keenly desiring it.'

'Really? I've never yet come across a village which has so much as heard of it. Tell me, in which village did you find this enthusiasm for collective farming?'

'To tell you the truth, sir, I haven't been about much in this district, so can't at present name any particular village here.'

Lightfoot smiled good-naturedly. 'Well,' he said, 'if ever you find one, just let me know, as I'm very much interested. But I don't believe it will all be quite such plain sailing as you imagine. The peasants are still totally incapable of organizing themselves or throwing up effective leaders. Look at your political peasants at the present time. What are they, most of them, but glorified dacoits,[2] carrying on their old trade under a new political cloak? They call themselves communists, socialists or kisan[3] workers, but really they're just preying upon society, as they always have done—wild, unruly elements, ready to rob and murder anyone, a legacy from India's immemorial past. At best they can only create confusion, and I doubt whether they're even capable of doing that without other forces to help them. In order to achieve any of your aims you'll need a strong political party led by bourgeois intellectuals. And where are you going to find it? Can you name a single one of the established political parties that is seriously interested in

[1] Boys.   [2] Armed robbers.   [3] Peasant.

your programme of socialized industry and collective agriculture? Why, the Muslim League hasn't even got a social and economic policy. It's a purely communal middle-class party, interested in securing posts and power for middle-class Muslims. In so far as it takes any notice of socialism it is wholly opposed to it.'

'What about Congress, sir?'

'Well, what about it? Congress is just an omnium gatherum held together only by dislike of British domination. Once that unifying bond is gone, it will break into a thousand fragments. At the moment social and economic questions are subordinated to the political struggle, and the deep divisions within Congress over these questions are more or less successfully masked. But if you look below the surface, you'll find that Congress, as a whole, has no definite social and economic policy; only a few vague and contradictory yearnings. One can discern at present three main incompatible elements in Congress. First of all there's Gandhi with his archaistic views. He wants to turn back the onrush of modern machine civilization and perpetuate the old, self-sufficing, village-community with its primitive agriculture and simple hand industries. It is in many ways a charming ideal. I myself often feel that what we want to evolve in India is a comparatively simple civilization, based on the village and untainted by the material, urban civilization of the West. But no purely village civilization that I know of has ever advanced much beyond the level of bare subsistence, such as you find in India to-day. If you cut yourself off from modern science and industry you condemn yourself to a narrow, limited, essentially static way of life—the life which has continued in the villages of India with little change or interruption for at least four or five thousand years. I must own that I have an affection for it; and as a matter of fact I believe that in our day this age-old village life will go on as before, indestructible alike by calamity or by progress. But I doubt whether it is the correct ideal; I doubt whether a life of bare subsistence, a sort of idealized poverty, is what we ought to aim at for millions of human beings. "Allow not nature more than nature needs, Man's life is cheap as beast's." In any case it's an impracticable ideal. It does more credit to Gandhi's heart than to his head. You cannot permanently stem the tide of machine civilization.'

COMMUNISTS AND CONGRESS

'Sir, we communist workers don't believe in Gandhi's doctrine of non-violence, hand spinning and poverty. Gandhi is exploited by the bourgeois capitalists. They find him useful because of his influence over the people. They don't really care a fig for his moral and social doctrines; but they consider them harmless and even useful; for they deter the masses from any violent effort to achieve their own liberation.'

'That may be. But however much he may be exploited by capitalists, you must admit that he has a profound feeling for the poor. He himself is sincere in his views, though his capitalist backers may not be. And he and his little group of genuine disciples are an element and, for the time being, an important element in Congress.'

'We don't doubt, sir, that Gandhi is sincere. But his ideas are out of date. They won't survive his death.'

'Well, then, let's leave him and come on to the second main element in Congress, the Hindu bourgeoisie. This is made up of the big industrialists, who finance Congress and exploit it for their own ends, and the petty traders and shopkeepers—the rank and file and real backbone of Congress. None of them have any interest in your socialist programme. Money is their God, and they think they'll make more money with the English out of the way. Those big Hindu capitalists have no sympathy with the masses. They simply want to exploit them, and to have the whole field of exploitation to themselves. And pretty hard and oppressive they'll be, too. Worse than English capitalists, I should say. Not that I hold any particular brief for English capitalism and its system of economic exploitation. One sometimes hears Englishmen saying that they're damned if they see why they should hand over the helpless masses of India to such bloodsuckers as the Indian capitalists. But of course everyone knows that to the people of India even the scorpions of Indian capitalists are better than the whips of foreigners. In any case this English apologia is three parts humbug. If people who talk like this really had the welfare of the Indian masses at heart, they would be doing all they could to back the third group in Congress, which we've not yet mentioned—the socialist wing of Congress. But that's the last thing they would think of doing.'

'Sir, the socialist wing of Congress is the most important of all the groups. With their help we'll be able to rally all the dynamic forces of India—the industrial workers and the awakening masses of the peasantry. Jawaharlal Nehru, the most prominent figure in the socialist group, is certain to succeed Gandhi as the principal national leader.'

'Yes, but he'll never have Gandhi's influence; he'll never be able to dominate and dictate to Congress as Gandhi has done. And he'll never have the same hold over the masses; for he is not, like Gandhi, a faqir and holy man. I should say that he is too intolerant, impatient and doctrinaire to be a really successful popular leader. He may continue to lead the socialist wing of Congress; but I fear that in so far as they retain their socialism they'll become increasingly impotent. They'll go down before the bourgeois, capitalist group. For this group has all the money, and, when it comes to social and economic questions, the backing of the politically conscious classes. You socialists and communists haven't a ghost of a chance against them. You haven't yet got a properly organized party or any real backing in the electorate. Your talk about dynamic forces and awakening masses is, if you'll pardon me for saying so, sheer bunkum. The most you'll be able to rouse the peasants to will be a little misdirected looting. And that will be easily suppressed by even only a moderately competent government. But let us suppose for a moment that your awakened peasantry really got the bit between its teeth and caused considerable disorder. There would at once emerge in full force all those sinister, criminal elements which lurk in the shadows of India. Do you imagine that a few socialist intellectuals and college students would be able to ride the storm and settle the peasants down to collective farming which none of them care about in the least? It's unthinkable. Lenin and the Russian communists spent years planning, plotting and preparing themselves, and then in the end they had to have a disastrous war to help them.'

'But, sir, you're forgetting the industrial workers. We shall be able to form them into a strong party.'

'I'm not forgetting the industrial workers, but at present they're a minute fraction of the population and they've hardly got the semblance of an organization. The trades unions are still in their infancy, and pretty pathetic at that. Take the railway union here. About every six months the secretary decamps

178

with the money, or there's a split and a rival union is formed. Then for a bit we have two unions; then perhaps none; and then there's a general reshuffle. A new set of men come in, the name of the union is changed, fresh notepaper is ordered, a new secretary gets to work; till after a few months he too decamps with the money and we start all over again. But perhaps I oughtn't to say all this to you, for haven't you and some of your pals just started a rival union here in the engineering workshops?'

'The other union had fallen into bad hands, sir. The secretary and president were in the pay of the employers and were cheating the workers.'

'There you are! In the pay of the employers! Can you beat it? And those are your industrial workers, one of your dynamic forces, to which you pin your faith. It's absurd. It is going to take years to build up a sound, honest trades union movement in this country. The capitalists will go on corrupting you with their money and disrupting your organizations, while they get hold of political power and do what they like. And mind you, once the Indian moneyed classes get control, they won't care much about our English liberal ideas to which you've all grown accustomed—a free press, free speech, the rule of law, democracy and all the rest of it. If people like you, Salig Ram, begin squeaking too much, you'll be popped into gaol and probably never be heard of again. You've only to look at the Native States to get an idea of how things will be. Or consider the two big political parties, Congress and the Muslim League. You've seen how mercilessly they crush opposition. Anyone who raises his voice against Gandhi or Jinnah is just broken. They're dictators. Not that I blame them. When people are divided and factious and unaccustomed to give-and-take, dictatorial methods are inevitable. But they show you what to expect when the Congress capitalists get a free rein. You communists, I know, approve such methods, but you'll find yourselves hoist with your own petard.'

'You're prejudiced against us, sir; that's why you think we'll fail and won't be able to organize the peasants and workers. English officers can't be expected to like our ideas.'

'On the contrary I like many of them very much. And at the moment we're officially supposed to like *you* also, because

179

you're supporting the war effort. That, I gather, is why you communists have been let out of gaol.'

'Yes, sir, we're supporting the war effort because we believe that this is now a People's War and that we must help the Soviet Union in its struggle against the Nazi oppressors. That is what we are explaining to the people. As a result of our propaganda they're becoming very eager to join in the war effort.'

'There you go again, Salig Ram, drugging yourself with meaningless phrases and talking complete nonsense. A People's War indeed! What on earth can the illiterate peasants of India understand about a People's War? To the Russian peasant this may be a People's War. At any rate he's fighting for his hearth and home which is something he has done before and can understand. But what do our zemindars know or care about Soviet Russia? You can get a measure of their interest by the amount they contribute when you ask for help for the Soviet Union. Though prices are good and the zemindars at the moment have plenty of money, you only manage to collect three or four rupees from them at your meetings. As for talk about Nazism, Fascism, Totalitarianism and all the other highfalutin stuff you pour forth, it simply has no meaning for them. That's why your meetings are such a flop and your audiences drift away, unless you serve them out some of the usual hot stuff about the wickedness of the Government and the tyranny of the police. I should very much doubt whether as a result of your propaganda a single recruit has joined the army. The best that can be said for it is that it is not so positively mischievous as it used to be.'

'But, sir, recruits are coming in fast. Our propaganda is having a wonderful effect.'

'Recruitment is determined by quite other factors than your propaganda; nor, if you take India as a whole, can you say that recruits are coming in fast. So far, somewhere near two million men have been taken into the forces, including the ancillary services. Out of a population of 400 million this isn't much; and over half a million of these come from a single Province, so you can judge what the rest of India is doing. Recruitment is mainly determined simply by economic factors. No doubt there are a few small areas where the people regard soldiering as a profession. They've been serving in the Indian army for nearly a century, and when opportunity occurs, they join up in large numbers because that's their trade. They're hereditary soldiers, and damned fine soldiers too—well disciplined in peace and brave in war. Magnificent men in their simple way. India should be proud of them. But barring these, your other recruits join the army not to fight Hitler, to help Russia, to defend India, or to protect their homes, but simply to make a livelihood. Most of the hereditary soldiers were all mopped up months ago. If you go round with recruiting officers now, you'll find that we're just getting the dregs of the countryside, outcasts, village menials, landless labourers, who've no stake in the country but want to fill their bellies and earn a pension. In the prosperous parts of the country down in the canal colonies for instance, you simply can't get recruits. The people are too well off. And those folk down there who hope for titles, jagirs[1] or grants of land as a reward for bringing in recruits, have to import them from elsewhere—from other poorer districts. There are regular agents in the business. They purchase potential recruits, say, in this district, for eight or ten rupees a head, rail them down to the colonies and sell them there for forty or fifty rupees. Meanwhile Mr. Amery talks in the House of Commons of two million "volunteers" and you communists prattle about a People's War. Bah! It makes me sick!'

'But, sir, it *is* a People's War, and we find that even the villagers are beginning to understand it. They're prepared for sacrifices. We've been explaining to them the scorched earth policy, and, if the Germans or Japs should come here, they'll be ready for it.'

'Salig Ram, you're an intelligent man. How can you talk such rubbish? The attitude of the rural masses towards war is just the same as it was more than 100 years ago when a wise man said, "They consider defeat and victory as no concern of their own, but merely as the good or bad fortune of their masters." This being so, no responsible person who has the welfare of the people at heart can dream of applying the scorched earth policy in India. You can't ask illiterate peasants to destroy their crops and bring upon themselves untold sufferings for the sake of something to which they are quite indifferent. Their best course,

[1] The right to receive the land revenue of a certain area of land.

181

if the Japs or Germans came, would be to lie low, and hope that the tide of war would sweep over them. It doesn't really matter to them whether Japs, Germans or English rule the country. Their meagre existence will go on much the same, and the less they annoy whoever happens to have the upper hand the better off they'll be. Officers like myself, who are in some sense responsible for the welfare of the people of their district, feel strongly in this matter. People up in the clouds in Simla may babble what they like about scorched earth and rousing India to resistance; but they don't know what they're talking about. They're quite out of touch with India, living in a dreamland of their own. I entirely agree with Gandhi's attitude. He understands your "dumb millions"; instinctively he senses their feelings; and he knows that, in reply to the threat of invasion, to talk of scorched earth is madness. I wouldn't be surprised if this irresponsible talk hadn't influenced him in launching Civil Disobedience. By the way, have you heard that he and the Working Committee were arrested early this morning?'

'Your orderly mentioned it to me as I came in. I hadn't heard the news till then. In the interests of the war effort it was necessary to arrest them.'

'Absolutely necessary. I was getting a little anxious at the delay; but I think action has been taken in time. Nevertheless it's a disaster.'

'Certainly it's very bad to have to shut up all these national leaders. It doesn't look well.'

'Yet I suppose that in a few days' time the Viceroy and Mr. Amery will be getting kudos for their firm handling of the situation. As though anyone in his senses could possibly at this stage have acted otherwise! Not to have arrested Gandhi and co. now would have been criminal folly. On the one hand there'll be these childish encomiums, while on the other hand you, Salig Ram, having told me that Gandhi had to be arrested, will be making speeches and passing resolutions demanding his release. What people you are!'

'Sir, we have to say these things, or no one would care to listen to us.'

'Perhaps that's because you're not worth listening to. But never mind, Salig Ram, *I've* enjoyed listening to you' (Lightfoot omitted to notice that he had done most of the talking) 'and

I'm sorry I can't go on. But I ought to have been in Court at 10.15 and must hurry along. I've already spent too much time gossiping to you. What with Civil Disobedience and these arrests I'll have a good deal to attend to. Now what was it you really came about? Urgent business, so the orderly said.'

'I wanted to request you to withdraw the case against Narain Singh. He's one of our best workers. In his speech at Awan he said absolutely nothing against Government. The case is quite false. He was simply urging the people to help in the war and explaining the communist aims.'

'I've seen the report of his speech. It was full of the most violent anti-Government and anti-British stuff. It was a direct incitement to murder British officers. I myself gave orders for his prosecution.'

'He was quite wrongly reported by the head constable. He could never have departed from the party line and party instructions and made such a speech at this time.'

'From what I know of Narain Singh I should say he is a wild youth who once he begins haranguing a mob doesn't know what he's saying.'

'I can promise you, sir, he was wrongly reported. The head constable just wanted to impress his officers and get a good name.'

'That's most unlikely. The police know perfectly well that Government have recently released communist workers from gaol and aren't at present out to catch them. The head constable couldn't hope to get any special credit for roping in Narain Singh at this time. I see no reason to suppose that he has reported him wrongly. He could have had no motive for so doing.'

'Sir, I can't tell you his motive just at present. I haven't made full inquiries. But I assure you he's innocent. For some reason or other the head constable has falsely entangled him. There are all sorts of enmities which may be at the bottom of it.'

'This is all utterly vague, Salig Ram. You can't expect me to withdraw the case just because Narain Singh happens to be useful to you and you say he's innocent. However, if you can convince me that the head constable had some motive for reporting him wrongly, I'd be prepared to talk to the magistrate concerned and see what he thinks about it. Possibly then something could be done.'

'I've heard that you are a very just officer,' said Salig Ram with adroit flattery. 'You always hear people. I know that if I can convince you he is innocent you'll release him.'

'Well, of course—— But I'll probably need a good bit of convincing. However, you're quite at liberty to try. Now, I must say good-bye to you. I'll look forward to seeing you again and having another talk.'

Lightfoot bustled off to the District Courts with a certain air of fuss and importance. But there really were a good many things to occupy his mind. The arrest of Gandhi was bound to cause a stir in Nanaksar. There would be meetings and violent speeches—possibly worse. A good many arrests would have to be made, and made as unobtrusively as possible. But Lightfoot had splendid Indian police officers under him—loyal, intelligent, well-informed and wise men. He had full faith in them, and he liked and admired them. What rot people talk, he would think to himself, about Indians not being fit to govern themselves. A stock remark of ignorant Englishwomen. How little they know! And what harm they do! They live their lives in India and never discover what pearls of great price it contains —able and honest men, quite ready to take responsibility, but so often—all too often—overlooked, because they won't bow and scrape and flatter. The pearls are few, but they are there and of rare quality.

In the course of the morning Lightfoot learned from the police that there was to be a meeting that evening in Nanaksar, to protest against Gandhi's arrest. The police did not want to disturb it. They would be conspicuous by their absence. Any arrests that might be necessary would be made later at night. Lightfoot went home to tea fully satisfied.

At 6 p.m. he decided to take a walk right through the centre of the city. Most of the shops were closed and the shutters down. But the narrow bazaars were crowded. Groups of young men were standing about, chattering or reading scurrilous vernacular newspapers, while the fat Hindu shopkeepers lounged about on the low wooden platforms which projected in front of their shops into the street. It was stiflingly hot and oppressive. Bathed in perspiration, Lightfoot made his way through the crowds, glancing vaguely at the shuttered shops. The hartal[1] was pretty complete, but there were a few people

[1] Closure of shops and cessation of business as a protest.

184

doing business in a half-hearted manner. He wandered on till he came to the main bazaar and then stopped in front of a largish cloth shop. It appeared to be only partially shut and through the half-open shutters could be seen rolls and rolls of cloth of every shade and variety. A fat, greasy, sour-looking Hindu was lying on the floor right in front by the street, his head and shoulders propped up against one of the walls and his legs sprawled out across the entrance. He was wearing an open white shirt, chewing betel, and reading a newspaper. Drops of perspiration trickled down the sides of his face and over his bulging neck. The Hindu bania at his worst! Lightfoot addressed him. 'I want some stuff for some pyjamas. Would you kindly show me what you've got?' The shopkeeper gave him a disagreeable look and continued reading his newspaper. Lightfoot repeated his question. The shopkeeper heaved himself over on one side, gave a vigorous chew, displaying a tongue and teeth foully discoloured with betel, and grunted, 'The shop is shut.' But Lightfoot was not going to be put off by these offensive manners. He sat down next to the Hindu on the low wooden platform and peered through the half-open shutter into the interior. 'It seems to be more or less open,' he said, 'I should be much obliged if you would kindly let me select some material for pyjamas.' The Hindu turned away rudely. 'The shop is shut,' he repeated. But Lightfoot persevered. He was determined that this deliberately insulting Congress-wala should sell him some material, even though Gandhi had just been arrested. 'I really don't want to inconvenience you,' he said 'but I can't often find time to come out all this way to the city, so I should be very much obliged, now that I've got here, if you would kindly just attend to me. It will only take two or three minutes.' The Hindu continued to read his paper. But meanwhile a small boy of about eleven, with a bright eager face, had come out from the interior of the shop and was standing looking at Lightfoot. 'Are you the Deputy Commissioner?' he inquired nervously. Lightfoot nodded his head. 'Uncle, Uncle!' cried the little boy in a state of great excitement, 'it's Lightfoot Sahib, the Deputy Commissioner! Quick, bring a chair for him.' Then turning to Lightfoot, 'Sir, my uncle didn't know who it was. He didn't recognize you. Kindly excuse him, sir. May I fetch you some water or some lemonade?' The fat Hindu scrambled to his feet, reached for a coat that was hanging on a peg, mopped his face and brow, and began straightening himself out and trying to look respectable. 'Please excuse me, sir,' he said, 'I never thought it was the Deputy Commissioner.' He waddled off heavily on his heels into the inside of the shop and brought out a chair. He had known all along quite well who it was, and his rude, disobliging manner had been deliberate. But his little nephew's spontaneous enthusiasm and eager hospitality had shamed him and at the same time awakened in him all the Hindu's instinctive reverence for authority. It was proper, it was wise to be respectful to officers of Government. Otherwise they might put the police on to you. He was now all smiles and obsequiousness. In spite of Lightfoot's protests, he sent off the small boy with a glass to fetch some iced lemonade, and himself bustled about his shop, pulling out rolls and rolls of cloth for Lightfoot's inspection. 'No trouble at all, absolutely no trouble,' he kept on saying in reply to Lightfoot's apologies. 'It's a pleasure. It was my good fortune that brought your Honour to this humble shop.'

The lemonade, or what passed for it, was brought—a highly sweetened drink of brilliant green. Lightfoot sat in the chair sipping it and selected some stuff for his pyjamas. By this time a knot of idle bystanders had collected, nearly all of them Hindu shopkeepers or young Hindu shop assistants. Several were wearing Gandhi caps. They stared at Lightfoot as though he were some interesting exhibit in a zoo, and nudged each other and giggled. Presently a short, stout Hindu, wearing khaddar and a Gandhi cap and carrying an umbrella, came along the bazaar, and with an air of some authority pushed his way to the front of the cluster of idlers so that he was standing right opposite Lightfoot. He had a keen, intelligent face and wore large, round, steel-rimmed glasses. Lightfoot recognized him at once as Ram Saran Das, a prominent local Congress leader.

'Well, Lalaji,[1] are you taking your umbrella for a little evening walk?' he inquired.

'I'm on my way to the meeting to protest against the arrest of Gandhi and our other leaders.'

[1] A polite form of address applied to Khatris and other Hindu castes.

186

'I hope you won't say anything too violent. You surely can't really be angry at Government's action. With the Japanese on the borders of India how could people be left at large who have openly announced their intention of helping the enemy?'

'We were dragged into this war against our will. We were not consulted.'

'True, you weren't consulted. But was it against your will? Before the war began most of the Congress leaders were girding at England for not standing up to the Nazis. Now that we're fighting, why should they change their tune? Besides, their own recent conduct and utterances show that they are not really opposed to the war. At the time of the Cripps mission they negotiated on the assumption that India had to defend herself against Japan, and they talked about rousing India to resistance.'

'India can't resist while she is enslaved. Why don't you give us our freedom? Then we would fight.'

'Well, we've already promised you complete independence after the war. It has been clearly stated that the Cripps offer still holds.'

'You're always making us promises and holding out hopes. But you always disappoint us. We don't trust you. We don't believe in the Cripps offer. After so many bitter experiences we can't have faith in you.' Ram Saran Das was working himself up into a temper. But he paused and calmed down a little. Then with a rather cold, malignant look he said, 'Why does everybody hate you English?'

Lightfoot was a little taken aback. 'To tell you the truth, I didn't know they did,' he replied.

'Well, we Indians hate you, the Irish hate you, the Germans and French hate you.'

'I'm very sorry to hear that *you* hate us. I don't think you all do. I even doubt whether Gandhi does, though he may want to be rid of us. As for the Irish, they have long memories. They can't forget what happened in Cromwell's time, and even earlier. The Germans perhaps dislike us because we've long been the principal obstacle to their ambitions. The French, perhaps, because they feel they've let us down. And it may be that everyone has long been a little envious of us. That might account for a good deal.'

187

'No,' said Ram Saran Das emphatically, 'there must be something about you which makes everyone dislike you. I don't know what it is, but there must be something.'

'Well, I'm afraid I can't tell you what it is. Possibly it's because we seem rather superior and aloof. But, having answered your question to the best of my ability, perhaps I might ask you one. Why has Gandhi launched this Civil Disobedience movement?'

'He had to do it.'

'But what has happened in the last few months to compel him to take this step? And what good can come of it? It can't possibly succeed. It will be easily crushed. Now that a war's on, Government is armed with such tremendous powers.'

'We have to fight for our freedom. The National struggle must go on.'

'Yes, but I should have thought it was better to fight when there was more chance of success and when you might hope to win the sympathy of the outside world. As it is, you'll lose it.'

'We have to win freedom by our own efforts and not rely on the sympathy of other people. Gandhi has given the call and we Congressmen must obey it.'

'I hope that your loyalty to Gandhi won't make you go to too great lengths.'

'I must play my part. When others are going to gaol and making sacrifices for the country, I cannot hang back. I must certainly go to gaol with them.'

'I am sorry to hear it. Well, you haven't exactly answered my question, but perhaps I couldn't expect that. And now, I suppose, you ought to be going on to your meeting, taking all these people with you, including our friend here who has so kindly sold me some cloth and given me a glass of lemonade.'

The fat shopkeeper folded his hands, smirked obsequiously, and made deprecating noises. 'No, no, your Honour', he said. 'I am quite a harmless person, absolutely loyal and obedient to the benign British Government. I've never been to any political meeting. I've never said or done anything against Government and never shall do so.'

A general titter greeted this obviously false speech. The shopkeeper looked a bit sheepish, but, having embarked on the policy of propitiating Lightfoot he decided he had better go through with it. 'When your Honour is controlling everything here so smoothly,' he said, 'why should I say anything against Government? These people are making fun of me without any reason. I am absolutely obedient to your Honour and have full confidence in your Honour's justice.'

Lightfoot rose to go. 'All right, that's quite all right, Lala-ji,' he said. 'It was very kind of you to attend to me and give me some lemonade. I'm much obliged to you. Your little nephew was also very kind. Thank you both very much.' The crowd made way for him to go. Ram Saran Das, grasping tightly his umbrella, looked a little disappointed. The Deputy Commissioner was going off without taking any further notice of him. 'Good-bye,' he said a little awkwardly.

'Oh, good-bye, Ram Saran Das,' said Lightfoot. 'I hope the meeting's a success and that you'll remain strictly non-violent.' He walked away homewards, while Ram Saran Das, short, stout, and determined marched off with his umbrella, at the head of a band of followers, to his meeting. His desire to make sacrifices and to go to gaol was about to be gratified. Lightfoot had already given orders that he should be arrested that night.

Lightfoot was gloomy and dispirited. He sat alone in his drawing-room after dinner, puzzling over the question he had put to Ram Saran Das. Why had Gandhi started Civil Disobedience, announced that it was 'open rebellion', that it would be the last struggle of his life, and exhorted his followers 'to do or die'? Many of the Congress leaders, many of the rank and file thought it foolish and were unmistakably opposed to it. Like Ram Saran Das, they would join the movement out of loyalty, but not from any conviction. And after needless bloodshed and embitterment of feelings it would be suppressed. The whole thing seemed pointless and inexplicable. Ever since the outbreak of war Gandhi had said that he didn't want to embarrass the British; and for three years he had kept his word. The Civil Disobedience which he had started in October 1940 had been entirely innocuous, and designedly so. A few individuals had wandered about shouting pacifist slogans, but nobody took much notice of them, and the effect on the war effort was precisely nil. Again and again he had expressed his sympathy for Britain, and even his admiration for the British people in the dark days of 1940. What had happened in the last few months to make him change his mind? Could it be that he felt he had lost prestige in the country by the decisive part he had played in securing the rejection of the Cripps offer, and hoped to rehabilitate himself by an appeal to sentiment and emotion? Yet even if this motive had in fact influenced him, he must have justified his conduct to himself on some other ground. For Gandhi, whatever one might sometimes think of his political manœuvres, had a strong moral sense. He could hardly admit to himself that he was acting from a purely self-regarding and quite unethical motive. But what other motive could there be? Perhaps the Japanese menace had something to do with it. There was Jawaharlal's evidence that he believed the Japanese were going to win. Had he been alarmed by the talk of rousing India to resistance? Was he determined that India should in no circumstances become a battleground, that his countrymen should be spared the miseries of war, and did he hope to ensure this by paralysing Government so that resistance would be impossible? This would be in accordance with his pacifist principles, with his feeling for the illiterate masses, who would be suffering in a cause they couldn't understand, and, perhaps, with the natural Hindu instinct to bow before superior force? Yet, Lightfoot thought to himself, what an extraordinary miscalculation! It discounted altogether the possibility of beating off a Japanese attack before they could land or otherwise gain a foothold in India. Moreover, the gravest Japanese menace had passed. The worst moment had been in the spring, a few weeks after the fall of Singapore. The general position and prospects were decidedly better now.

Lightfoot couldn't make it out. He turned on the wireless for news. Reports were obscure, but already there seemed to have been trouble in Bombay. All the hooligan element in India was certain to make the most of the opportunity. There would be precious little non-violence. He went into his office and worked away at his files for a couple of hours.

But his mind kept running on the same topic. So at last the break had come—the decisive break, avoided during three years of war, but now, perhaps, irreparable. And Congress appeared to have put themselves so clearly in the wrong. What a golden opportunity for all those Englishmen in India who

190

had been brought up to think of Congress as the 'enemy' and had spent their lives fighting Congress and Congress movements! Senior officials, from Governors downwards, would be swept away by irrational emotion and do things which later, in a cool hour, they would see to be unwise and indefensible. All their accumulated resentment would now have full rein. They would inflame themselves and one another with war-time patriotism, and brand the 'enemy' with stock terms of abuse—rebels, Quislings, fifth columnists. Treat them rough. That would be the motto. And to it all would be added a subconscious touch of fear—the fear that had more than once overtaken Englishmen in India, finding themselves a handful of foreigners amid a hostile population. The English, normally so phlegmatic, tolerant and humane, under the influence of an angry fear would repeat the story of 1857 and 1919. There would be hooligan atrocities which would call down fearful and sometimes misdirected vengeance. Government officers, stung to fury by the murder of their colleagues, would themselves acquire something of the hooligan mentality and glory in a violence miscalled firmness. And all would recoil on their own heads, like a veritable boomerang. For the 'enemy', despite his follies, had the sympathy of Hindu India. Eventually the Congress-walas must again come to the front as the active leaders of the country. These would be the men who would have influence in the India of to-morrow, when England would want her friendship and co-operation, as a willing, voluntary partner in the Commonwealth. Did not wisdom require that they should be shut up quietly, with the minimum of harshness. and without taunts, strong language and abuse?

Lightfoot wiped the perspiration from his face. The night was unbearably hot and stifling. There was not a breath of air. He went into the drawing-room and sat down at his piano. Handel! Handel, the best antidote to all the madness of the world. Handel, whose music had soothed the madness of poor old George III. He began to play and to sing; in a few moments he was in another world, on another plane of existence, his mind a blank, his spirit untroubled. His voice floated out through the open windows into the still, steamy night, rising above the ceaseless croaking of the frogs. At the gate the police sentry stirred and shifted his rifle. At the back of the house his servant,

191

lying in the open on his string bed, turned over half asleep. The Sahib is singing, the Sahib is happy, he thought to himself. And still far into the night, Lightfoot went on singing, 'Piangero, piangero la sorte mia'. And still the frogs croaked.

XI

CONCLUSION

'We cannot expect to hold India for ever. Let us so conduct ourselves . . . as, when the connection ceases, it may do so not with convulsions but with mutual esteem and affection.'

HENRY LAWRENCE

' I am not one of those who think that we have built a mere fragile plank between the East and the West which the roaring tides of Asia will presently sweep away. . . . To me the message is carved in granite, it is hewn out of the rock of doom—that our work is righteous and that it shall endure.'

LORD CURZON

A writer on India is expected not merely to state problems but to solve them. But solutions to practical problems are not to be found ready-made like answers to crossword puzzles. What can be done and what ought to be done varies with the daily flux of events. While broad aims may be constant the appropriate means are inconstant.

In the preceding pages of this book some of the major Indian problems have been touched on. In the course of the discussion, criticism of mistakes has sometimes by implication suggested certain general principles of policy. Here and there, too, facts and tendencies have been cursorily noted as possible sources of danger or possible means of salvation. This is the nearest one can get to meeting the reader's desire for ready-made solutions. It may, however, be convenient to bring together in a more compact form some of these scattered hints and implications.

Greenlane was struck by India's poverty. Great poverty is a feature of nearly all oriental countries. It is not peculiar to India. But to lessen it is certainly for India one of the most urgent tasks. The prospects of doing so are perhaps brighter than they have been for some time. India is making money out of the war. The debtor-creditor relation between her and England, which Lightfoot deplored and which has been the source of so much mistrust, has been completely reversed. England has been

193

generous in the extent to which she has undertaken to shoulder the cost of India's defence. She has already, in consequence of this generosity, ceased to be India's creditor and become her debtor; and the debt is steadily piling up. The result will be that by the end of the war India will be owed at least £1,000,000,000. The war has also given a fillip to India's industries and increased the number of her skilled workmen. There seems, therefore, to be an opportunity, such as there has never been before, for a reconstruction of India's economic life and a raising of the whole standard of living. A five- or ten-year plan for industrial and agricultural development, based on a rapid extension of hydro-electric and irrigation schemes, appears to be the necessary foundation of material progress. Agreement between the major Provinces and States of India on the outlines of such a plan is, for the Indian masses, as important as the settlement of the communal problem, and may not be any less difficult.

Even if such agreement were reached, it must be recognized that the industrial development of India might easily prove a doubtful blessing to the mass of the people. Indian capitalists are certainly not more enlightened, more public-spirited, more scrupulous, and more mindful of the rights and interests of others than their prototypes in Europe. Their influence in India's strongest political party, Congress, is already great; and the forces which might be ranged against them are at present politically unorganized and helpless. Lightfoot's disparagement of these 'progressive forces' was well justified. Ruthless exploitation of the weak by the strong is still the rule in India. The capitalist class will follow that rule.

Agricultural development, if it is effectively to raise the general standard of living, involves the almost superhuman task of reorganizing the whole of village life. On the purely material side electricity is fundamental. For it solves the two major problems of fuel and water. But more difficult and far-reaching changes of method and outlook are also required. The old idea of the village 'community' must replace the individualism fostered by English rule and English conceptions of property. The aim should be to transform faction-ridden villages of struggling tenants or peasant proprietors into 'co-operative societies' employing modern methods of agricul-

194

ture and running small-scale village industries ancillary to agriculture. The experience of Soviet Russia, where a not dissimilar problem is being tackled, should be invaluable. And, as Lightfoot pointed out, there is excellent opportunity in India for small-scale experiment in places where new irrigation schemes enable virgin soil to be brought under the plough. A comparatively few instances of successful 'co-operative villages' might possibly make the idea catch on. Simple people quickly recognize a good thing when they see it.

In Russia reform of village life has been accompanied by a great spread of education. The illiteracy of the villagers of India was frequently mentioned by Greenlane and Lightfoot. But neither of them showed any particular concern about it; for they realized that illiteracy is natural and proper to the life of bare subsistence which most of the people are living. Until the economic conditions of their life are changed, education exceeds both their means and their needs. Even if it were possible to teach them all to read and write, a large proportion would quickly relapse into illiteracy, because illiteracy suits the simplicity of their present existence. If once the character of that existence is radically changed, literacy will not only be desired and, therefore, retained when once acquired, but will also through increase of wealth become possible. At present India has not the resources, human or material, to provide elementary education for her whole population. The cost would far exceed existing revenues; and trained teachers (especially women teachers) could not be made available. While therefore a new and more comprehensive system of education must ultimately form part of the reorganization of village life, it is not the first part. More material foundations must first be laid.

A reorganization of village life is intimately connected with what appears to be the true line of political development in India. Parliamentary democracy is far removed from the present needs and wishes of the people. Like the English legal system when applied to India, it has to be perverted in order to function at all. It corrupts and is itself corrupted. Those who believe in democratic liberty, instead of hoping to conjure it all at once out of nothing, should try to plant the seeds of it in soil where they may be capable of natural growth. Allah Dad rightly observed that the mass of the people should be made to

CONCLUSION

attend 'to their own quite petty affairs in their villages'. Democratic institutions should develop gradually out of village Councils managing the common concerns of co-operative village communities. For many years these Councils would have to be subject to a good deal of bureaucratic control both as regards their actions and their personnel (as village panchayats are at present), and the part which they could play, directly or indirectly, in the larger affairs of a District or Province would be small. But the aim should be to link them, by a system of indirect election, first with District Councils and then with Provincial Councils. Broadly speaking, membership of a community which has shown its capacity for corporate action would be the necessary qualification for any wider political activity. Here again Russian experiments with 'Soviet Democracy' may be a valuable guide.

But in British India there is not a clear field. The ground is already encumbered with inferior replicas of unsuitable English institutions; and there is no obvious method by which this useless lumber can be quietly disposed of. In the immediate future we must look elsewhere for the possibility of sound development. We must look to the Native States. Here, for the most part, it is still practicable, without much preliminary clearing of the ground, to lay the foundations of democratic institutions, which will fit the life and conditions of the people of India. And here, therefore, in the backward obsolete States, the objects of so much misplaced scorn, there perhaps lies the secret of India's future and her best hopes.

The States, besides being in the main free from exotic political forms, give expression to the deep-seated Indian respect for authority and for hereditary right. A hereditary monarchy is a most valuable political institution and is not incompatible with a gradual change-over from an authoritarian to a democratic form of government. It makes for continuity and stability; it can produce unity amid diversity. India is fortunate in still possessing this institution and still retaining her veneration for it. In course of time she may find it wise to extend its scope and, in the Provinces of British India, to transfer the traditional respect for an all-powerful but fleeting English Governor to an Indian Governor, less powerful, but less transient.

CONCLUSION

But in all these matters Englishmen are not likely to have much voice. Whether India elects to remain a willing partner in the British Commonwealth or whether she turns away in anger, there will be little room left for Englishmen as administrators or as political advisers. Technical and scientific experts, specialists of all kinds, will be needed in plenty. But it is improbable that India will desire or require any more non-specialist officers such as abound in the Indian Civil Service and Indian Police. Even those who are already there, if they are without faith in or affection for the people of India—and there are many such—would be best removed. For they will do no good to England or to India.

Is it still permissible to hope that the imminent change in the relations between the two countries will take place 'not with convulsions but with mutual esteem and affection'? In considering this question, Englishmen must recognize an unpleasant fact. Indians have lost faith in us. We are no longer trusted. Even the promise of complete independence, at the end of the war, first made on behalf of the British Government by Sir Stafford Cripps and since reaffirmed, is viewed with suspicion. Indians do not believe that we really mean it. And do we?

We are not trusted because we seem untrustworthy. And we seem untrustworthy because, as Lightfoot remarked, we are, and long have been, in two minds. For more than a generation we have been proclaiming that full self-government for India is our goal. But instead of ourselves leading the way to it we have been pushed reluctantly towards it. We have appeared in India to be fighting an obstinate rearguard action, stubbornly defending each position before withdrawing to the next. The reasons for the inconsistency between our words and actions have been twofold. To withdraw from India, where for a century and a half we have been dominant, is painful to our pride and may be damaging to our pocket. It is not easy to give up power. Our reluctance to do so has been natural. Added to this, there has been a genuine and well-founded belief, expecially among Englishmen with Indian experience, that we were setting India on quite a wrong path. We proposed to give her self-government in the form of parliamentary democracy of the Westminster pattern. Anyone acquainted with India, however much he might sympathize with her aspirations, could not help

197

doubting whether self-government in this form would be attainable within a century—if indeed ever. It is not that Indians are congenitally incapable of governing themselves—any such proposition is ridiculous—but merely that they cannot govern themselves in the particular way which we had proposed. For it is not consonant with India's past history or present stage of social development.

In these circumstances it was inevitable that we should falter, uncertain of our aim. We ceased to lead, because we had lost faith in our avowed intentions. The first essential now is that we should regain a sense of definite purpose. Without it we cannot regain India's confidence; and without India's confidence we can do nothing—we cannot help her to resolve her own internal difficulties, still less persuade her to co-operate as a free and willing partner in the Commonwealth.

What then is our purpose? Do we mean to make India independent as soon as possible? Or do we mean to hang on as long as posssible?

Many people can still be heard saying, 'Indians can't do without us. They'll never agree among themselves.' Such people plainly believe, and perhaps even hope, that the pledge of independence at the end of the war will not be fulfilled. No doubt there is much that could be said for a diehard policy—for retracing our steps and reverting to the old paternal rule which India both understood and liked. Perhaps India would be happier. Certainly many Indians would welcome it, if only because the future would seem more certain. But it is essentially a sterile policy. It affords no scope for change and growth. And it is not now a practicable policy. Quite apart from Indian opposition, neither English public opinion nor the public opinion of the world could now be reconciled to it. It must be rule out and banished altogether from the mind. There must be no nostalgic harking back to a vanished past. It will only confirm Indian distrust.

The only possible course now is for us to honour our pledge. For better or for worse we have to proceed 'immediately upon the cessation of hostilities' to put India in charge of her own destiny. If this were all, it might seem simple enough. But it is not all. Whether Indians and the rest of the world see it or not, we cannot suddenly disclaim further responsibility and, as Lightfoot put it, abdicate in favour of Chance or Chaos. India contains too large a portion of the human race to be allowed to drift into anarchy. In entrusting India with her own destiny we must see to it that her ordered life will not at the very outset break down. And because this appears so difficult, there is a danger that we shall flinch from the task, lose sight of our aim, and so continue to be distrusted.

To regain India's confidence then we must resolve to hold fast to our purpose, however difficult its fulfilment may seem. We must no longer falter and be in two minds. We must also in other ways try to put our relations with India on a sounder footing. Instead of harping on the communal problem and reproving India for her divisions, we should consider what change in our own attitude might be helpful.

The Civil Disobedience movement of 1942 has left a legacy of bitter memories. Details of the excesses—of which neither side has been guiltless—have been suppressed. It is not necessary to supply them here. But it is necessary to realize that excesses took place. Nor is it merely Congress partisans who resent what was said and done in the excitement of the moment.

Neither side will easily forget and forgive. And Englishmen are in a particularly difficult position; for they owe a debt, which they cannot forget, to those elements in India which have unfalteringly stood by them throughout the war. Nevertheless, Englishmen will perhaps do well to remember just who the men are who have gone to gaol in India. Whatever may be thought of them, they are, and are likely to remain, national leaders, and only a few years ago they formed the Governments of seven of India's Provinces. A small number of them, no doubt, are bitterly anti-British. To gratify their hatred they would gladly intrigue with Britain's enemies. But many of them are in gaol simply out of loyalty to Congress. Like Mr. Rajagopalachari they did not approve of the Civil Disobedience movement, but, unlike him, they had not the courage to break with the party. India is not likely to regard them as fifth columnists; and if we so regard them our relations with India will not be on a sound footing.

It may be said that a clear conception of our purpose and a change of attitude towards the nationalist leaders will do nothing to remove the real obstacle to Indian self-government, viz. the Hindu-Muslim quarrel. It is true that they will not solve the communal problem, but they may facilitate its solution. Once we have firmly made up our own minds and also made it unmistakably clear to others that India is to be independent, Congress and the League will at last be forced to attempt to reach agreement. So far they have not even seriously tried, because the pressure of compulsion has been absent. Congress would not deny this. For they have repeatedly claimed that a settlement with Britain must precede a communal settlement. We have said that it must be the other way round. This, rather than the communal conflict itself, was the real cause of the deadlock during the first three years of the war.

Might it not now be a good plan to take Congress at their word and concentrate our attention, not on the communal problem, but on those many questions which must form the subject of an agreement or treaty between a self-governing India and England? This would be evidence of the sincerity of our intentions, and a discussion of general principles could take place without prejudging the question of partition; for they would apply equally whether there is a single Indian Federation or more than one. The final settlement of some of these questions, e.g. defence and economic development, would be found to involve not merely England, but other members of the Commonwealth and other countries. As has already been suggested,[1] in the effort to reach agreement with these other countries the specifically Hindu-Muslim conflict might tend to disappear. In any case, once such discussions were initiated, political leaders would at last realize that we meant business. They would see that the settlement of their own differences could no longer be shelved. And our suggestions (if any) for their settlement would carry more weight.

This is only a suggested approach to the problem. As regards possible settlements, there are two broad alternatives, each with several variants: (a) Partition, (b) an arrangement for the sharing of power between Hindus and Muslims at the Centre, and possibly in the Provinces also. For the present we should keep an open mind, prepared to implement whichever alternative and whatever variant Indians may themselves agree upon. Only if they fail to agree need we commit ourselves to any

[1] Page 117.

particular plan. In such an event our judgment of what plan is best and fairest would have to be influenced not only by Indian opinion, but also by the opinion of leading nations of the world. For if Indians cannot themselves reach a settlement of their differences, we shall need the moral and perhaps the material support of the outside world in imposing a settlement.

It is probable that a settlement which seemed to us and to the world the best and fairest possible in the circumstances would in practice be accepted by the major elements in India's national life. If it were not, we should be compelled to do the very thing which in August 1940[1] we said we could not do, viz. coerce the dissentient elements into submission. To have to do so would be deplorable; and its ultimate consequences are hardly likely to be satisfactory. But of a choice of evils such a course may be the least bad; and the actual difficulties should not be overestimated. It seems likely that for some years after the war military bases and considerable armed forces (some of them, no doubt, Indian) would have to be maintained in India under the general supervision of Great Britain or the United Nations as part of the defence of Southern Asia. It is also reasonably certain that any constitutional plan which we propounded for a fully self-governing India,[2] even if rejected by certain important elements, would receive a considerable measure of Indian support. There would be no lack of persons to work the Constitution and run the Government. In these circumstances, if it were known that in the last resort these persons had the backing of the United Nations, the dissentient elements, though they might cause some temporary disorder, could not effectively challenge them. For they would not be able to organize the requisite force. And a system of government once established might tend more and more to command general acceptance.

An independent India, whatever its form and however it comes into being, will inevitably pass into the orbit of some great power. For India cannot at present stand alone. Partner-

[1] In the statement issued by the Governor-General with the authority of His Majesty's Government on 8th August 1940—known as the 'August Offer'.

[2] There would, of course, be more than one if Partition was found to be the best plan.

201

ship with some stronger organization will for some years be essential. The choice will probably lie between Great Britain, Russia and China—if China establishes herself as a great power.

Broadly speaking—and this is only the roughest generalization—Hindu India feels attracted to China, Muslim India to Great Britain, and intellectuals of all classes and communities to Russia. There is no certainty what the choice will be. Natural evolution points to the continuance, in a changed form, of the partnership with Britain. If India remains a member of the British Commonwealth, her safety, while she transforms herself from a backward oriental country into a modern State, can be most easily and cheaply secured. In any programme of economic development British technical skill and experience and the products of Britain's heavy industries will be valuable to India. And, owing to the decline of Britain's financial power, the assistance of British capital will be obtainable on terms which will not mean its dominance. The existing ties with Great Britain, political, economic, linguistic, cultural, and sentimental, which have been formed during an association of over 150 years, cannot be severed in a day. They ought to be decisive in keeping India within the orbit of the Commonwealth.

But passions and prejudices may distort natural evolution and even override calculations of self-interest. For more than a generation some of the best elements in India have been estranged. They have spent their lives fighting the British, and they cannot now easily conceive of them as friends instead of foes. They may desire to sever all ties with Britain as fast as possible; and they may be strong enough to make their views prevail and to bring about a separation harmful to both countries and also to the world.

At best one can still hope that this will not be the case. The hope is not great; rational calculation of probabilities affords no ground for optimism. But it is true that many, even of those who are most bitter and critical, are so steeped in Britain's thought and culture that they can never feel wholly alien from her. Undying hatred is still confined to a few. The world hears the angry invective of politicians. It forgets the numberless unrecorded friendships between Englishmen and Indians; it forgets that over the length and breadth of India English and Indian officials are working side by side, often in remote and

CONCLUSION

lonely stations; it forgets the long and happy record of comradeship between Englishmen and Indians in the Indian army —a record creditable to both nations which only prejudice will deride. Anyone who has had personal experience of these ties of emotion and sentiment will believe that they have not all been casual and purposeless, but are really part of something larger, significant, and destined to endure. But this belief has little rational foundation. It is a faith, which may be merely wishful thinking.

NOTE ON THE BRITISH SYSTEM OF ADMINISTRATION IN INDIA

The administrative unit is the district. The average district is considerably larger in area than an English county. Its population may be taken to be 1,000,000, but there are considerable variations.

The executive head of a district is variously known as the District Magistrate, the Collector, or the Deputy Commissioner. He is also sometimes loosely referred to as the District Officer.

As District Magistrate he is head of the magistracy, has a large measure of control over the police, and is responsible for law and order. As Collector he is head of the revenue staff, and responsible for the collection of land revenue and the maintenance of land records. As Deputy Commissioner he has a large number of miscellaneous administrative functions, e.g. he controls the working of local bodies (which are very largely responsible for education, medical relief, and public health), and is the channel of communication between them and the Provincial Government; he supervises the work of the Treasury; issues licences for motor vehicles, cinematographs, etc.

To assist him he has a number of magistrates with varying powers. In large districts a senior magistrate is sometimes posted out to some outlying region as Sub-Divisional Magistrate with somewhat enhanced powers. Usually one of them specializes in revenue work. Another is in charge of the Treasury.

For revenue purposes a district is divided into three or more tahsils, each under a tahsildar who has an assistant known as the naib-tahsildar. There is a sub-treasury in each tahsil into which the land revenue is paid by the headmen of the villages. Though primarily a revenue officer, the tahsildar has limited magisterial powers, and, like the Deputy Commissioner, combines the functions of magistrate, revenue collector and general factotum.

In most Provinces of India groups of five or six districts are formed into Divisions, each under a Commissioner. This arrangement is a survival from bygone days when communication with the headquarters of a Provincial Government was difficult. It makes the administration unnecessarily cumbersome.

The general schemes can be seen at a glance from the table below.

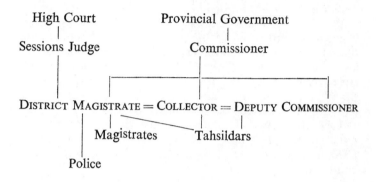

NOTE ON RECENT CONSTITUTIONAL
DEVELOPMENTS IN INDIA

1909 *The Morley-Minto Reforms*

There had for many years existed both a Central Legislative Council and Provincial Legislative Councils consisting of both official and non-official members; but all of them were nominated and not elected. By the Morley-Minto Reforms the principle of election was recognized, and in the Provincial Councils, though there was still a large 'official bloc', the non-officials (some of them elected) became a majority.

These Legislative Councils had the right to advise and criticize, but they had no effective control over the acts of the Executive Governments which continued to consist almost entirely of officials.

1919 *The Montagu-Chelmsford Reforms*

The Provincial Legislative Councils were enlarged, elected on a wider franchise, their powers increased, and the 'official bloc' reduced. Executive work was divided into two classes: (i) Reserved subjects, e.g. Law and Order and Finance; (ii) Transferred subjects, e.g. Public Health, Education, Local Government.

Reserved subjects continued to be managed by the Governor of the Province with the help of Councillors not responsible to the Legislature.

Transferred subjects were entrusted to 'responsible' Ministers. The Governor of a Province was expected to accept the advice of the Ministers on transferred subjects, but was not bound to do so.

At the Centre two Chambers (the Council of State and the Legislative Assembly) replaced the previous Legislative Council. In both of them, the 'official' and 'nominated' members were outnumbered by the elected members, but the Governor-General was given the power of 'certifying' any legislation which he considered necessary and which the Legislature would not pass. The Governor-General's Executive Council remained virtually unchanged—responsible not to the Legislature but to the Secretary of State. In practice, however, more Indians were appointed to it than previously (three out of seven in place of one out of seven). *This scheme of Government at the Centre remains substantially the same to-day.*

The reforms included provision for review of the position after ten years. Hence the appointment of the Simon Commission.

1930 Report of the Simon Commission.

1930 Round Table Conference (First Session).

1931 Round Table Conference (Second Session, attended by Gandhi).

1932 Round Table Conference (Third Session).

1935 *The Government of India Act*

This Act provided a new constitution for India. The sections dealing with the Provinces came into force on 1–4–1937 and are still in force. The sections dealing with the Centre—the federal portions of the Act—have never come into force.

(i) The Provinces were granted practically full self-government, i.e. government by Ministers responsible to an elected legislature. The Governors were to become 'constitutional' Governors acting on the advice of their Ministers, unless in the discharge of their 'special responsibilities' they felt it necessary to act otherwise. These 'special responsibilities' included (a) The prevention of any grave menace to the peace and tranquillity of the Province; (b) The safeguarding of the legitimate interests of minorities; (c) The protection of the rights of Civil Servants; (d) The protection of the rights of the States and their Rulers.

The powers reserved to the Governors for the discharge of their special responsibilities were known as the 'safeguards'. In practice they have been very little used.

In the event of a breakdown of the constitutional machinery, the Governors were empowered themselves to assume control of government. This had to be done in the seven Congress Provinces when in 1939, just after the outbreak of war, the Congress ministries resigned and no other ministries commanding the confidence of the legislatures could be formed.

The Provincial Governments deal with most matters which touch the life of the ordinary man, e.g. Civil and Criminal Justice, Police, Education, Public Health, Land Revenue.

(ii) The Act contemplated the creation of a Federation of India in which both British Indian Provinces and Indian States would participate. Broadly speaking 'Dyarchy', which was now being abolished in the Provinces, was to be reproduced in the Federal Government at the Centre. 'Foreign Affairs' and 'Defence' were to be 'reserved' subjects. Other central subjects were to be 'transferred' to Ministers responsible to the Legislature, subject to certain 'safeguards'.

As this part of the Act has never been brought into force, the system introduced by the Montagu-Chelmsford Reforms continues to operate at the Centre with slight modifications.

DATES MARKING THE RISE AND FALL OF THE MOGUL EMPIRE AND THE ESTABLISHMENT OF BRITISH DOMINION IN INDIA

1525 Babur invades India.

1556–1605 Akbar, grandson of Babur, establishes the Mogul Empire based on religious toleration.

1599 Foundation of the East India Company.

1658–1707 Reign of Aurangzeb, the last effective Mogul Emperor. But his bigotry undermines the empire.

1707 Beginning of the Mogul Empire's rapid decline.

1757 Battle of Plassey. The East India Company becomes master of Bengal.

1798–1805 Lord Wellesley Governor-General. Defeat of Tipu Sultan of Mysore and of the Marathas. The Company is firmly established as the strongest power in India.

1817–19 Final defeat of the Maratha Chiefs. The Company assumes its obligations as the dominant Power in India.

1805–35 Pacification of India. Malcolm, Munro, Metcalfe, Elphinstone.

1843 Conquest of Sind.

1845–9 First and Second Sikh Wars. Annexation of the Punjab. Completion of the Company's conquests.

1857 The Mutiny.

1858 The Government of India transferred from the Company to the Crown.

INDEX

211